THE FAMILY
Handyman.

Home Improvement
2010

THE FAMILY Handyman.

Home Improvement
2010

by The Editors of *The Family Handyman* magazine

THE FAMILY HANDYMAN HOME IMPROVEMENT 2010
(See page 288 for complete staff listing.)
Editor in Chief: Ken Collier
Project Editor: Mary Flanagan
Contributing Designers: Joel Anderson, Bruce Bohnenstingl, Teresa Marrone
Contributing Copy Editors: Donna Bierbach, Peggy Parker
Indexing: Stephanie Reymann

Vice President, Publisher: Lora Gier

The Reader's Digest Association, Inc.
President & Chief Executive Officer: Mary G. Berner
President, U.S. Affinities: Suzanne Grimes
Senior Vice President, Chief Marketing Officer: Amy J. Radin

Warning: *All do-it-yourself activities involve a degree of risk. Skills, materials, tools, and site conditions vary widely. Although the editors have made every effort to ensure accuracy, the reader remains responsible for the selection and use of tools, materials, and methods. Always obey local codes and laws, follow manufacturer's operating instructions, and observe safety precautions.*

ISBN 978-1-60652-130-4

Address any comments about *The Family Handyman Home Improvement 2010* to:
Editor, Home Improvement 2010
2915 Commers Drive, Suite 700
Eagan, MN 55121

To order additional copies of *The Family Handyman Home Improvement 2010*, call 1-800-344-2560.

For more Reader's Digest products and information, visit our Web site at rd.com.
For more about *The Family Handyman* magazine, visit thefamilyhandyman.com.

Printed in the United States of America.
1 3 5 7 9 10 8 6 4 2

INTRODUCTION

The June 2009 issue of *The Family Handyman* was our 500th issue, and we didn't let the occasion pass without a celebration. We gathered our current staff plus a group of former editors for a noontime BBQ picnic complete with a big chocolate cake. In true DIY fashion, our editor-in-chief, Ken Collier, grabbed a reciprocating saw from our studio/workshop, wiped off the blade and began slicing into the cake!

We also marked the accomplishment of 500 issues with a large poster showcasing *The Family Handyman* covers from the 1950s to 2009. Sara Koehler, our design director, worked her magic and created a beautiful tribute to the many outstanding covers we've published, including the Geraldo Rivera cover from March 1981!

In the last 55 years, *The Family Handyman* has helped a generation of WWII veterans build, maintain and improve their homes. We've been there with our readers as they navigated through the energy crisis in the '70s, and we've continued to provide energy- and money-saving projects right into the new millennium. We strive to be helpful to young first-time homeowners as well as seasoned do-it-yourselfers. On the cover of the very first issue appears this note: "Memo to Reader. Here is the first issue of the best friend your home will ever have."

During the past year we've all enjoyed looking back and seeing how the magazine has evolved, while at the same time creating 10 new issues. *The Family Handyman Home Improvement 2010* is a compilation of the best projects, hints, tips and techniques from the past year. We hope you find inspiration and useful information within, and wish you the best of luck with all of your DIY projects.

—The staff of *The Family Handyman* magazine

Contents

5 EXTERIOR MAINTENANCE & REPAIRS

6 OUTDOOR STRUCTURES & LANDSCAPING

7 AUTO & GARAGE

BONUS SECTION

SAFETY FIRST–ALWAYS!

Tackling home improvement projects and repairs can be endlessly rewarding. But as most of us know, with the rewards come risks. DIYers use chain saws, climb ladders and tear into walls that can contain big and hazardous surprises.

The good news is, armed with the right knowledge, tools and procedures, homeowners can minimize risk. As you go about your home improvement projects and repairs, stay alert for these hazards:

Aluminum wiring

Aluminum wiring, installed in about 7 million homes between 1965 and 1973, requires special techniques and materials to make safe connections. This wiring is dull gray, not the dull orange characteristic of copper. Hire a licensed electrician certified to work with it. For more information visit inspect-ny.com/aluminum/aluminum.htm.

Asbestos

Texture sprayed on ceilings before 1978, adhesives and tiles for vinyl and asphalt floors before 1980, and vermiculite insulation (with gray granules) all may contain asbestos. Other building materials, made between 1940 and 1980, could also contain asbestos. If you suspect that materials you're removing or working around contain asbestos, contact your health department or visit epa.gov/asbestos for information.

Smoke and carbon monoxide (CO) alarms

On average, forty percent of all home fire deaths result from fires in homes with no smoke alarms. Test your smoke alarms every month, replace batteries as necessary and replace units that are more than 10 years old.

As you make your home more energy-efficient and air-tight, existing ducts and chimneys can't always successfully vent combustion gases, including potentially deadly carbon monoxide (CO). Install a UL-listed CO detector, and test your CO and smoke alarms at the same time..

Lead paint

If your home was built before 1979, it may contain lead paint, which is a serious health hazard, especially for children six and under. Take precautions when you scrape or remove it. Contact your public health department for detailed safety information or call (800) 424-LEAD to receive an information pamphlet.

Buried utilities

A few days before you dig in your yard, have your underground water, gas and electrical lines marked. Just dial 811 or go to call811.com.

Five-gallon buckets and window covering cords

From 1984 to 2003, more than 200 children drowned in 5-gallon buckets. Always store them upside down and store ones containing liquid with the covers securely snapped.

According to Parents for Window Blind Safety, more than 768 children have died after becoming entangled in looped window treatment cords since 1973. For more information, visit windowblindskillchildren.org or cpsc.gov.

Spontaneous combustion

Rags saturated with oil finishes like Danish oil and linseed oil, and oil-based paints and stains can spontaneously combust if left bunched up. Always dry them outdoors, spread out loosely. When the oil has thoroughly dried, you can safely throw them in the trash.

Working up high

If you have to get up on your roof to do a repair or installation, always install roof brackets and wear a roof harness.

Vision and hearing protection

Safety glasses or goggles should be worn whenever you're working on DIY projects that involve chemicals, dust and anything that could shatter or chip off and hit your eye. Sounds louder than 80 decibels (dB) are considered potentially dangerous. Sound levels from a lawn mower can be 90 dB, and shop tools and chain saws can be 90 to 100 dB.

For additional information about home safety, visit homesafetycouncil.com. This site offers helpful information about dozens of home safety issues.

1 Interior Projects, Repairs & Remodeling

IN THIS CHAPTER

HomeCare&Repair
TIPS, FIXES & GEAR FOR A TROUBLE-FREE HOME

STOP DRAFTS AROUND ENTRY DOORS

With heating costs going through the roof, here's an easy way to keep heat from slipping out your doors, too. Take 30 minutes and replace the weather stripping and door sweeps around your steel entry doors. (To do the same job on a wooden entry door, go to thefamilyhandyman.com and search for "stop drafts.") Plan to do this project on a warm day since you'll have to remove the doors. Steel doors use a compression-style strip for the hinge side and a magnetic one for the knob side and the top. But look at the door and confirm the style of weather stripping on all three sides and the type of door sweep before you head to the store. You'll find replacement weather stripping for less than $20 and sweeps for $10 in a variety of lengths and colors at home centers and hardware stores.

To remove the door, close it and use a hammer and a pin punch or a thin nail to tap out the door hinge pins. Turn the knob, open the door slightly and lift it off the hinges. When you rip out the old weather stripping, you might find that it's tacked into place with small brads from the manufacturer. Leave them in place after removing the old weather stripping or you'll damage the doorjamb. Then shear off the shanks inside the groove with an old chisel (**Photo 2**) or drive them deeper into the groove with a screwdriver. Press the new magnetic weather stripping firmly into the groove on the knob side and top of the door frame and do the same with the compression strip along the hinge side. To ensure that the strips won't pull out, pin them with a few 1-in. brads, especially in the magnetic strips (**Photo 3**).

The sweep on the door bottom is even easier to replace. Pry or slide out the old sweep. Run a bead of caulk along the bottom edge of the door, tap the sweep into place and then staple it at the ends (**Photo 4**). While you're at it, you might as well do a quick fine-tune of the adjustable threshold. Adjust all four screws until the door opens and closes without too much drag and any drafts have been eliminated (look for light between the sweep and the threshold with the door closed). Turn the screws clockwise to lower the threshold and counterclockwise to raise it (**Photo 5**).

1 "Unzip" the old, damaged weather stripping, pulling it through the brads that hold it in.

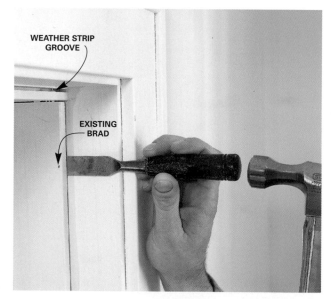

WEATHER STRIP GROOVE

EXISTING BRAD

2 Cut off the old brads or push them all the way back into the groove with an old chisel.

3 Cut the new weather stripping to length and reinstall it, pinning it with new brads positioned near the old ones.

NEW WEATHER STRIPPING

NEW 1" BRAD

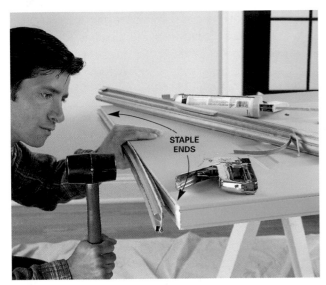

STAPLE ENDS

4 Peel out the old door sweep and caulk the ends of the door frame. Tap in the replacement sweep and staple the ends with 1/2-in. staples or the fasteners provided with the sweep.

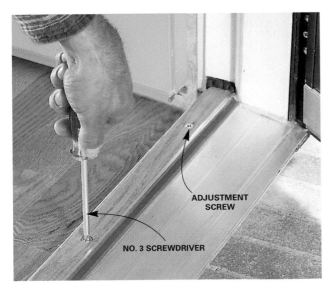

ADJUSTMENT SCREW

NO. 3 SCREWDRIVER

5 Adjust the door threshold with a No. 3 Phillips screwdriver. Move it up or down until the door closes smoothly with no light seeping through.

FINE-TUNE YOUR MECHANICAL THERMOSTAT

If you have a mechanical thermostat and your gas- or oil-burning furnace cycles on and off a lot, or the room gets too hot or too cold before the furnace kicks on, you may be able to fix the problem with a couple of simple adjustments.

First, remove the thermostat cover and make sure the subbase is mounted level on the wall. If it's not, the mercury switch inside won't work properly, which can affect the accuracy of the temperature readings. Your subbase will either have leveling posts where you can lay the level, or a flat area at the top or bottom where you can set the level (**Photo 1**). Move the subbase around until it's level and then tighten the mounting screws.

Next, adjust the heat anticipator, which fine-tunes the point at which the thermostat turns off the furnace burners. Locate the heat anticipator adjustment lever arm (**Photo 2**). If the furnace is cycling on and off too often, move the heat anticipator adjustment lever away from the "longer" setting by one calibration mark. If the room temperature is either too hot or too cold for long periods, move the lever closer by one calibration mark. Let the furnace run for two to three hours and, if necessary, repeat the above adjustment. If the problem persists, you may need to replace your thermostat (go to thefamilyhandyman.com and look for "replacing a thermostat.")

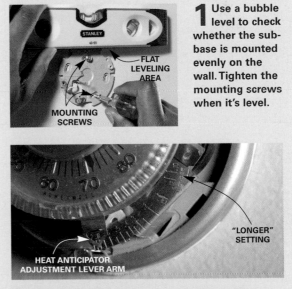

1 Use a bubble level to check whether the subbase is mounted evenly on the wall. Tighten the mounting screws when it's level.

FLAT LEVELING AREA

MOUNTING SCREWS

"LONGER" SETTING

HEAT ANTICIPATOR ADJUSTMENT LEVER ARM

2 If the furnace is cycling on and off too often, move the heat anticipator adjustment lever arm away from the "longer" setting by one calibration mark. If the room temperature is either too hot or too cold, move it closer by one calibration mark.

WET BASEMENT BLUES?

Cheer up. We'll show you simple fixes that are easy on your pocketbook, too.

If your basement leaks when it rains or is damp and musty smelling in the summer, don't throw in the towel. There are all kinds of ways to dry up a wet basement, ranging from simple weekend fixes to more difficult repairs that you may want to hire a contractor to do. In this article, we'll show you how to diagnose your wet basement problem and give you a bunch of solutions you can try yourself. We won't go into detail on how to complete some of the more difficult jobs, like installing an interior drainage system, but we'll show you how they work and what's involved in their installation.

Where's the moisture coming from?

Water or moisture in basements comes from two sources. One source is indoor humidity that condenses on cold surfaces, much like water droplets form on a cold drink on a humid day. The other is water—or water vapor—that comes from outside. Rainwater, melting snow or groundwater can saturate the soil around your foundation and leak in. Water can leak through cracks, or it can penetrate porous concrete or masonry walls in the form of water vapor. And basements can be wet from a combination of indoor humidity and water from outside. So your job is to figure out what's causing the problem and, starting with the simplest fixes, work on solutions. **Photo 1** shows a simple test to help diagnose your basement moisture problem. But before you go to the trouble, read the rest of this article for other clues. The problem may be so obvious that you can skip this test and get right to solving the problem.

Get rid of excess humidity

When humid air in the basement comes in contact with cool surfaces like concrete or block walls, concrete floors or cold water pipes, it condenses into water. Then the condensation drips off pipes and runs down walls, leaving your basement wet and clammy. The humid air that causes condensation can come

from outdoors, or indoors from a leaking dryer vent, an unvented shower or even a humidifier left on by mistake. Water droplets forming on cold water pipes or the outside of your toilet are a clear indication that at least part of your wet basement problem is caused by condensation.

Eliminating the sources of humid air will help dry out your basement. Repair and seal your leaking dryer vent (**Photo 2**, p. 14). Add a vent fan to your basement bathroom and make sure your family turns it on during showers. Keep your basement windows closed during humid weather. And if you're still getting condensation on cool surfaces, run a dehumidifier to lower the indoor humidity. Air conditioning also dehumidifies air, so if you have central air conditioning, make sure the basement registers are open. Consider adding air conditioning ducts to the basement if you don't have any.

Insulate cold surfaces to prevent condensation

Condensation dripping from cold pipes or collecting on cool basement walls can contribute to basement water problems. Reducing the humidity level in the basement is the first step, but in addition, try insulating cool surfaces. Wrap cold water pipes with foam insulation (**Photo 3**). Install a toilet tank insulating kit (search online for "toilet insulating kit") or replace your toilet with one that has an insulated tank. Reduce condensation on exterior walls by insulating them (Photo 4, p. 14, shows one method). For more information, go to thefamilyhandyman.com and enter "insulate basement" in the search box. But don't cover the walls with insulation if water is leaking in from outside; you'll just create a potential mold problem.

Direct water away from the foundation

If your basement leaks after heavy rains or after snow melts, making sure water is diverted away from your foundation may solve the problem. It's common for the soil alongside your house to settle over time, creating a moat that collects runoff and directs it down your foundation wall and into the basement. Lawn edging and gravel along the foundation can make things worse. The edging acts like a dam, and the gravel can hide the fact that the ground slopes toward the house (Figure A). The fix isn't technically difficult; it's just a lot of backbreaking work.

Start by inspecting the ground around your house to find areas that are level or sloping toward the foundation. If only one side of your basement leaks, then start your inspection on that side of the house. Figure B shows how to slope the ground away from the foundation. Unfortunately, this solution may require you to dig up existing foundation plantings, remove gravel and landscape edging, and haul in additional soil to raise the level

next to the house. But it's worth the effort because there's a good chance this fix will prevent additional water problems in your basement.

Start by creating a 6-ft.-wide slope that drops about 4 in. away from the foundation. For extra insurance, cover the sloping soil with a layer of 6-mil poly. Then hide the poly with mulch, gravel or a layer of soil covered with grass. This will keep water from soaking in near the foundation.

MOISTURE

ALUMINUM FOIL

1 Tape aluminum foil to your basement wall and inspect it a few days later. Moisture on the outside surface of the foil indicates high indoor humidity. Moisture behind the foil means moisture is leaking through the walls.

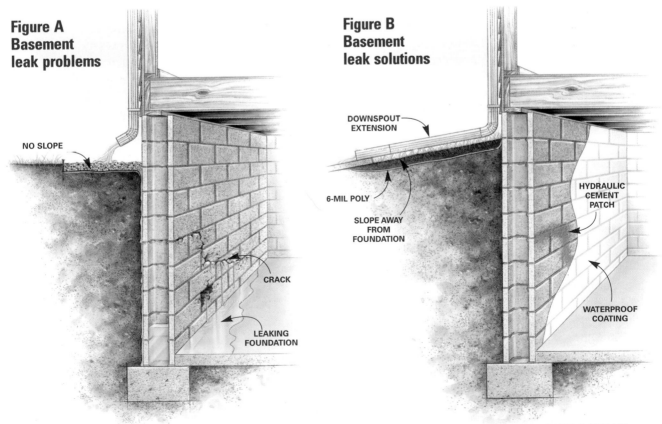

**Figure A
Basement
leak problems**

NO SLOPE

CRACK

LEAKING
FOUNDATION

**Figure B
Basement
leak solutions**

DOWNSPOUT
EXTENSION

6-MIL POLY

SLOPE AWAY
FROM
FOUNDATION

HYDRAULIC
CEMENT
PATCH

WATERPROOF
COATING

Add gutters and extend downspouts

If your basement leaks after it rains and you don't have gutters, consider adding them. Gutters catch the rain and channel it to the downspouts, which direct it away from the house. Whether you're installing new gutters or already have them, be sure the downspouts have 4- to 6-ft. horizontal extensions to move the water away from the house (**Photo 5**).

The next time you get a heavy rain, put on your raincoat and go outside to see if your gutters are doing the job. If water is gushing from your downspouts and still overflowing the gutters, you should install additional downspouts or replace your standard 2 x 3-in. downspouts with larger, 3 x 4-in. downspouts to increase the capacity. Also notice where the water is going after it leaves the downspout. If it looks like water is pooling in the yard, one solution is to install drainage tubing that leads to a dry well.

Plug holes and cracks in the foundation

Holes and cracks in your foundation can let moisture and water seep into your basement. Plugging them probably won't solve basement-leaking problems, but along with the other solutions we've suggested, it'll help. Hydraulic cement works great for patching holes in a foundation because it can set up even under water, and it expands as it sets to seal the hole and lock the plug in place. Drylok Fast Plug is one brand. Use a cold chisel or an angle grinder fitted with a masonry-cutting disc or diamond blade to enlarge the hole or crack into an inverted "V," with the narrow part of the "V" on the surface of the wall. Then follow the package instructions for mixing and using the hydraulic cement (**Photo 6**).

Coat the walls with masonry waterproofing

If your basement leaks periodically after it rains or when snow melts, or if the aluminum foil test (**Photo 1**) reveals that water vapor is seeping in from outside, waterproofing the walls on the inside can help (**Photo 7**). Waterproofing materials that go on like paint fill the pores in the concrete or masonry walls and prevent water from leaking in. Drylok Masonry Waterproofer is one brand, and it costs about 50¢ per square foot. To be effective, these coatings must be applied to bare concrete or masonry walls. Start by removing loose material with a wire brush. Then clean off any white powdery "efflorescence" with Drylok Masonry Cleaner or other masonry cleaner. Follow the safety and application instructions carefully.

A common mistake when using masonry waterproofing products is to spread them too thin. The goal is to fill every pinhole to create a continuous waterproofing membrane.

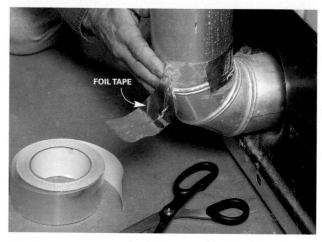

2 Seal leaky dryer vents with foil tape to prevent unwanted humid air from entering your basement. Don't just use duct tape; it'll eventually fall off.

3 Cover cold water pipes with foam pipe insulation to stop condensation. The foam insulation is inexpensive, about $3 per 4-ft. section, and easy to cut with scissors.

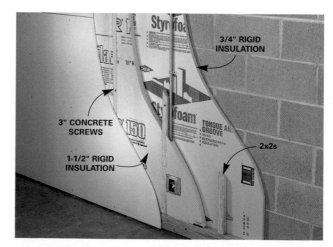

4 Insulate exterior walls to prevent condensation. In cold climates, insulating basement walls also saves energy and reduces your heating bill.

Crystalline waterproofing material is another type of waterproofing coating. One brand is Xypex. Xypex penetrates the surface and reacts with chemicals in the concrete to form water-blocking crystals. You'll spend 55¢ to $1 per square foot for this option, depending on how porous the walls are. You'll find ordering information by going to www.hi-dry.com or calling (888) 443-7922.

Install a drainage system

If you're still getting water in the basement after sloping the ground away from the house and adding gutters and downspout extensions, then a drainage system may be the only solution. Drainage systems installed below the basement floor level on the outside of your foundation are very effective, but this approach is only practical while the house is under construction and access to this area is easy.

There are two other options for existing basements. You can buy a channeling system that glues to the floor around the perimeter of the basement. For information on one brand, go to waterproof.com or call (651) 644-2000. The channel diverts water that leaks into the basement into a sump pump. This system is easier to install than one that's buried under the floor. The disadvantages are that the channel is visible above the floor, and the effectiveness of the system relies on creating a waterproof seal between the channel and the basement floor. You'll also have to install a sump basket and sump pump. The channel costs about $4.50 per foot; the sump pump kit, about $200.

The second option, drainage tubing below the basement floor that's connected to a sump basket and pump (**Photo 8**), is more expensive and difficult to install, but it's the best permanent fix for chronic basement leaks. You can install a system like this yourself, but breaking out the concrete floor, burying the tubing, and patching the floor are a lot of backbreaking work. Materials to do an average basement will cost $600 to $1,000. Expect to spend $3,000 to $8,000 for a professionally installed system in a standard-size basement.

5 Add downspout extensions to carry rainwater at least 6 ft. away from the foundation.

6 Patch cracks and holes in basement walls with hydraulic cement. Chisel out cracks first to allow space for the cement.

7 Brush a waterproof coating onto basement walls. Brush the coating in all directions to completely fill every pinhole. Add a second coat after the first dries.

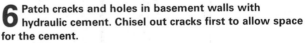
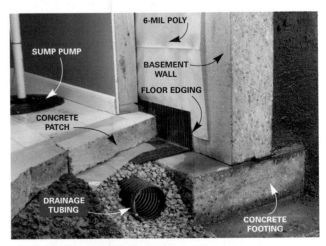

8 An interior drain system channels water from the base of the wall into a drain tube that leads to the sump basket and pump, which pumps it to the outside.

HomeCare&Repair

STOP STAIR SQUEAKS COMPLETELY

Squeaky stairs are easy to fix from underneath—provided they're exposed. A simple fix is to tap shims into voids between the treads and the stringers and add some glue. Then screw the stringer to each stud. But most stairs are finished underneath with drywall or plaster. Squeaks in these stairs need to be fixed from the top. That's why the perfect time to fix them is when you're replacing the carpeting—you can remove the treads and get at the squeaky culprits. Here are four easy steps to permanently fix the treads that squeak and keep the rest from ever starting.

After you've removed the carpet, use a flat bar to pry off the treads, working from the top down (**Photo 1**). Since you'll be reusing the treads, remove the nails and any leftover carpet pad and staples. Screw the outside stringers

to each stud with 4-1/2-in. screws (**Photo 2**). Starting with the bottom tread, apply a bead of subfloor adhesive (two brands are PL 400 and Liquid Nails) along the top of the riser, the stringers and the back of the tread, and press the tread back into place. Next, drive three 2-1/2-in. screws through the top of the same tread into each stringer (**Photo 3**). Then, drive a 2-in. screw through the riser into the back of the tread between the stringers (**Photo 4**). Repeat these steps with each tread, working your way to the top of the stairs.

Note: Your stairs will be out of commission for a couple of hours, so let everyone in the house know what's going on. Make sure you cordon off the top to keep someone from tumbling down the steps while you're working!

1 Pry off each tread with a flat bar. Remove the nails and clean off any carpet pad or staples.

FLAT BAR

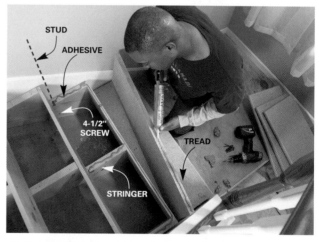

STUD

ADHESIVE

4-1/2" SCREW

TREAD

STRINGER

2 Apply a bead of subfloor adhesive along the top of the riser, the stringers and the back of the tread. Press the tread back into place.

2-1/2" SCREWS

3 Drive three 2-1/2-in. screws through the top of the tread into each stringer.

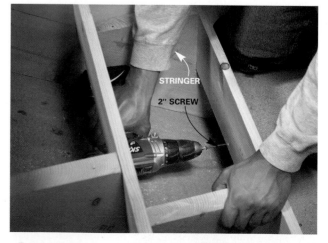

STRINGER

2" SCREW

4 Drive a 2-in. screw through the riser into the back of the tread.

16

ADD STYLE WITH ARCHES

If you want high style on a low budget, you can't beat a drywall archway. It takes a few hours to frame and finish an arch, but the materials cost is usually less than $20. And an arch looks like a million bucks. This isn't a complex job; if you've done some basic wall framing and drywall taping, you can handle it. To see how to frame an arch in a new or existing wall opening, go to **thefamilyhandyman.com** and search for "drywall arch."

BE YOUR OWN LOCKSMITH

If you need to change your deadbolts or doorknob locks for security reasons, you have three options. You can buy all new locks (ka-ching!) or hire a locksmith to rekey the locks (ka-ching). Locksmiths charge anywhere from $35 to $100 just to show up and then $25 and up for every lock they rekey. But there is a third, really cheap option: rekeying the locks yourself with the help of an $11 rekeying kit. Find the kits at home centers, hardware stores or online at changealock.com (866-546-2957). Just be sure to get the kit for your brand of lock.

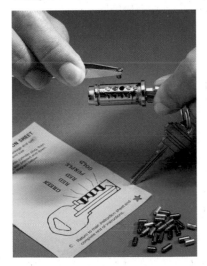

For complete instructions on how to use the kit, go to thefamilyhandyman.com and search for "rekey lock." It's mostly just a matter of taking apart the lock and replacing the internal pins with the ones from the kit. One kit will upgrade six locks. The first lock will take you about 20 minutes, but you'll pick up speed after that.

CHEAP PAINT IS NO BARGAIN

Buying low-quality paint may save you five or ten bucks a gallon, but it's one of the worst moves you can make. It not only leads to lots of extra work, but can actually cost you more money. Cheap paint—whether interior or exterior—doesn't cover as well as pricier paint, so you end up buying more for extra coats. Even worse, cheap paint doesn't stand up to Mother Nature for long. A high-quality exterior paint typically lasts two to three times as long as cheap paint. So over time, the cheap stuff costs you at least twice as much money—and days of paint-scraping drudgery. To find high-quality paint, look for "100 percent acrylic" on the label. Price is usually a good indicator of quality, too. Spend at least $15 per gallon for interior paint and $25 for exterior. That's a true bargain.

REVIVE TRIM THE EASY WAY

Renew dull trim in one weekend
by **Jeff Gorton**

Time takes a toll on your home's woodwork. Moldings get dinged up, window stools lose their luster, and doors show the wear and tear of everyday use. But you can dramatically improve the appearance of stained and varnished woodwork without all the work and mess of a complete stripping and refinishing job. We'll show you a much easier process here—and you may even be able to eliminate some steps if your woodwork is in better shape than ours. Just gather the supplies in a 5-gallon bucket and tackle the renewal project one window or door at a time whenever you have a few spare hours. Start in a corner or in an inconspicuous area—better to learn from your mistakes there than on the front door.

Start with a thorough cleaning

The first step in renewing your woodwork is cleaning it to remove grease and grime and create a contaminant-free surface for the new finish. Wash the woodwork with a TSP substitute. Use just enough cleaner to wet the surface. Scrub with a sponge dipped in the cleaning solution. Then rinse with a sponge and clear water and wipe off the wood with a dry rag.

If there's paint slopped onto the edges of your trim or spattered on the surface, now's the time to clean it off. A rag dampened with denatured alcohol will remove most paint spatters (**Photo 1**). Alcohol won't harm most finishes, but it will dissolve shellac. Don't worry if some of the finish comes off. You can touch it up later (**Photo 7**). Protect the walls with masking tape to prevent the alcohol from damaging the paint. For tougher paint spatters, use a fine synthetic abrasive pad (such as a 3M Wood Finishing Pad) dipped in denatured alcohol.

Scrape and sand badly damaged areas

Window stools and other areas exposed to moisture and sunlight may need to be completely refinished. In spots such as these where the wood is discolored and the finish worn away, you'll get the best results by scraping and sanding to expose bare wood (**Photos 2** and **4**).

If the wood has dark water stains that scraping and

sanding won't remove, you can remove them with oxalic acid (Photo 3). **Caution:** Wear protective gear, including goggles, rubber gloves and a long-sleeve shirt, when you work with oxalic acid. Mix the oxalic acid in a plastic container. Add 1 oz. of oxalic acid powder (about 2 tablespoons) to 1 cup of hot water and stir it until the powder dissolves. Then brush the solution onto the stain with a disposable sponge brush and let it work for 20 minutes. You can repeat the process to further lighten the stain. Wipe the bleached wood with a sponge and clear water. Then neutralize the oxalic acid by applying a solution of 3 tablespoons of borax to 1 gallon of water with a sponge. Finally, rinse the bleached wood with water again and let it dry overnight. Then sand it with 120-grit followed by 180-grit sandpaper (Photo 4) and stain it to match the rest of the woodwork.

Fill small holes with wood putty

To make new finishes stick well, slightly roughen the old finish

Round up your supplies

Below we've listed the essential supplies you'll need for a basic wood renewal project and some optional materials and supplies you may need if you're refinishing window stools or removing stains. Most of the tools and supplies are available at paint stores, full-service hardware stores and home centers. Visit an art supply store for the artists' markers. Oxalic acid is available online at rockler.com or at woodworking stores and some hardware stores and lumberyards.

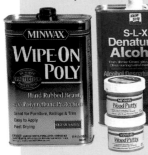

Supplies you'll need:

TSP-PF (phosphate free)

Fine synthetic abrasive pads

Denatured alcohol

Disposable gloves

Safety glasses

Stain to match

Wood putty to match

Wipe-on polyurethane for varnished wood

Rags

Mineral spirits

Optional tools and materials:

Paint scraper

Oxalic acid

Sandpaper

Wood filler

Felt tip markers

Goggles

Rubber gloves

Spar varnish for window stools

1 Soften old paint along the edges of trim with alcohol. A rag wrapped around a putty knife lets you scrub the trim without slopping alcohol onto the wall.

2 Scrape away badly weathered finish. A carbide paint scraper removes the old finish much faster than sandpaper. But be careful not to gouge the wood.

3 Bleach away deep stains that scraping or sanding won't remove. You don't have to scrub; just let the oxalic acid penetrate and lighten the stain.

4 Sand the bleached wood after it dries. Start with 120-grit sandpaper. Then sand with 180-grit. Vacuum the dust before staining and finishing.

5 Rub the wood with an abrasive pad to create a slightly roughened surface for the new finish. Vacuum the dust from the surface before wiping on a new coat of finish.

6 Fill holes with perfectly matched putty. Just knead different colors together until you get an exact match.

first (**Photo 5**). Synthetic finishing pads are the best choice because they conform to profiles and aren't as aggressive as sandpaper. Buy medium and fine and experiment in an inconspicuous area. Use the pad that roughens the finish without removing any stain.

Fill holes left by nails or screws with soft wood putty. Wood putty is available in many colors that you can blend for a perfect match. Application is easy. You just push it into the hole and wipe it off (**Photo 6**). There's no sanding required. Buy several shades of putty, ranging from dark to light, that are similar to the color of your trim. Then mix them to match the wood surrounding the hole. Push the putty into the hole and wipe off the excess with your fingertip. Then remove residue from around the hole by wiping over it with a clean rag. If your woodwork has filled nail holes that have darkened and no longer match, pick the old filler out and replace it with soft putty. Buy water-based putty if you plan to use water-based polyurethane.

Apply stain to hide dings and scratches

Completely refinishing the area may be the only way to make flawless repairs to badly damaged doors, windows and moldings. But you can greatly improve the overall appearance of worn or damaged wood with less drastic measures.

Disguise large areas where the stain is worn away by dabbing stain over the light areas to blend them in. The patched area may not match exactly, but at least the spot will be less obvious. Or simply wipe the surface of the wood with a rag dipped in stain to fill in small scratches and imperfections—you'll see a big improvement (**Photo 7**). Wipe the stain on. Then wipe off the excess with a clean rag. Allow the stain to dry overnight before you apply the finish.

One of the trickiest parts of a wood restoration project is finding stain to match. You can pry off a small piece of trim and ask the paint department to mix stain to match. Some paint stores and home centers offer inexpensive sample packets of stain. You can choose several samples that are close to the color of your wood and experiment in a hidden area to find the best color match. Then buy a larger con-

7 Hide scratches, chips and worn-away finish with a fresh dose of stain. Then wipe the woodwork with a clean rag to remove the excess stain. Let the stain dry overnight.

8 Restore the shine with a fresh coat of polyurethane. Wipe-on poly gives you a faster, smoother finish with less mess than brush-on poly.

tainer. Another approach is to buy two or three cans of stain that are close to the color of your woodwork and mix them to get the right color. Use an eyedropper and disposable plastic cups to mix small batches until you get the proportions right. Keep notes so you can reproduce the results in a larger batch.

Refresh the finish

The final step in your trim renewal project is to apply a fresh coat of finish. Wipe-on polyurethane is a good choice because it's fast and easy to apply. You simply wipe it on with a soft rag and let it dry. Each coat is very thin and dries quickly. You can recoat in two or three hours if you want a thicker finish for extra protection. Several coats of wipe-on polyurethane are required to equal the thickness of one coat of brushed-on varnish, but it's easier to get a smooth, drip-free finish with wipe-on poly.

Fold a cotton rag to create a pad. Then dip an edge of the pad into a container of wipe-on polyurethane and press it against the side to wring out the excess. Wipe the polyurethane onto the wood in long strokes in the direction of the wood grain as you would if you were using a brush.

For window stools or other trim exposed to sunlight, consider using spar varnish. Spar varnish has built-in ultraviolet protection and is more flexible, so it holds up better in areas exposed to sunlight and water. Experiment on a scrap of trim or in an inconspicuous area to see if the slightly amber tint darkens the color too much. When you've completed all of the steps above, your woodwork will look like new and be protected by a fresh layer of finish. If you don't have time to do an entire room from beginning to end, just tackle one door or window whenever you have a few spare hours. You'll be done with a room before you know it. ⌂

Question&Comment

SEE VISITORS ON A BIGGER SCREEN

I have a peephole in my front door. But as I get older, I'm finding it harder to see through it. I'm guessing lots of baby boomers have this problem. Is there something better for us "old folks"?

Replace your old peephole with one of the newer in-door viewers. It's a low-cost solution ($30) that uses prisms and a lens to project the visitor's image onto a 2-in. screen. The large screen allows you to see visitors from 5 to 7 ft. behind the door. You can get an in-door viewer at SecurityProductsinc.com.

You'll have to drill a new 2-3/8-in. hole. Place it so the new hole eliminates the existing hole at the same time. You can probably leave the old peephole in place while you drill the new hole (to provide a firmer surface and prevent pilot bit wandering). Make sure the drill is level and drill until the pilot bit comes out the other side of the door. Then remove the hole saw and drill from the opposite side (to prevent splintering). You'll also need to drill two 1/8-in. holes for the retaining ring anchor pins (use the template to mark the location for the small holes). To finish the installation, insert the viewer and screw it onto the lens prism.

The new viewer provides a much brighter image, but since it uses prisms, be aware that the image will be flopped left to right. As an added benefit, the viewer optics prevent visitors from peering into your house (a flaw in old-style peepholes) or from noticing that you're even using the viewer.

Chuck up a 2-3/8-in. hole saw and cut a large opening for a new door viewer. Screw it in place and see who's at the door from 7 ft. away.

ALUMINUM BODY, GOLD FINISH

TILE BACKER BOARD AROUND A BATHTUB

I'm installing new cement tile backer board around my bathtub. I tried overlapping the tub lip, but then the board angled away from the wall, leaving a gap behind. What's the proper method here?

The best approach is to keep cement board out of the lip area. Apply it to the wall with the bottom edge about 1/4 in. above the lip of the tub. Then apply a generous amount of thin-set to the bottom tile and position it 1/8 in. above the tub. Fill the gap between the tile and the tub with caulk.

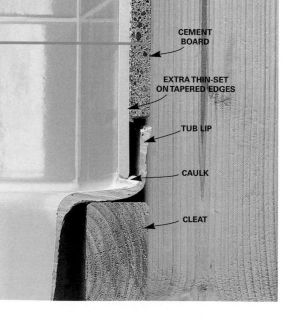

CEMENT BOARD

EXTRA THIN-SET ON TAPERED EDGES

TUB LIP

CAULK

CLEAT

INSULATE CRAWL SPACE DUCTS

The forced-air heating/cooling ducts in my crawl space aren't insulated, and I know I'm losing heat. How do I insulate them, and what type of material should I use?

Uninsulated ducts that run through unconditioned spaces can lose more than 30 percent of their heating or cooling capacity. So you'll save money by insulating them. The Residential Building Code calls for R-8 insulation for these ducts, but check with your building inspector for local code requirements. Before you insulate, however, plug any air leaks by sealing all the joints with caulk or tape.

Look for "duct wrap," a fiberglass product with an outer foil vapor barrier. The foil barrier prevents condensation (and mold) from forming on the duct.

Unfortunately, R-8 duct wrap can be difficult to find. We checked three home centers and found only R-3 duct wrap. That didn't meet our local codes, so we contacted a heating equipment supply house (look in the yellow pages). That company knew exactly what we were looking for and had it in stock.

We bought a roll of Owens Corning SoftR 3-in. duct wrap for our installation. The 48-in.-wide by 50-ft. roll cost $193. We also bought a few rolls of UL181 aluminum duct tape to seal the insulation seams.

You'll be handling fiberglass, so wear long sleeves, goggles, mask and leather gloves. Measure the circumference of the duct, add 2 in. to the total, and cut the insulation to that length. Remove a 2-in. strip of fiberglass to create an overlapping flap for taping (**Photo 1**). To finish the job, butt the insulation edges together along the bottom of the duct, overlap the 2-in. strip of foil, and secure it with aluminum tape (**Photo 2**). Wrap wire around the insulation to relieve seam stress and prevent the seam from separating (**Photo 3**).

You'll save lots of cutting and fitting time on rectangular ducts by removing the hanging brackets one section at a time. Remove the screw from the joist and rotate the bracket. Once the insulation is in place and taped, cut a small hole near each bracket, rotate it back up through the hole and reattach it to the joist. Seal around the bracket with tape.

FOIL BACKING

DISCARD

1 Cut the insulation to match the circumference of the duct, plus 2 in. Then peel away the foil backing and cut off 2 in. of fiberglass.

2 Remove several duct hanger brackets and slide the insulation around the top of the duct. Overlap the 2-in. foil tab at the seam and seal with aluminum tape.

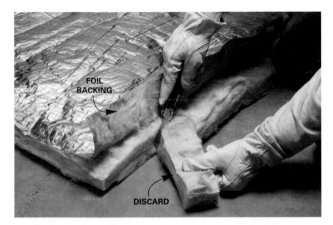

3 Relieve stress on the seam by wrapping wire around the insulation. Place two wires on each 4-ft. section.

WAX PAPER LINER

FOIL TAPE

4 Repeat the cutting, tabbing and taping procedure for each round duct.

Question&Comment

CAN I TILE OVER TILE?

The tile in my entryway is in great shape—no cracks or loose grout—but the style and color are outdated and I want to replace it. Removing it and starting over will be a huge job because it was installed with an epoxy adhesive on a concrete floor. Can I just tile over the existing tile?

As long as there are no cracks in the existing tile (indicating underlying problems in the concrete), you can tile on top of it. In fact, pros do it all the time.

Surface preparation is paramount. Start by making sure all the tiles are solidly bonded to the floor. Tap them lightly with a wood mallet or a chunk of 2x4. A hollow sound is an indication that a tile is loose. Remove and reset any loose ones with thin-set. Next, use a 4-ft. level to find any high spots and grind those down using a right-angle grinder with a masonry wheel. Then sand all the tiles with a belt or orbital sander (80-grit) to scratch any surface glazes. Remove any moldy or loose grout with a rotary tool or carbide scraper. Vacuum the tiles and clean with detergent and water to remove dirt, sealers and wax. Rinse the surface with clear water and let it dry.

Buy a latex-modified thin-set (one brand is FlexBond) and mix it in small batches. Complete adhesive coverage is critical on large tiles (12 in. or larger) and even more important when you're tiling over tile. Some installers prefer to "flatback" each tile with the flat edge of the trowel before applying the tile to the combed thin-set. Others prefer to use a larger-notched trowel (1/2 x 1/2 in.) to apply the thin-set. Whichever method you use, always comb the adhesive in one direction (no swirls). Then set the tile on the floor and slide it perpendicular to the combed thin-set to knock down the rows and spread the adhesive.

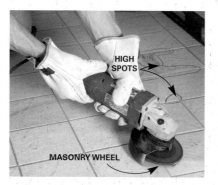

1 Lay a level on the old tile and mark any high spots. Grind them down with a grinder. Roughen the tile with 80-grit sandpaper.

2 Spread a flat layer of thin-set on the back of large tiles for better adhesion. Or, use a larger-notch trowel.

3 Press the tile onto the floor thin-set and slide it perpendicular to the combed lines.

QUIET CREAKING PIPES

My water pipes creak every time I fill the tub, take a shower or run the dishwasher. How can I stop the creaking?

Usually the hot water pipes do most of the "talking" because they expand and contract as the water temperature changes inside them. That movement eventually loosens the nails at some pipe straps. The pipes then rub against the floor joists, making that annoying creaking sound. The best way to solve the problem permanently is to add more pipe straps (they're cheap, so add one per joist) and replace all the existing nails with screws.

Replace pipe strap nails with 1-5/8-in. coarse-thread drywall screws.

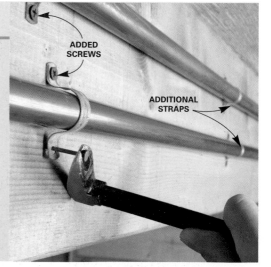

24

RADIOACTIVE COUNTERTOPS?

I saw a report that some granite countertops give off dangerous levels of radon gas. Should I have my new countertops tested?

There's a lot of controversy but very little hard-core research on the topic. We do know that very few granite slabs "outgas" levels of radon high enough to register on lab equipment. And even with those, room size, amount of ventilation and other factors may prevent any buildup to levels the EPA considers a health hazard. But if you want to test your counters, purchase a do-it-yourself test kit. One source is Air-Chek Inc., (800) 247-2435, airchek.com. Its countertop test kit is $80 and includes laboratory analysis.

Follow the kit instructions for test packet placement. Leave the packets in place for the recommended amount of time and record all requested room sizes on the return envelopes. Then mail them in for analysis. If the results show a higher concentration of radon in the kitchen, contact a local testing laboratory for a more thorough analysis before you start ripping out your new countertops.

Radon gas can pose a serious health threat. But you should keep the issue of radon and granite countertops in perspective. Radon is far likelier to enter your home through cracks in your basement slab or foundation. If you're concerned about the possibility of radon in your countertops, test them. But check your basement or lower level first. Airchek.com sells those test kits as well.

AIR TEST POUCH

ARE CHEAP DUST MASKS OK?

I want to protect myself while I sand some drywall joints, and I know I need to wear a mask. But I see dust masks ranging in price from 25¢ to $26. Is there really a difference between the cheap masks and the more expensive ones?

There's a huge difference between a 25¢ mask and the expensive ones. A cheap mask may filter out bees and mosquitoes, but it won't reduce your exposure to small particles.

Dust masks are officially called "Particulate Filtering Respirators" and are certified by the National Institute for Occupational Safety and Health (NIOSH), a department within the U.S. Department of Health and Human Services. The certification markings denote the respirator's filtering efficiency and ability to handle oil mists or oil-based particles. An N95 marking on a respirator means that it has at least a 95 percent filtering efficiency and shouldn't be used in the presence of oil mists or oil-based particles. If you check the label on the 25¢ masks, we bet you won't find any NIOSH markings.

First look for a NIOSH-certified respirator with a minimum rating of N95. Then consider the comfort features of the different respirators. Respirators with multiple headbands, soft nose foam and a foam face seal may cost a bit more, but they're also more comfortable. Since a large drywall sanding project involves a lot of physical exertion, consider a respirator with an exhalation valve. The valve makes breathing a lot easier. It's well worth the extra cost. For the ultimate in comfort and protection, consider a "half mask" rubber/silicone respirator with replaceable filter elements. Make sure you read the instructions and put the respirator on properly for the best performance.

**The respirators shown below:
3M 8210 N95 Particulate Respirator, $6.
3M 8211 N95 Particulate Respirator with exhalation valve, $7.
MSA 817664 P100 Toxic Dust Respirator, $26.**

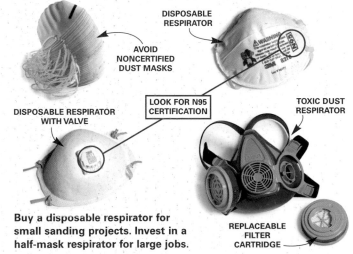

DISPOSABLE RESPIRATOR

AVOID NONCERTIFIED DUST MASKS

DISPOSABLE RESPIRATOR WITH VALVE

LOOK FOR N95 CERTIFICATION

TOXIC DUST RESPIRATOR

REPLACEABLE FILTER CARTRIDGE

Buy a disposable respirator for small sanding projects. Invest in a half-mask respirator for large jobs.

MAKE YOUR CARPET LAST

3 strategies that double the life of your carpet and save thousands **by Elisa Bernick**

Carpet cleaning—not exactly cocktail party conversation, right? But basic carpet care is one of the best financial moves you can make. If you care for it properly, that 1,500 sq. ft. of wall-to-wall carpeting that you paid $6,000 to $10,000 or more for should last 15 years or longer. Unless you maintain your carpeting properly, you might need to replace it in half that time. This article will lay out three strategies for protecting your carpet from everyday wear and tear. We'll tell you about free and effective cleaning products, how to get your money's worth when you hire a pro, and the best methods and products to use when you clean your carpet yourself. Our tips will help you keep your carpet looking beautiful for years to come so you get the most out of your big buck investment.

STRATEGY 1

Banish dirt

Dirt is like thousands of little blades that cut carpet fibers. When you walk across a dirty carpet, you grind sharp dirt particles against the yarn, making tiny nicks in the fibers. All that fuzz mixed in with the dirt in your vacuum cleaner bags is your beautiful carpet headed out the door one bag at a time. When dirt scratches the fibers, it dulls the sheen, which is why high-traffic areas appear duller than the rest of the carpet. Over time, grinding dirt wears away the fibers too, which mats them down and makes them stain more easily. Follow these tips to keep your carpet as dirt-free as possible.

Vacuum often

To protect your carpet, vacuum entrance areas and high-traffic areas twice a week and the rest of the carpeting at least weekly. Oily soils attract oily soils, and frequent vacuuming will reduce soil buildup.

Start with a clean bag or filter

A dirty bag, dirt cup or filter can cut a vacuum's suction power in half. The main reason bagless vacuums stop working is that the filters aren't changed often enough. Replace or wash (if possible) the filters on bagless vacuums every three months. Replace vacuum bags when they're three-quarters full.

Vacuum at the right speed

Vacuum slowly enough to get out as much dirt as possible. Make one quick pass over low-traffic areas and two slow

Set the vacuum at the right height

If your vacuum is set too low, you can damage the carpet as well as the vacuum's roller brush and drive belt. If it's set too high, you won't pick up any dirt. To set the vacuum's ideal height, raise it to its highest setting, turn it on and lower it until you can feel the vacuum trying to tug itself forward.

passes over high-traffic areas. Two slow passes removes ground-in dirt more effectively than several fast passes.

Use walk-off mats

Use walk-off mats inside and out to keep dirt off the carpeting. Coarse-textured mats outside your doors remove soil. Water-absorbent mats inside prevent wet shoes on the carpeting.

STRATEGY
2 Use a pro wisely

Most carpet manufacturers recommend professional hot water extraction as the primary cleaning method for synthetic carpets. Although it's often referred to as "steam" cleaning, there's no steam involved. The carpet is pretreated with a detergent solution, and then a very hot rinse solution under high pressure is forced into your carpet and vacuumed out. When done correctly, this process cleans deep and doesn't leave behind a soap residue. Quality pros charge $300 to $500 to deep clean 1,000 sq. ft. of carpet. At that price, you might be tempted to skip professional cleanings altogether and just rent a machine to clean the carpet yourself. Don't. Or at least don't do only that. A rented or purchased carpet-cleaning machine will remove the surface dirt. But deep cleaning to remove allergens, dust and greasy residues requires the specialized equipment and training of a pro. The best strategy is to use our DIY cleaning tips most of the time (see p. 28) and hire a professional every 12 to 18 months.

Don't take bids over the phone

Quality pros will provide references, an in-home inspection and a written estimate based on the square footage, type and condition of the carpeting rather than the number of rooms cleaned, and a written guarantee of their work.

Beware of "discount" carpet cleaners

Discount pros depend on making volume sales rather than establishing ongoing client relationships. They typically spray soap on your carpet, suck up the water and are gone in 30 minutes. These services leave behind a soap residue that will actually attract dirt to your carpet. Those "three rooms for 50 bucks" offers also get them into your house so they can sell you high-priced add-ons like spot removal and deodorizers—services that quality pros include for free.

You get what you pay for

Quality pros charge 35¢ to 65¢ per sq. ft. of carpet depending on the type of carpeting, the services you need and the size of the job. The entire process can take one to three hours.

Four ways to recognize a quality pro:

1 Truck-mounted equipment is a better choice than portable steam cleaning equipment because it exhausts the dirty air and humidity outside. Its stronger suction leaves carpets drier, too.

2 Quality pros include furniture moving, vacuuming (some charge extra for this, so check), routine spot removal, preconditioning and deodorizing as part of a standard cleaning package.

3 To agitate the pile and neutralize the carpet's pH, pros force a hot, high-pressure rinse solution into the carpet and then extract it.

4 After cleaning, quality pros set furniture on blocks or pads to prevent stains from transferring from furniture legs to the damp carpet.

3 DIY right

Carpet pros do a more thorough job than you can, but hiring a pro is expensive. So the next-best approach is to alternate between DIY and pro cleanings. DIY "steam"-cleaning machines can be effective if you understand how to use them and take the time to clean your carpet carefully.

You can rent a steam cleaner from a grocery store or home center for $20 to $40 per day. If you pick the machine up late in the day, many stores will charge you a half-day rate and let you keep the machine until the next morning. The detergent costs another $15 per half gallon (and typically you should use a tablespoon or less per gallon of water).

If you prefer to buy a steam-cleaning machine, plan to spend $60 to $300 or more. The pricier models have more powerful water jets and suction, and some even have a heating element to keep the water hot. The reviews on these machines are mixed, and some are prone to breakdowns. Do some online research (type "carpet cleaning machines" into your browser) before you buy.

Most rental machines weigh more, hold more water and come with a wider wand than purchased models, making them useful for larger, high-traffic areas. Purchased models are usually smaller, more portable and easier to store. They're good for spot cleaning and are easier to drag up and down stairs. Whether you rent or buy, avoid damaging your carpets and make your cleaning last longer by following our tips.

Clean the carpet before it becomes really dirty

How often your carpet needs cleaning depends on the kind of carpet traffic you have (think kids and pets). Clean the carpet when the color starts looking dull. If you wait until the carpet is filthy, cleaning it will be much more difficult, take much longer and cost more.

Use DIY machines carefully

Hurrying through a cleaning will leave soap residue, a soaked carpet and a pad that can mold or mildew. Larger rental machines require you to pull them across the floor rather than push.

Use less soap than directed

The soap used in DIY machines foams a lot and leaves behind a lot of residue, which acts as a dirt magnet. Despite what the directions say, use a tablespoon or less of soap to 1 gallon of hot water to prevent soap residue.

Vacuum well before and after cleaning

Vacuum beforehand to remove large particles of soil. Vacuum again after you clean and the carpet is completely dry to pick up soil that wicks to the surface during drying.

Pretreat stains and high-traffic areas

Mix a drop of detergent with hot water in a spray bottle and lightly mist the dirtiest areas. Let sit 5 to 10 minutes before starting the general cleaning.

Use a mild acid rinse to neutralize soap residue

DIY machines are often sold with a neutralizing rinse, or you can make your own using 1 cup white vinegar to 1 gallon hot water. Rinse after you make one pass with the detergent solution.

Remove or elevate furniture

If your furniture is too heavy to move, put aluminum foil squares, wood blocks or plastic film under and around the legs of all furniture to prevent rust from metal casters or stains from paint and finishes from transferring to damp carpet.

Don't overwet the carpet

DIY machines put a lot of moisture into the carpet, and most don't have strong enough suction to extract it thoroughly. Make only one pass with the soap and water solution. Make one pass with the neutralizing rinse solution. Then make two or three drying passes with the water off.

Let it dry thoroughly

Wet carpet is a perfect environment for mold and mildew. After you clean your carpets, open the windows, use fans and a dehumidifier, or put the AC on a moderate setting (72 to 78 degrees) to remove excess moisture from the air. Don't replace the furniture or walk on the carpet until it's completely dry. This can take up to 12 hours, although six to eight hours is typical.

Clean stains right—right away

Act quickly

If you get to a stain immediately, there's a 99 percent chance you can remove it. The longer a stain reacts chemically with the carpeting, the harder it is to remove.

Try water first

Eighty percent of stains can be removed using plain tap water. To remove a stain, press a clean, dry, white cloth over the stain to absorb the spill. Repeat until the spill is absorbed. Then gently work water into the stain with a damp white towel and blot until the stain is gone. Change cloths when necessary. For a particularly stubborn spot, go to the "spot solver" resource at carpet-rug.org to find your stain and a suggested solution.

Blot—don't rub or scrub

Scrubbing a stain will damage the fibers and create a fuzzy area. Always blot from the outer edge toward the center of the stain to avoid spreading the spot and creating a larger problem.

Be patient

Work water gently into the spill and then blot with a dry cloth. Repeat until the stain is gone and all the water has been absorbed. If you're patient, you'll almost always be able to remove the stain.

Try vinegar or club soda

If water alone doesn't remove a stain, try a white vinegar and water solution (equal amounts) or club soda before trying stronger commercial cleaning products.

Test commercial products first

Some products can cause carpet to get dirty faster or damage the carpet's color and texture. For a list of carpet manufacturer-approved spot and stain cleaners, go to carpet-rug.org and under the residential customer tab you'll find a "Seal of Approval Products" search box. Test carpet-cleaning products on an inconspicuous area before using. 🏠

Don't dig or scoop food spills

Digging or scooping can work the stain into the carpet. If there are solids on top of the stain, use a spoon or dull knife to carefully scrape the food toward the middle of the spill and into a white towel and then treat the stain.

Use a shop vacuum on wet spills

Keep vacuuming until no more liquid can be removed. If the spill was a colored liquid, treat it as you would a stain, after vacuuming.

Spot removal and more

The Carpet and Rug Institute, a nonprofit trade association of carpet manufacturers, has a great Web site (carpet-rug.org) for consumers. It's filled with information about carpet care, including a list of CRI-approved, off-the-shelf cleaning products, a state-by-state list of member service providers and lots of stain removal advice in its "spot solver" database on the residential customer tab. You can type in your specific stain for advice about how to remove it.

HandyHints®

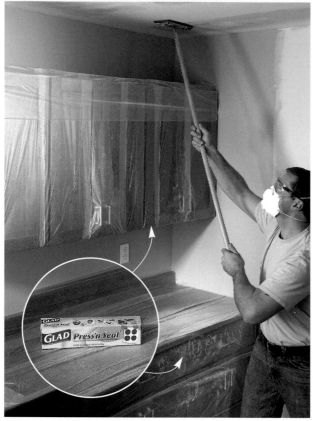

KEEP KITCHEN CABINETS CLEAN DURING REMODELING

Knocking down old walls or sanding drywall creates a fine dust that coats everything in the house, but you can keep it out of cabinets by sealing them temporarily with a self-sticking plastic wrap (one brand is Glad Press'n Seal).

PERFECT WALL PATCH EVERY TIME

Next time you have to patch a hole in your wall, instead of squaring it up or struggling to get the exact measurements, just trace the hole on wax paper to use as a guide to cut the new piece. Tape the wax paper over the hole, then run a permanent marker around the edges of the hole. Cut out the shape, then tape it to the new drywall and cut it out.

WAX PAPER

CABINET HANDLE JIG

When we remodeled our kitchen, we put new door fronts on all the cabinets. To make sure I installed each of the new cabinet door handles in the right spot, I made a jig from a 4 x 7-in. plywood scrap. I nailed a piece of 1x2 over two ends of the plywood. Then I marked the handle screw locations on the jig and drilled guide holes. I was able to screw perfectly placed holes for each door handle in each door. This works great for both two-hole and one-hole handles.

JIG

DOOR HANDLE

FILL HOLES WITH DRYWALL ANCHORS

If you have holes in your wall from large nails or old anchors, make filling go faster by screwing in drywall anchors first. Sink the heads just below the surface of the drywall—locking the anchor tightly into the wall—then fill with spackling compound. Sand the surface flat after it dries. If the holes already have screw-in anchors, leave them in place and just sink the heads a bit more.

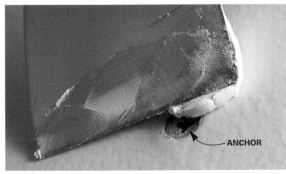

← ANCHOR

WINDSHIELD ICE SCRAPER

BETTER WALLPAPER SCRAPER

Scraping off wallpaper is no picnic. Wallpaper scrapers are tiring because you can only use one hand. Putty knives have the same problem and can also damage the drywall surface. And neither gives you much of a reach. Here's a way to make the chore easier and faster. After wetting the wallpaper with a sponge, use a long-handled windshield ice scraper to remove it. The handle makes reaching high spots a breeze, and the scraper won't gouge the wall unless you get too aggressive.

TAKE THE WORRY OUT OF CHOOSING TILE

Deciding on tile colors and layouts for a whole room on the basis of a few samples can be a little scary since you'll have to live with the results for years. To get a better sense of what a wall or floor will look like before you buy anything, make color copies of the samples and tape them in place. Then live with the look for a week.

PIPE INSULATION

SCREWS AND NAILS RIGHT AT HAND

Instead of strapping on a big tool pouch just to carry a few fasteners, fit a piece of pipe insulation on your wrist. Then poke your fasteners into it. This is really handy for working on the roof or in a crawl space, where a tool pouch would get in the way or slow you down.

HandyHints

MASKING TAPE

SCREW GRIPPER

Here's a classic hint we love. If you need a simple way to get a screw started in a hard-to-reach place, poke the screw through a piece of masking tape with the sticky side of the tape toward the head. Place the tip of the screwdriver in the slot and fold the tape up onto the shaft. Once you start the screw, pull the screwdriver loose and remove the tape.

HINGE LEAF

HINGE BARREL

FINISH SIX SIDES OF A DOOR AT ONCE

Staining or sealing a door takes a while if you set it on sawhorses to do one side, then let it dry before flipping it over to do the other. Here's how to cut the drying time in half. Hang two chains from the open joists in your garage and put an S-hook on each of the ends. Hang the door by sliding the hooks through the door's hinge leaf or barrels. Then you can stain the entire door at one time.

SIMPLE CARPET PROTECTORS

To prevent heavy furniture like a filing cabinet or grandfather clock from leaving big dents in new carpet, cut leftover carpeting into squares the same size as the furniture. Place the squares on top of the carpet and put the furniture on top of them. The carpet squares blend right in with the carpet and keep the wall-to-wall carpet dent-free.

CARPET SQUARE

STAY-PUT SOAP DISH

Here's a tip for installing a ceramic soap dish on a tiled wall. Put a couple of strips of double-face foam tape on the back of the soap dish. Align the dish and press it against the tile backer board. Then apply silicone caulk around the edges. The foam tape will hold the dish in place until the caulk cures. This works better than putting tape across the front and prevents the dish from sagging while the caulk cures.

TILE BACKER BOARD

DOUBLE-FACE FOAM TAPE

InstantProject

INDOOR
FOUNTAIN

Create this indoor water fountain using a planter, rocks and a small pond pump for under $100.

Plug the drain hole of a large glazed ceramic or resin planter with plumber's epoxy putty. After it cures, fill the planter with water for a day or two to confirm that it won't leak. Place the planter exactly where you want it before adding the rocks and water. It'll be very heavy once it's done.

Stack bricks or stones around and above a small pond pump (about 40 gph) to about two-thirds the depth of the vessel. Then cut the water line to length and add a restrictor valve. We used a 3/8-in. PEX valve (clamp it if the hose comes loose under pressure). Or choose a "pinch"-type valve, found with pond accessories at home centers. You can change the look and sound of the water fountain by tinkering with the water flow rate and the shape, size and arrangement of your stones. That's the fun part!

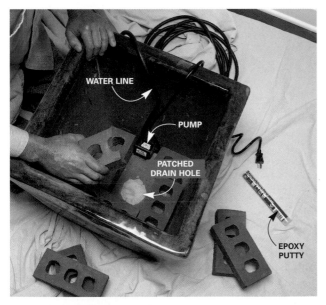

1 Place the pump in the bottom of the container with the tubing attached and the switch on. Fill around and above it with bricks or stones.

2 Create a ledge with a flat stone for a mini waterfall. Adjust the flow with the valve and orient the water line until you achieve a pleasing result. Hide the line with more stones.

A **BETTER BATH**
FOR YOUR BUCK

Get a new look and stay on budget

by **Brett Martin**

If you plan your design, shop smart and invest some sweat equity, you can have a $25,000 bathroom remodel for a fraction of the price. Don't believe us? Well, we updated this bathroom with new wall and floor tile, a new vanity and top, and new plumbing fixtures. Then we framed the mirror and added glass shelves above the toilet—all for less than $3,000 (see Buyer's Guide, p. 37). And we did it all with materials purchased at home centers. For this story, we worked with kitchen and bath designer extraordinaire Lori Jo Krengel. The following pages feature Lori Jo's advice for dramatic bathroom improvements that are easy on the wallet.

Tips from an expert designer

Lori Jo Krengel is a Certified Master Kitchen and Bath Designer and the president of Kitchens by Krengel, Inc., an award-winning design firm in St. Paul. Lori Jo combines style and function to create bathrooms that meet specific budgets. She recommends consulting a designer before remodeling a bathroom to avoid common mistakes. Expect to pay $100 to $125 for a one-hour meeting.

Use extended light fixtures over medicine cabinets

Light fixtures that sit close to the wall won't cast adequate light over a medicine cabinet. Installing a light fixture with a long neck is an easy solution. Buy one that places the light bulb above and in front of the mirror.

Cost: $20 and up

Check out granite vanity tops

Granite tops used to be for big-buck bathrooms only. But now you can get one for less than $200 at home centers, including an attached, under-mounted sink. (The top shown cost $465.)

If you need a vanity for a corner, buy one with a backsplash along the back and one side to protect the walls from water spills. Mount the faucet in the vanity top before setting the top in place. Then you won't have to lie on your back inside the vanity and reach up under the faucet.

Cost: $180 and up for granite

"Light fixtures, plumbing fixtures and hardware don't have to match, but they should have complementary finishes and styles."

Frame the mirror and side-light it

A tile or wood frame adds style to a plain mirror. Any tile will work (we used a mosaic glass tile). Apply the tile to the wall using mastic adhesive. Tape off the mirror and use unsanded grout to avoid scratching the mirror.

You can also buy a wood mirror frame at a framing store, or buy wood molding with a rabbet cut into the back and build your own frame. Paint or stain the frame before installing it. A third option is the mirror framing system from Moen (see p. 40).

"A frame gives the mirror a strong element of design and really dresses up the room," Lori Jo says.

Sconces placed on both sides of a mirror will give you better illumination than overhead lights. Light cast from opposite sides eliminates shadows on

your face. And two lights reflected in the mirror can brighten the entire room.

"New lights give you quick appeal and add a lot of ambience to the space," Lori Jo says.

Cost: $30 and up for mosaic tile; $20 for wood frames you make yourself; $26 and up for two sconces

Install a curved curtain rod

Besides giving the bathroom a sleek look with its gentle radius, a curved curtain rod gives you more elbow room in the shower. You can use your current shower curtain, or buy a new curtain and new rings ($10 and up) in the same finish as the curtain rod to complete the new look.

"Installing a shower rod instead of glass doors is a great way to save money," Lori Jo says. "If you really want doors, you can always add them later when you have the budget."

Cost: $40 and up, depending on the finish

"Choose your vanity first, then the top. Next, choose your flooring and any tile. Then pick your plumbing fixtures and finally your wall paint. It's easier to match paint to the vanity and tile than the other way around."

Crown the room

Crown molding makes a big impact in bathrooms. And since bathrooms are small, you can add a lot of elegance for $50 to $100. For painted crown, urethane is a good choice because unlike wood, it won't expand and contract with changes in humidity. Urethane molding is lightweight and easy to install with adhesive caulk and nails. Available at home centers, 8-ft. sections are $3 to $15 less expensive than wood the same length.

If you want to use wood, make sure the bathroom is well ventilated. Also seal the back side with a wood conditioner ($6 a pint) if you're staining the wood, or a primer if you're painting it. Sealing the back side reduces warping.

Cost: $13.50 and up per 8-ft. section of urethane molding

Add a shower shelf

Home centers and tile stores sell shelves that you adhere to tile walls with all-purpose construction adhesive (Loctite Power Grab is one brand; $8 for 6.7 ozs.). Apply adhesive to the shelf back, tape the shelf in place and then let the adhesive set for 24 hours. This only works for tile walls, not fiberglass surrounds.

Or buy shelving that sticks with suction cups or tension bars. Prices start at $9 at discount stores.

Cost: $15 and up per tile shelf

Give old faucets a new look

New plumbing fixtures give the shower a fast and easy face-lift. Use a shower trim kit when you replace your single-handle shower faucet. These remodeling kits have all the necessary parts——a new handle and wall plate—to update the look of your faucet while leaving the old valve in place. That means no hassling with any in-the-wall plumbing. Make sure to buy the same brand as your existing faucet. Some models are available at home centers. If you don't see your brand, contact your faucet manufacturer to find out where to buy one.

Trim kits are available for single-handle faucets only. To convert from a two-handle faucet to a one-handle, install a shower cover plate (also called a "remodeling" cover plate; $18 and up). The wide plate covers the handle openings so you don't have to install any tile to patch the hole.

Cost: $25 and up

Measure your vanity footprint

When bathrooms are built, vanities are installed before the flooring. That means your flooring ends at your vanity. If you're replacing the vanity, buy one that's the same length and width as your existing vanity (or larger). Otherwise, you'll end up with gaps between the vanity and the flooring. Or replace the flooring too. Then you can install a new vanity (any size!) and butt the flooring against it.

"Vanities take a beating from water spills, bathroom humidity and everyday use, so new cabinetry can make a dramatic improvement," Lori Jo says.

Cost: $100 and up.

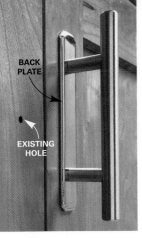

BACK PLATE

EXISTING HOLE

Install hardware from this century

If you're keeping your vanity, give it a subtle update with new handles. Replace any visible hinges too. To change from knobs to handles, or vice versa, install back plates under the hardware to cover the existing holes. Back plates start at $3 each. Home centers carry a limited selection, but you can special-order them or buy them online (topknobsusa.com is one source).

"Back plates cover up the sins of hardware past," Lori Jo says.

Cost: $1 and up for knobs; $4 and up for handles

Test a paint color

A new coat of paint can make a world of difference by brightening up the room or adding color. Stick with white for the ceiling—it makes the room appear bigger. Satin and eggshell finishes are good choices for bathrooms. They're easy to clean and don't show every imperfection in the wall.

Paint stores and home centers sell paint samples for about $4, so you can test out a color before painting your entire bathroom. A test sample lets you see the true color on your walls so you won't have to guess.

Toss the bar—hook your towels instead!

Installing hooks instead of towel bars helps you keep your bathroom organized. That's because they're super simple to use, especially for kids, so the towels don't end up on the floor. Plus, you can fit in several hooks—and hang more towels—in the same space a towel bar would take. Don't worry; your towels will still get dry. The hooks are called utility hooks or robe hooks in home centers.

Cost: $1.20 and up per hook

Mix in mosaic

Mosaic tile accents give shower surrounds a custom look while letting you use mostly inexpensive tile. Plan the layout on paper first to identify any design problems.

Shopping around for tile can save you a fortune. We bought this gray/blue tile on clearance for 80¢ per tile and mixed in mosaic glass tile ($10 per sheet). ⌂

"Find colors you like to punch up the bathroom, then add those colors with new dispensers and new towels. Those things can make a huge difference."

Splurge on the faucet

The sink faucet is one item it's OK to splurge on (it's even recommended!). You want your faucet to last and look good. One way to judge faucet quality is by weight. Heavier ones are better—they're solid metal. For optimal durability, buy a fixture that uses a ceramic disc valve (it'll say so on the packaging) instead of rubber washers (the washers wear out). And be sure to buy a faucet that fits the hole pattern in your sink.

"The faucet is the most frequently used thing in the house, but it's where people don't want to spend money. When you think about it, it's where you should spend money," Lori Jo says. "Buy a quality faucet and look for a lifetime warranty."

Cost: $90 and up for a quality faucet

Buyer's Guide

Here's what we used:

Floor and wall tile: Lowe's. Florence Gazebo porcelain tile, $16 for a box of 18. Note: This was a clearance item. Similar tile is available at home centers and tile stores.

Mosaic tile: $10 per sheet at Home Depot. No longer available, but similar tile is available at tile stores and theglassmosaicoutlet.com.

Vanity: Home Depot. Pegasus Exhibit. Model No. TRIA4822D. $489.

Vanity top: Home Depot. Pegasus Blue Pearl Granite Top with white bowl. Model No. 49905. $465.

Sink faucet: Price Pfister Falsetto 8-in. double-handle, hi-arc faucet in brushed nickel. Model No. 049FLKK at Home Depot. $128.

Shower faucet: Price Pfister Sedona single-handle tub and shower faucet in brushed nickel. Model No. 808LT0K at Home Depot. $144.

Glass shelves: Home Depot. Décor Bathware Greenwich Satin Nickel Glass Shelf. Model No. 74528SN. $40 each.

New Tools & Gear

GREAT VALUE COMBO KIT

Craftsman's NEXTEC combo kit offers a 3/8-in. drill/driver, a multi-saw and an LED work light for only $100. The kit comes with two 12-volt lithium-ion batteries (which charge in 30 minutes) and a charger.

My favorite tool in the bunch is the cleverly designed multi-saw, which functions as a jigsaw and a mini reciprocating saw for tight spaces. It uses T- and U-shank saw blades (not standard recip saw blades). An electric brake quickly stops the blade when you release the trigger. Buy the kit (model No. 11890) at Sears stores or sears.com.

Craftsman, craftsman.com

LOW-TECH STUD FINDER

The company (Biary Innovation) calls it "magic." We call it low tech. Or to be precise, magnets. Two round magnets fit inside the Magic Stud Finder Plus, then as you sweep the holder over the wall, the magnets stick to drywall screws or nail heads. It's brain-dead simple. When you hear a clicking noise, you pull away the holder, leaving magnets in place to mark the stud.

There are no electronics to read or batteries to replace—ever. But at $20, the stud finder costs as much as some high-tech electronic versions. So it's no bargain, but it might appeal to anyone who hates electronic gadgets. The Magic Stud Finder comes with three magnets. A four-pack of additional magnets costs $13. Buy the stud finder online from the company.

Biary Innovation, (877) 582-7961. magicstudfinder.com

A COMPACT DRILL DRIVER WITH A CHUCK

The problem with most compact drivers is that they only have hexagonal sockets at the end, with no chuck. That means they'll only accept screw drives, tips or drill bits that have matching hex shafts. Ridgid's drill driver gives you something more. It has a chuck, so you can use conventional drill bits as well as screw drive tips. A compact design means the driver can slip right into your tool belt. A small but powerful 12-volt lithium-ion battery packs a punch while keeping the tool lightweight. And here's another reason to buy it—Ridgid offers free parts, free service and free batteries for the life of the tool (just be sure to fill out the paperwork and send it in!).

At $100, the drill driver costs about the same as high-end drivers that don't have chucks. Buy the Ridgid driver at Home Depot.

Ridgid, (800) 474-3443. ridgid.com

1 BOX WRENCH, 4 SIZES

Take a close look at the Craftsman 4-in-One wrenches and you'll notice that there are actually two fastener sizes in each box end. Most ratcheting wrenches have only one in each end. Reversing levers allow for quick reverses for the 12-point hex openings. Two wrenches are available in metric sizes and two in standard sizes. The metric wrenches fit heads between 8 mm and 19 mm. The

SAE models handle heads from 5/16 in. to 3/4 in. Each two-piece set costs $30. Buy them at Sears stores and sears.com.

Craftsman, craftsman.com

REVERSING LEVER

18 MM
19 MM

PRECISION CIRCULAR SAW

Table saws aren't always the easiest solution for cutting large sheets of plywood or MDF, especially if you're crosscutting. For long, clean, perfect cuts in sheet goods, Makita's new 6-1/2-in. plunge circular saw (model No. SP6000K) has you covered. Finish carpenters are buying it to avoid hauling around a table saw (and it gives you a much cleaner edge than a table saw). It's ideal for specialized tasks like cutting off door bottoms. And if you don't have space for a table saw, this tool is the perfect alternative. The dust collection system captures most of the dust for a cleaner shop.

Clamp the rail to the material using the special clamps that fit in a track on the underside of the

CLAMPS

Makita's plunge saw slides along the rail to give you a crisp cut with minimal tear-out. A plunge release lever makes plunge cutting easier.

rail. Although this type of saw has been available for years, Makita offers a more affordable version. The saw costs $345. A 54-in. rail costs $80, a 117-in. rail $200. That's about what you'd pay for a decent portable table saw, but this tool is a better choice for some DIYers. Find retailers on the company's Web site.

Makita, (800) 462-5482. makitatools.com

LOW-COST TOOL LIGHTS

When you have to work in dark recesses, built-in lights on power drills can light your way. If your drill isn't equipped with lights, check out the Magnetic Tool and Flash Light ($9 at rockler.com; item No. 22115). Slide it over a screw drive shaft or drill bit, or stick it to a metal surface. Rotate the yellow ring for an incredibly bright light from three LEDs. The downside: It can be tricky to peer around the disk to line up the driver and the screw head.

The three 1.5-volt batteries last about 5-1/2 hours. You can replace them for a $5 shipping fee at the Web site below.

ufo-toollight.com, e-mail to info@ufo-toollight.com

New Tools&Gear

EASY WAY TO PULL ANY NAIL

We put the Nail Jack ($30) through its paces while demolishing old sets in our studio. Our set builder—who usually gives a thumbs down to any new products I give him to test—really liked this one. The nail puller can pull any size nail or staple, even if the nail head gets popped off. The head is rounded (like nippers), so the tool can roll forward or backward to pull the nail. It doesn't take long to learn how to use it efficiently.

A gripping head between the jaws grabs the nail's shank, so you don't need to pry against the nail head. A hammer tap behind the tool head lets you whack the tip of the jaws under staples or buried nail heads to pull them out. Our only complaint is that the wide handles require both hands to get started. If you only have to pull a few nails occasionally, this tool isn't for you. But if you're doing serious demo work, go for it.

Nail Jack, (877) 785-5624. nailjack.com

30-MINUTE MIRROR MAKEOVER

Framing a mirror is a fast, simple way to add flair to a dull bathroom. And Moen's new Mirrorscapes lets you add a frame in about 30 minutes—without taking the mirror off the wall or cutting a single miter. The system comes with brackets that attach to the mirror and hold the corner pieces in place. Straight pieces of frame (which you cut to length; best done on a miter saw) fit between the corners and are also attached with brackets (a short video on the company's Web site shows the installation process).

A wide variety of metallic and wood frames are available. You can also paint the frame to match your bathroom. To order, simply enter your mirror's dimensions and pick the frame you want on the company's Web site. Prices start at about $130 to frame a 24 x 36-in. mirror.

Moen, (800) 289-6636. buymirrorscapes.com

BRAD NAILER COMBOS

Are you still nailing by hand? Maybe it's time you treated yourself to a compressor/brad nailer combo kit. Brad guns drastically reduce the time spent assembling projects—we usually recommend them in at least one or two stories per issue. Now that you can buy an air compressor, hose and brad gun for less than $200, it's time to add these crucial tools to your arsenal—especially since buying a combo kit saves you a few bucks over buying the pieces individually.

The 18-gauge guns typically shoot 5/8-in. to 2-in. nails to handle a range of projects, and the compressors are lightweight and easy to carry. It's one of those tools that makes you wonder how you ever got along without one. Look for the kits at home centers and hardware stores.

Porter-Cable, (888) 848-5175. deltaportercable.com

Senco, (800) 543-4596. senco.com

Bostitch, (800) 556-6696. bostitch.com

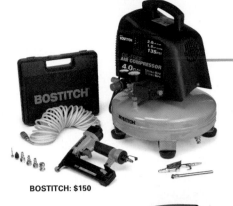

BOSTITCH: $150

PORTER-CABLE: $180

SENCO: $220

RX FOR DULL DRILL BITS

The Drill Doctor drill bit sharpener means never having to buy new bits again. A few years ago, I bought myself one—and I haven't bought a bit since (except to replace the ones I've snapped off!). Every few months, I grab my jar of dull bits and plug in the Drill Doctor. In about 15 minutes, those old bits are as good as new—better, actually, because I can grind a sharp "split point" on the tip. Split points, which are common on more expensive bits, dig into wood faster and wander less on metal. In addition to standard twist bits, the Drill Doctor sharpens masonry bits.

Drill Doctor models start at about $80, but you have to spend about $110 to get a version that grinds split points. Before you buy, go to drilldoctor.com to compare features, locate retailers and watch the online videos showing how Drill Doctor works. Drill Doctor is available at most home centers and many hardware stores.

Professional Tool Manufacturing, (800) 597-6170. drilldoctor.com

ONE HANDLE, 10 OPTIONS

Screwdrivers with interchangeable bits have been around for ages, but Lee Valley added a new twist with its saw and screwdriver handle (model no. 88K11.20). The handle accepts 6-in. reciprocating saw blades (included), which are great for cutting holes in drywall or in tight spots. The handle, which locks in place for in-line use or at a 60-degree angle, also accepts a 4-in.-long hex extension that holds driver bits (extension and bits also included). It's a handy tool for around-the-house projects and inexpensive, too: $14.50 on the Lee Valley Web site.

Lee Valley & Veritas, (800) 267-8735. leevalley.com

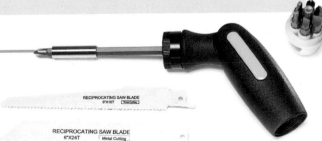

RECIPROCATING SAW BLADE 6"X10T

RECIPROCATING SAW BLADE 6"X24T Metal Cutting

BEAM & PANEL CEILING

A quick, inexpensive way to transform a room—and a beautiful cover-up for damaged ceilings

by **Travis Larson**

Paneling a ceiling is a great way to add character to a plain room. And if the existing ceiling is cracked or water-stained and in need of a makeover, all the better. Covering it with panels and beams is more elegant and less expensive than hiring a pro to restore a damaged ceiling to its original condition.

A paneled ceiling like this normally calls for expensive tools and lots of carpentry skill, but we designed this project to be DIY-friendly. It's made easy by a homemade circular saw ripping jig, the installation of a simple 2x4 framework and miter-free joinery (**Figure A**). The visible finished material over the framework is MDF. It's inexpensive ($30 per sheet), readily available at home centers, and smooth and easy to work with. However, cutting, sanding and routing MDF is extremely dusty, so do all your power tool work outside or at least in the garage with the overhead door open, and be sure to wear a dust mask.

While the ease of construction is a big plus, the real

Three shortcuts make it DIY-friendly

1. Miter-free joints: There is no such thing as a miter on this project. Every end joint is a straight-forward square cut. Just get the length right, cut at 90 degrees on your miter saw, and all the joints will look like a million bucks.

2. Chamfered edges: Small 45-degree chamfers routed on the edges of all the exposed trim hide all but the worst imperfections.

3. Overhangs: The vertical side trim overhangs the ceiling panels to hide any sloppy cuts. And the caps overhang the side trim, so small gaps there will be hidden as well.

beauty of this project is its low cost. The materials for this 12 x 12-ft. ceiling cost less than $350, including the paint.

Which ceilings are candidates?

Our system is ideal for dressing up any ceiling whether it's damaged or perfect, textured or flat, drywall or plaster. If your ceiling is flat and in good shape, you can omit the MDF panels and simply paint the ceiling and apply the grid work and trim right over the existing material. But keep in mind that you'll have to make the side trim strips 1/2 in. wider to account for the missing panel thicknesses.

The nine-panel pattern works for rooms up to 13 ft. wide and 33 ft. long. The use of materials is efficient and the shape of the panel will automatically be proportional to the shape of the room. A square room will have square panels; a rectangular room will have rectangular panels.

Laying out the grid

The first step in laying out the grid work is to chalk lines around the perimeter of the room 4-1/2 in. away from the walls. That will allow the full 5-1/2-in. cap to fit against the wall and match the rest of the finished trim. Then measure the length and width of the space inside. It's up to you how many panels to use and how big to make them. Most average-size rooms work well with nine panels. In other words, divide both room dimensions by three. You'll only be able to have perfect square panels if the room is square. Otherwise, you'll have rectangles, which is fine—they'll look great as long as they're a consistent size. And you can *always* make the panels exactly the same size. Make them as large or as small as you wish, as long as they're under 4 ft. wide and 8 ft. long, as much as the sheets will allow.

Once you figure out the panel sizes, snap the grid layout on the ceiling (Photo 1). To avoid some confusing math (accounting for the width of the 2x4 grid), just snap center lines to lay out the grid and then snap lines 1-3/4 in. on both sides to mark the outsides of the 2x4s. It's a good idea to snap lines marking all the ceiling joists at this point so you'll know where to put the fasteners for the grid and ceiling panels.

Attach the grid framing

Start by screwing on the uppermost layer of 2x4s oriented perpendicular to the ceiling joists (Photo 2) with 3-in. screws. That way you'll have great support. Toe-screw the ends through the drywall into the wall top plates. Next, screw the 2x4s in the opposite direction with two screws at each intersection (Photo 3). Lastly, add a second layer of short 2x4s over the 2x4s against the ceiling. That will give you a continuous flat surface for the caps and hubs (Photo 4 and Figure A).

Figure A: Ceiling cross section

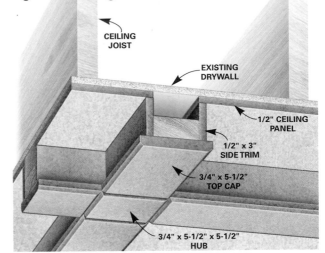

CEILING JOIST

EXISTING DRYWALL

1/2" CEILING PANEL

1/2" x 3" SIDE TRIM

3/4" x 5-1/2" TOP CAP

3/4" x 5-1/2" x 5-1/2" HUB

STAINS FROM BATHROOM DISASTER

1 Mark out the beam pattern with chalk lines. Then make it easy on yourself by marking the joists with a different color chalk.

JOIST DIRECTION

2 Screw 2x4s to the ceiling perpendicular to the joist direction with a couple of 3-in. screws into each joist.

3 Screw the overlapping 2x4s to the first ones at each intersection. Fill the spaces between the lower 2x4s to complete the grid work. Space screws every 16 in.

SECOND 2x4 LAYER

1/2" CEILING PANEL

2-1/4" BRADS

SUPPORT CRUTCH

4 Cut the panels to size, prime them and then nail them through the drywall into the joists.

FENCE

3/4" STOP

40-TOOTH BLADE

TOP CAP

5 Rip the top cap trim using a ripping jig. The simple three-part jig gives you straight cuts and perfect widths.

TAPE UNDER TRIM

CEILING PANEL

2" BRADS

SIDE TRIM

6 Nail the side trim to the framing. Paint and mask the panels with painter's tape first to avoid fuss when you paint the trim.

Cut and install the panels

Cut the panels 1/2 in. shorter than the grid openings to make them easy to slip into place. Cut them to width first and set aside the 8-ft.-long waste pieces to use for trim caps and hubs. Then cut them to length. You can just snap chalk lines and cut the panels "freehand" since the side trim pieces will hide imperfections. Then roll on a stain-blocking primer (KILZ and BIN are two brands) with a 3/8-in.-nap roller sleeve. If you're working alone, make yourself a support crutch (**Photo 4**) to hold the panels tight against the ceiling while you nail them into each floor joist with 2-1/2-in. nails spaced every 8 in.

Fill the nail holes with wood filler. Sand down any excess filler and surface imperfections and spot-prime those areas. Then roll on two coats of latex paint.

Make a trim cutting jig

MDF panels are heavy—90 lbs. for a 3/4-in. sheet! So even if you have a table saw, you're better off cutting side trim and caps with a ripping jig (**Photos 5** and **9**) and a circular saw.

Here's how to make a jig that will accurately cut the trim pieces you need for the ceiling:
1. Rip an 8-ft.-long, 3-in.-wide

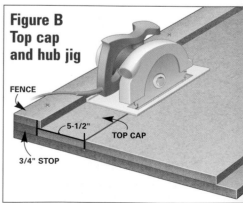

Figure B
Top cap and hub jig

FENCE

5-1/2"

TOP CAP

3/4" STOP

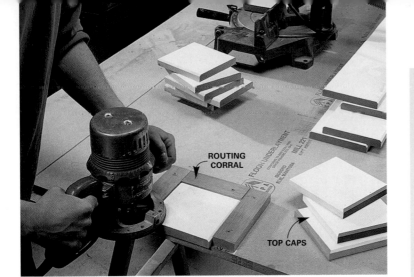

ROUTING CORRAL

TOP CAPS

7 Cut the hubs to length, then rout the edges using a "corral" tacked to your workbench to safely hold the small pieces in place.

HUB

8 Center and nail the hubs at each intersection. Don't forget to prime the freshly routed edges.

TOP CAP

45° CHAMFER BIT

9 Use the top cap ripping jig to hold the caps in place while you rout the edges. Cut them to length and nail them to the grid with 2-in. brads.

You've got options

If you love the natural look, you can panel your ceiling with any type of wood and still use the techniques we show. Use painted MDF for the panels and solid natural wood for the beams, or go all out and use matching veneered plywood for the panels. To save money when you use this technique, rip plywood for the side trim pieces. That'll look fine since the plywood edges will be hidden. You can also use any type of wallpaper or covering on the panels, or on the existing ceiling drywall if it's in good shape.

WALLPAPER OVER DRYWALL

MDF

PAINTED MDF

CHERRY

Figure C
Side trim jig

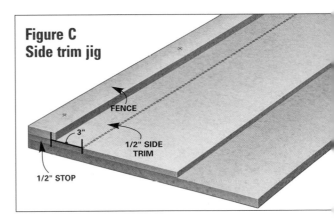

FENCE

3"

1/2" SIDE TRIM

1/2" STOP

10 Patch the nail holes, lightly sand, spot-prime and then paint the grid-work trim.

SCORED

11 After you paint the trim, slice through the tape at the inside corners and peel it away.

"fence" for a top cap ripping jig (**Figure B**).

2. Rip one 2-1/2-in.-wide "stop" out of 1/2-in. material for ripping the trim strips for the side trim (**Figure C**) and a 3/4-in.-thick stop for ripping the caps and hubs. Rip the stop and fence from the edges of new sheets, and always face the factory edges toward the saw for straight, true guide surfaces.

3. Screw each stop to the jig base with countersunk 1-1/4-in. screws spaced every 12 in., and then screw the fence to each stop wherever it needs to be to match the width you're ripping.

The key to both jig setups is the distance from the left side of your circular saw's base to the edge of the saw blade (**Figure B**). That distance will determine fence placement.

You'll have to set up the ripping jig twice with two different fence locations and the stop that matches the thickness of the material you're cutting (1/2-in.-thick side trim or 3/4-in.-thick caps and hubs). The base of the jig is the same for both jig setups—a 1/2-in. or 3/4-in. sheet of any flat sheet good. Or use one of the MDF sheets and make panels with it later. Hubs are cut from the 5-1/2-in. cap strips, so while you still have the jig set up, make sure you rip enough stock for those, too.

Cut, paint and install the hubs and caps

Figure out roughly how long the caps will be and cut and rout the hubs from the extra material. Sand off any saw

blade marks on the edges of the cap stock and rout those edges (**Photos 7 and 9**). Prime the pieces. Cut the side trim pieces to length and nail them to the grid sides. Then nail on the hubs. Cut each top cap to length. Chamfer the ends and nail each into place. ⌂

Improve your lighting

Since you're covering the drywall with panels, this is a great time to add or move ceiling light fixtures. If you have a floor above, just cut channels in the drywall and drill holes through the middle of joists, or staple the cables on the sides of joists to get the cables to the new electrical boxes or recessed light canisters. If you have an attic above, you'll have to crawl up there to run the cables. Just remember that when you mount the new boxes, they should be flush with the finished MDF surface. You'll need to add 1/2-in.-deep plaster rings to existing boxes before you install the finished ceiling.

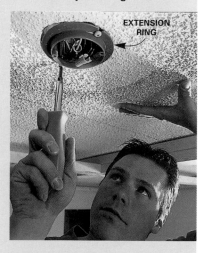

EXTENSION RING

Do's&Don'ts

TIPS FOR **TIGHT MITERS**

It's not hard to cut pretty good miters. But why settle for "pretty good" when you can create perfect miters with just a bit more effort? First you'll need a power miter saw fitted with a sharp carbide blade. Choose a blade with 40 or more teeth for the cleanest cut. After that it's just a matter of learning a few techniques for measuring and cutting miters so they fit perfectly. We'll show quick and easy ways to mark, cut and tweak your miters for furniture-quality joints.

Mark, don't measure

Whenever possible, hold your trim in place and mark where the miter cut should be. It's quicker and more accurate than measuring, and you'll avoid measuring mistakes. A sharp pencil works fine for marking window and door moldings where the reveal (a thin strip of exposed jamb; **see photo**) allows you a bit of lee-way. But for super-accurate marks where there's no margin for error, such as for baseboards and crown moldings that go around outside corners, use a sharp utility knife.

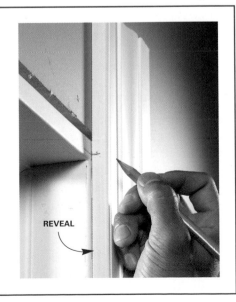

REVEAL

Do's&Don'ts

Test the fit, then fine-tune the miters

Start by cutting your moldings a little long so you'll have material to trim off if the fit is bad. Then hold the miter joint together, making sure the trim pieces are held parallel to the door or window jambs, and check the fit. If you're lucky, the miter will fit perfectly and you can trim a bit using the same miter saw setting. If the miters have gaps, like the ones in the photo, adjust the miter saw slightly and recut the miters. Then check the fit again. You may have to repeat this process several times.

Adjust the angle of the cut slightly to remove a fraction of an inch from the part of the miter that's touching. Adjustments of 1/2 degree or less are usually all that's needed.

44-1/2 DEGREES

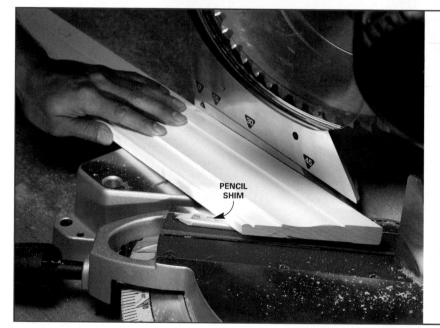

PENCIL SHIM

Use a shim to cut a back bevel

Cut a back bevel on miter joints that are open in front but touching at the back. To create a back-beveled cut on a standard miter saw, place a pencil under the molding. If you have a compound miter box, tilt the blade a degree or two to cut the back bevel.

OPEN MITER

Smash protruding drywall

Occasionally window and door jambs end up slightly recessed, which causes trouble when it comes time to install trim. Correct minor level differences by either bashing in or cutting out the drywall along the edge of the jamb. But be careful to avoid going beyond what will be covered by the trim. If the level difference is greater than about 3/16-in., nail thin strips of wood, called jamb extensions, to the jamb to bring it flush to the wall surface.

Use a brad gun for the best results

It's hard to beat a nail gun for perfect miters, especially if you're not skilled with a hammer. Trim nail guns allow you to hold the moldings in perfect alignment while you pin them in place. If you can afford only one trim gun, buy one that shoots thin 18-gauge nails up to 2 in. long. Fifteen- and 16-gauge nailers are good where more strength is needed, such as for nailing jambs, but the thicker brads make larger, more conspicuous holes and can crack thin moldings. Use shorter brads to nail the molding to the jamb, and long brads along the outside edges.

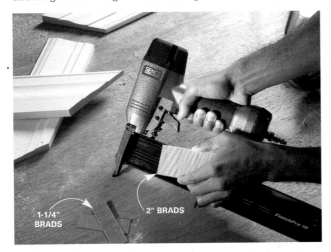

1-1/4" BRADS 2" BRADS

CRACKED MOLDING

Don't nail too close to ends or edges

Even with an 18-gauge trim nailer, you can split the molding if you're not careful. Avoid nailing less than 3/4 in. from the end of a trim piece or less than 1/4 in. from the edge.

Pin the miter before nailing the outside

In a perfect world, you could nail the trim flat to the wall and the miter would look great. But in reality, minor variations in level between the jamb and the wall often interfere. To solve this problem, start by pinning the inside edge of the trim, making sure the miter joint is pressed tight together. Then, while the miter is still tight, drive a pair of brads through the outside corners at opposite angles to pin it. To deal with gaps between the molding and the wall, see the tip at right.

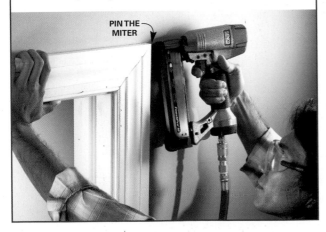

PIN THE MITER

THIN SHIM

Shim behind the miter

If there's a slight gap between the molding and the wall, don't press the trim tight to the wall and nail it; the miter joint might open up. Instead, slip a thin shim between the molding and the wall. Then nail the outside edge of the trim. If the gap and shim are visible, fill the crack with caulk before painting.

REMOVING **WALLPAPER**

It's an ugly job. We can't make it pretty, but we can make it easier.

by **Elisa Bernick**

I'm not going to sugarcoat it. Removing wallpaper is a messy, time-consuming and tedious job. I wish I could tell you there's a nifty new product that will make the whole thing easy. But there isn't. And if you don't know what you're doing or you start to get frustrated, you can damage your walls or stop before the job is done. The tips in this article won't make the job fun. But they will help you do it more efficiently, without damaging your walls. They'll also show you how to get a wall perfectly clean, ready for a fresh coat of paint or new wallpaper.

Do yourself a favor and take a full weekend to do the job right. Attack the messy and hard stuff (Steps 1–5) on day one and use the second day to prep the walls for paint or new wallpaper.

50

Protect the floor and woodwork

Everything is going to get wet and sticky, so carefully protect the floor, furniture and woodwork. Take everything off the walls, including vents, outlet covers and switch plates, and mask the openings with plastic and tape. Turn off the electricity to the room at the service panel and use high-quality work lamps on extension cords to light your work area. If possible, remove the furniture completely. If not, move it to the center of the room and cover it with plastic.

Glue and water are going to run down the walls, so you want to protect the floors and prevent the water from running behind molding, baseboards and chair rails. Do this by creating a plastic "gutter" to catch it. Top the plastic gutter with more plastic and then cover that with towels. Replace them with dry towels as necessary.

Pull off the face

Do this step without using any water. The point is to remove the top layer of paper and leave the backing on the wall. That way, the backing will easily soak

Take the whole weekend—do the job right.

up water, making the rest of the job faster and easier. Use a putty knife to get the edge of the paper started, if necessary, and pull the paper back slowly at a 45-degree angle, applying moderate pressure. You can sometimes pull down entire sheets of newer wallpapers with this technique. But the longer the paper has been up, the more likely it is to come off in smaller pieces (or not at all). If you just can't remove the facing at all, use a scoring tool before moving on to the next step (see "Tough Tools for Tough Situations," p. 53).

Apply hot water

Apply the hottest water you can tolerate (wear gloves!) to the wallpaper backing and the remaining facing to soften them and the adhesive underneath. The hard part is doing this without damaging the wall surface. Plaster walls can take a lot of hot water without a problem. But drywall has a paper surface that can be damaged by prolonged contact with water. It's OK to moisten drywall, but don't keep it

MASK OUTLETS

TOWELS

Step 1: Keep the floor and trim dry
Tape plastic to the baseboard, allowing it to overlap the floor about 2 ft. Press hard on the tape to create a watertight seal. Cover the draped plastic with more plastic and top that with towels to absorb the water as it runs down the walls.

WALLPAPER FACING

WALLPAPER BACKING

Step 2: Tear off the facing
Start at a corner near the ceiling or under a switch plate, where the paper tends to be loose. Use a putty knife to lift the edges of the facing, then pull the facing off the wall using steady, even pressure.

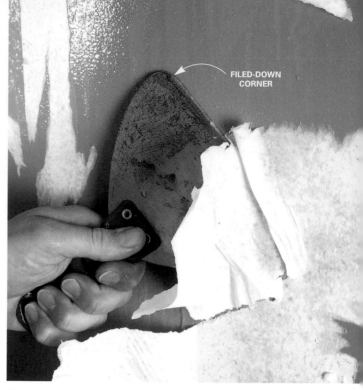

FILED-DOWN CORNER

Step 3: Soak backing to soften the paste

Apply water to the backing using a sponge or floor mop. This lets you control the amount of water you're applying each time. Let the backing absorb the water for up to 15 minutes. You may have to apply water several times to soften the paste.

Step 4: Scrape off the backing

Use a metal spatula or putty knife with a flexible blade and rounded corners to scrape the backing off the wall. If you don't have a rounded putty knife, file the corners. Don't be too aggressive with the scraper or you'll gouge the wall.

wet for longer than 15 minutes at a time. Work in small sections so the backing doesn't dry out before you have a chance to remove it.

Apply the water using a sponge (or a floor mop for the high spots). Let the backing absorb the water until it starts to pull away from the wall. When the backing softens (use your fingernail or a scraper to check), you're ready for the next step.

Scrape off the backing

Use an old, *very* flexible metal spatula or putty knife with *rounded* corners to scrape the backing and remaining facing off the wall. Don't use the spatula too aggressively—the drywall might be soft in spots and scraping too hard can easily gouge it. Using a flexible blade is key because it won't dig into the drywall as much. Plastic spatulas or scrapers don't work—they're too thick to get underneath the backing.

Remove every speck of paste. Really.

This is the most important step, but the one that typically gets short shrift. There's going to be a lot of paste on the wall once the backing is gone, and it's going to take a lot of effort to get it all off. Scrape off as much of the glue with a putty knife as you can. Then wash the walls thoroughly with a sponge and water.

OK. This is the moment when most people drop the

ball. You're tired, the wall looks clean and you just want to be done. So the temptation is to call it a (very long) night and "not see" the paste that's still there. Paste has a dark sheen to it and the wall will still feel sticky. Spray a light mist of water on the "clean" wall. Hold your work light parallel to the wall and you'll see the paste that remains. If you don't get it all off, when you paint the wall, the paint will eventually

Remove every bit of paste. Really.

flake and crackle. Wallpaper that's applied over it will bubble or fail to stick properly.

Use a gel stripper (see "Tough Tools for Tough Situations," p. 53) to get the last bits of stubborn paste and backing off the wall. You won't need a whole lot, so it's not going to break the bank. Since the gel clings to the wall, you can scrape off the gel and the paste at the same time with minimal cleanup. After the paste is completely gone, rinse the wall with water until it's smooth and squeaky clean. Now go to bed.

Repair, sand and prime the wall

The next day after the wall has dried thoroughly (and

Tough tools for tough situations

Chemical strippers

Some chemical strippers work as wetting agents that prevent the water from evaporating while you remove the paste. Others have enzymes (check the label) that actually break down the molecular structure of the paste, making it easier to remove. You can buy premixed liquid, powdered or gel chemical wallpaper removers at home centers and paint stores. (DIF by Zinsser is one brand. The gel formulation costs $19 per gallon or $6 for a 32-oz. spray bottle.) Strippers can get pricey on big jobs. To save money, use hot water to remove most of the paper and glue and then apply a small amount of the gel at the end to remove the most stubborn paste and backing.

Scoring tools

A scoring tool punches hundreds of tiny holes in the wallpaper facing so the water can penetrate the backing. If you can pull off the facing, you probably don't need to use one. But if you have a waterproof facing like a glossy paper or vinyl, a scoring tool can really help. But use it carefully. Plaster walls are impervious to abuse, but scoring tools used aggressively can easily punch tiny holes in drywall. You can find scoring tools at home centers and wallpaper stores. (The Paper Tiger, $8, is a popular model.)

PAPER TIGER

Electric steamers

Steamers are the tool of last resort. They're messy, difficult to work with and time-consuming to use. But in truly stubborn cases, they'll get the job done ... eventually. Steam removal is more dangerous than other methods because you can burn yourself, and you can also damage the paper drywall surface if you hold the steamer on the wall too long. But if nothing else is working, rent a steamer ($25 per day).

you've had a good night's sleep), prep the wall for paint or new wallpaper. Patch large gouges or holes from the scoring tools with joint compound. If you have really banged-up walls over a large area, trowel on a 1/16-in.-thick skim coat of joint compound over the entire wall. (For step-by-step instructions, go to thefamilyhandyman.com and type "preparing walls for painting" in the search box.)

Once your repairs are dry, sand the wall until it's smooth. If you plan to put up new wallpaper, use an acrylic primer that's formulated for wallpaper applications ($25 per gallon at home centers and paint stores) to make removing it easier the next time around. If you're going to paint, use a primer designed for that purpose. Always prime a wall, even if it's painted, before putting wallpaper on it. If you don't, you might remove the paper surface of the drywall when you try to remove it. 🏠

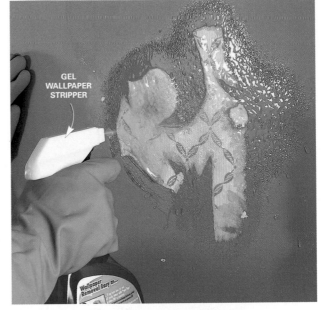

GEL WALLPAPER STRIPPER

Step 5: Use gel stripper on stubborn paste

Spray any remaining paste and backing with gel stripper and let it sit for 15 to 20 minutes. Scrape off the gel and paste underneath until all the paste is completely gone. Rinse the wall with water until it's smooth.

HAND SANDER

Step 6: Sand walls smooth

Patch any gouges or damage to the wall with joint compound. Sand the wall using a hand sander and 120-grit drywall sanding paper to smooth rough areas and remove any remaining backing or paste. Then prime the walls with an appropriate primer.

RemodelResources

GREEN REMODELING PRODUCTS

EASY, ECO-FRIENDLY CARPET TILES

Carpet tiles are a cinch to install: You just lay the tiles directly over a subfloor, vinyl or concrete. The backing keeps them in place, so you don't need adhesives or a separate pad. And the beauty of using carpet tiles is that not only can you clean or replace individual tiles, you can take the floor with you when you move!

Legato Fuse modular carpet tiles from Milliken are convenient to use as well as "green." Milliken uses alternative energy to produce the tiles, which are PVC-free and manufactured from recycled carpet. The company has generated zero landfill waste from carpet production since 1999.

Legato tiles are available in a range of styles that you can mix and match to design your own area rugs, runners or wall-to-wall carpets. Available in 20 x 20-in. or 22 x 23-in. sizes depending on the style, the tiles are available only at Home Depot for $2 to $3 per square foot. For installation steps, search for "carpet squares" at thefamilyhandyman.com.

sustainablecarpet.com, (800) 241-4826

AFFORDABLE LED LIGHTING

Light-emitting diodes (LEDs) produce the same brightness as incandescent bulbs but use two to five times less energy, last more than 40,000 hours and create significantly less heat. So, what's not to love? Well, until now, their price. But prices are finally starting to come down. Koncept's I-Tower LED floor lamp ($160) tops our cool list. It has a built-in dimmer and comes in two models: a daylight version and a warm white version. The lamp head adjusts to heights of 3 to 5 ft. and folds down when you're not using it. Available at Target, Wal-Mart and other retailers nationwide.

konceptech.com, (323) 261-8999

TOTALLY TUBULAR SKYLIGHT

Solatube's Tubular Daylighting System brings daylight to almost anywhere in your house, even rooms without direct roof access. Solatube's high-tech lenses and reflectors capture daylight from all angles and redirect it down a highly reflective tube that can run as long as 40 ft. It can even bend around obstacles if you use angled adapters and extensions. The tubing fits between rafters and requires no structural modifications, so it can be installed by a DIYer in a day. Add-on options include dimmer controls, incandescent and compact fluorescent lighting, and fan kits. Basic kits start at $300. Available at some lighting dealers and at greendepot.com.

solatube.com, (888) 765-2882

LOW-VOC PAINTS GO MAINSTREAM

VOCs (volatile organic compounds) are solvents that help paint stick, spread evenly and—whether you like it or not—give your home that new paint smell. But VOCs are bad for the environment and our bodies, so federal and state authorities have started regulating them. The first low- or zero-VOC paints to hit the market were expensive, hard to find, of questionable quality, or all three. But the quality of these paints has been steadily improving while prices are dropping. Olympic's zero-VOC interior paint and primer, for example, cost just $20 a gallon at Lowe's. And now you can find low- or zero-VOC paints at almost any home center or paint store. For more information, visit these Web sites.

afmsafecoat.com, benjaminmoore.com, freshairechoice.com, mythicpaint.com, olympic.com, sherwin.com

AFFORDABLE DUAL-FLUSH TOILET

Dual-flush toilets save water by letting you choose the right flush for the job: more water to flush solids, less for liquids. This idea has

KOHLER

been around for years, and several models are available (search online for "dual flush toilet"). Bathroom renovators on a budget should check out the Dual Force Sterling Rockton 402027 ($260 in white). The toilet features a two-button actuator that gives you the choice of .8 gallons to flush liquids or 1.6 gallons to flush solids. According to the manufacturer, this can save a family of four up to 6,000 gallons of water a year. Find the toilet (also available in almond and biscuit for $375) at Menards and Home Depot.

sterlingplumbing.com, (800) 783-7546

EVOLVE

TEMPERATURE-SENSING SHOWERHEAD

If you turn on the shower and then go make your bed while waiting for the water to heat up, you're sending water, energy and money down the drain. The low-flow Roadrunner showerhead from evolve is the perfect solution for morning multitaskers. Once the water reaches a perfect 95 degrees, the Roadrunner showerhead slows the flow to a trickle, letting you know the water's hot. Flip a switch on the showerhead and the flow returns to normal. According to the manufacturer, this simple idea can save you up to $75 a year on your utility bill. Saving money and water doesn't mean sacrificing a good strong blast. The Roadrunner showerhead may be low-flow and low cost ($40 for chrome; $46 for brushed nickel), but it's definitely not low pressure. Also available in rain, handheld and standard models at home centers and online retailers including target.com, samsclub.com and sears.com.

evolveshowerheads.com, (480) 496-2294

POWER-SAVING DIMMER

Any dimmer switch can save electricity and make bulbs last longer by simply reducing the power flow. But Lutron's Skylark EcoDim dimmer takes this idea a step further. It limits light levels to no more than 85 percent of full capacity at all times. That cuts energy use by 15 percent, and— according to the manufacturer —the human eye can't tell the difference. The EcoDim dimmer ($27) works with both incandescent and halogen bulbs and is available in up to four colors at Home Depot and Lowe's.

lutron.com, (800) 523-9466

LUTRON

RemodelResources

IKEA

GREENER BAMBOO FLOORING

Bamboo is considered a sustainable flooring material because it's a grass that grows quickly. Oak takes decades to grow to maturity, while bamboo can be harvested in three short years. Despite those "green" credentials, most bamboo flooring uses a urea-formaldehyde (UF) glue in the lamination process that's considered to be a human carcinogen. The amount of UF used in bamboo flooring is small compared with the levels found in materials like particleboard and MDF, but even when low, UF emissions can cause eye and throat irritation in sensitive people. In higher concentrations, they can cause nausea and asthma.

PlybooPure is a new line of formaldehyde-free bamboo flooring products manufactured by Smith & Fong. With its durability, easy installation and natural beauty, PlybooPure is an excellent flooring choice for health-conscious homeowners. PlybooPure is 100 percent bamboo—no fillers. It's available unfinished, or prefinished in a natural or amber color. The average price of PlybooPure edge-grain and flat-grain bamboo flooring is about $4 per sq. ft. For more information and to find state-by-state dealer locations, check out the Web site.

plyboo.com, (866) 835-9859

PLYBOO

BLOOMING WALL STICKERS

Ikea's Slatthult peel-and-stick wall decorations are perfect for walls that need a little visual wow. The flower-inspired designs come in a variety of colors and cost less than $20 each. To apply them, make sure the wall surface is smooth, clean and dry, then simply peel off the backing, stick them on the wall and you're done. Some of the designs are available at ikea.com, but you'll find the greatest selection at Ikea stores.

DIY VENETIAN PLASTER

"Venetian plaster" is a wall finishing technique in which thin layers of plaster are troweled on and then burnished to create the illusion of polished marble, rough stone or suede. It used to require a fair amount of skill and numerous steps to get these effects. But Behr's Premium Plus Venetian Plaster No. 770 simplifies the process into a single can ($35 per gallon). The heavy-bodied water-based product is specially pigmented to create the three-dimensional look of "old world" stucco. The best results come from applying two or more layers, and from practicing your trowel and burnishing technique on drywall scraps first. Behr Premium Plus With Style Venetian Plaster Topcoat No. 775 ($12 per quart) protects the faux finish and adds a lovely sheen.

Available at Home Depot stores.

BEHR

BRUCE

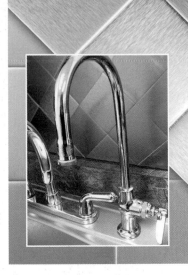

CH METAL (2)

DIY STYLISH METAL TILES

Do you want a stainless steel backsplash but hate installers' prices? Here's a frugal but beautiful DIY alternative. Interior 51's high-quality self-adhesive anodized aluminum tiles come in three styles: brushed, satin and light stainless. The 4-in. square tiles are packed 54 to a box, which is enough to cover 6 sq. ft., and they're a breeze to install using the peel-and-stick adhesive backer. The tiles aren't dirt cheap ($79 per box), but they're a lot cheaper than custom stainless panels and other metal tiles, which can easily run twice as much per square foot. The tiles cut easily with a utility knife, and the durable rubber-based adhesive is both heat and water resistant, so they work well behind the stove and as a kitchen and bath backsplash.
interior51.com, (800) 807-7341

EASY TO INSTALL RUSTIC HARDWOOD FLOORS

Distressed hardwood floors with highly defined grain patterns and wide planks are all the rage and with good reason: They're gorgeous. And for DIYers who love this look, Bruce Hardwood Floors' new Rustic Lock&Fold collection is worth checking out.

The collection combines the latest distressed flooring trends with a patented locking technology that reduces installation time and expenses by 30 percent, according to the company. The Lock&Fold technology means there's no need for glue, nails or staples. And unlike other click-together floor installations, Rustic Lock&Fold panels don't even have to be tapped together. All you do is fit the tongue-and-groove panels together, fold them down and lock them into place.

The collection includes two lines: American Originals, available in hickory (pictured), oak and maple; and American Vintage, available in cherry and walnut. Both are 100 percent engineered hardwood and come 3/8 in. thick and 5 in. wide with square edges and ends. They're also available in random-length planks that allow you to create dramatically different looks to suit any room. The flooring ranges in price from $5 to $8 per sq. ft. depending on the style. For a dealer locator, visit the Web site.
bruce.com, (800) 233-3823

AFFORDABLE GLASS TILE

Glass tile is eco-friendly and makes gorgeous backsplashes, countertops and bathroom walls, but it typically costs $30 to $60 per sq. ft. Here's a site that's easy on your eyes—and your budget. GlassTileStore.com stocks and ships more than 300 unique styles for just $12 to $20 per sq. ft. ($6 for closeouts!). Sold in 12 x 12-in. mesh-backed sheets, the tiles are available in styles such as brick, iridescent, and stone and marble mosaics.

GLASS TILE STORE

A sample quarter sheet costs $5. The style shown is Jelly Bean Blend.
glasstilestore.com, (866) 620-8453

GreatGoofs®

Safe, but sorry

I decided to buy a floor safe to protect my wife's jewelry. The locksmith wanted $200 to install it in my concrete floor—which was more than the safe cost! To do the job myself, I rented the biggest jackhammer known to mankind and bought some concrete mix for the patchwork. I fired up the jackhammer and it broke through the basement slab just fine. Then it hammered through the main water line, sending water shooting up like a geyser.

The project took some extra time and an emergency visit from my plumber, but you know what? That $200 locksmith would have caused the same disaster!

Try the hard way first

My parents were giving me a sofa and I had found the perfect spot for it—the downstairs family room. My dad and I maneuvered the heavy sofa through the front door and down the stairs, then discovered that it wouldn't fit through the door at the bottom of the stairs. So I removed the casing and jambs. Then it wouldn't fit through the family room door, so I took off those casings and jambs, too.

When we moved the sofa for the last time, we heard something rattling around inside it. I reached into the sofa and pulled out some loose change and the instructions on how to remove the sofa back. I thought about those instructions the whole time I was nailing on the casings and jambs.

New screen, take 2

We moved into a new house and needed to replace the torn screen on the doors opening up to the patio. My husband got out his tools, and I got excited to have a sliding screen door that would actually keep out the bugs. He did a superb job, then gathered up his tools to take them back to the shop. That's when he walked right through the brand new screen door, leaving a tangled mess of torn screen, tools and embarrassed husband lying on the floor. At least he now has the expertise to install another screen.

10 ft. of trim in a 9-ft. car

On my way to work one day, I stopped at my local home center to buy trim for my daughter's bedroom. I folded down the back seat in my car and ran the pieces of trim through the trunk, resting the front ends on the dashboard. I slammed the trunk shut, then recoiled in horror at the sound of breaking glass. The trim was too long for the car, and the slamming trunk acted like a battering ram, shoving the trim through the windshield. My little trim project suddenly got a lot more expensive—and my car was impossible to drive with a shattered windshield.

Nailed it perfectly!

To prepare for my new wood floor, I removed all the base trim. I labeled the trim to make sure the pieces would go back in the same order. I installed the floor in a single day, and in all modesty, it looked terrific. Then I got out my compressor and trusty nail gun to reinstall the base trim.

I had just nailed my last piece of base when my wife walked in and asked me why the pocket door wouldn't pull out of the pocket. I was baffled. After using every muscle in my body to try to pull the stuck door closed, I realized the problem: While reinstalling the base, I had shot nails through the trim, drywall, pocket door framing and into the door. Oh, well. Who needs to close a bathroom door anyway?

Two inches off the top

With the motto "measure twice, cut once" in mind, I borrowed my husband's tape measure and twice measured the closet floor where I was planning to install carpet. I wrote down the dimensions, grabbed my piece of carpet and headed to the garage.

I used a yardstick to measure the carpet in the garage since it held down the curling edges and provided a nice straight-edge. Soon my masterpiece was ready, and I hurried to the closet to install it. When I laid it out, I was shocked to find that it was 2 in. short on two sides. I double-checked my measurements. They were right, which left me more puzzled than ever. Then my husband walked in and solved the mystery with a laugh. Weeks earlier, he'd cut 2 in. off the end of the yardstick to use as a shim. I never even noticed.

Screw loose

To free up floor space in my kid's bedroom, I built a bed box to hold the mattress. Then I hung one side of the box from the ceiling joists with chains and screwed the other side to the wall studs.

To convince my skeptical family that the box was safely hung, I set down my tools, hopped up on it and started jumping around. As my family watched from below, the box pulled loose from the wall, dropping straight down and dumping me out onto the floor. The ceiling chains were sturdy enough, but the drywall screws pulled right out. I patched the wall and reinstalled the box with longer screws, but my family never lets me forget how I got thrown out of the bed.

SPECIAL SECTION Painting

TIDY PAINT MIXING

Mixing paint can get kind of messy, but here's a neat solution. Drill a hole through the paint can or bucket lid, insert a mixer through the hole and then put the lid back on the can. Now you can mix the paint without splashing it everywhere. This works great for driveway sealant and anything else you have to mix in large quantities.

LARGE-HEAD PIN

NAIL HOLE SPOT MARKING

I dreaded painting my hallway where I have 39 family portraits hanging. I knew that once I pulled all the hanger nails and repainted, the paint would hide the nail holes and it would take forever to reestablish each portrait's exact location. So as I took down each picture, I stuck a large-head pin into the nail hole. Then I rolled paint right over the pinheads. After the paint dried, I plucked out the pins, replaced the nails and hung my family back up on the wall.

GreatGoofs®

Tint-it-yourself paint

I wanted to surprise my husband by painting our bedroom. I waited until he had weekend Army Reserve duty and got right to work. Since our bedroom is small, I figured I could use the leftover gallon and a half of blue paint from a previous makeover project. To my surprise, it wasn't enough. As I was running out of paint—and time—I decided to get resourceful. I mixed what was left of the paint with some white paint, then added food coloring to get a close match.

The room turned out to be a light shade of blue fading into an even lighter shade of blue. I had the blinds closed when my husband came home, and kept them closed until I could go to the paint store, buy the right paint and finish the job. My husband never suspected a thing!

Do's&Don'ts

TRIM PAINTING TIPS

Repainting chipped, flaking, dirty moldings can transform a room. But for a crisp, professional-looking job, you have to go beyond just brushing on a coat of paint. From prep work to the final coat, here are tips for making your painted woodwork look like new.

Careful sanding is the key to a perfect job

If your woodwork is smooth, just give it a once-over with 120-grit sandpaper. But if your trim is in rough shape like ours, start with 80-grit sandpaper. Switch to 100-grit for smoothing and blending in the areas with layered paint. Finally, go over all the wood with 120-grit. Buy sandpaper labeled "no-load." No-load sandpaper won't clog as easily and is better for sanding painted surfaces.

NO-LOAD SANDPAPER

Fill holes and dents

To repair large dents or gouges on edges that are vulnerable to abuse, use hardening-type two-part wood filler (Minwax High Performance Wood Filler is one brand). Fill smaller dents and holes with spackling compound. Since spackling compound shrinks as it dries, you'll have to apply a second (and possibly a third) coat after the previous coat dries.

Shine a strong light across the woodwork to highlight depressions and ensure that you don't miss any spots as you're applying the filler. Let the filler dry and sand it smooth.

SPACKLING COMPOUND

Caulk for a seamless look

Here's a step that many beginners don't know about but pros swear by. Caulk every crack or gap, no matter how small. Use latex caulk or a paintable latex/silicone blend. The key is to cut the caulk tube tip very carefully to create a tiny, 1/16-in.-diameter hole. Fill all the small cracks first. Then, if you have wider cracks to fill, recut the caulk tube tip to make a larger hole. Move the caulk gun swiftly along the cracks to avoid an excess buildup of caulk. If necessary, smooth the caulk with your fingertip. Keep a damp rag in your pocket to clean caulk from your finger and to keep the tip of the caulk tube clean. If caulk piles up in the corners, remove the excess with a flexible putty knife.

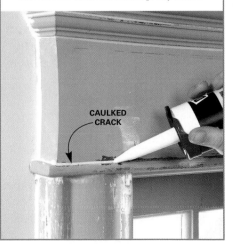

CAULKED CRACK

CAUTION: If your home was built before 1979, check the paint for lead. Call your public health department for instructions on how to test for lead and on what to do if you have lead paint.

Do's&Don'ts: Trim painting tips

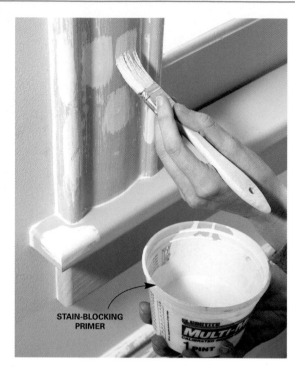

STAIN-BLOCKING PRIMER

Spot-prime to avoid blotches

Brush a stain-sealing primer (BIN is one brand of shellac-based primer) over the areas that you've patched or filled, and over areas where you've sanded down to bare wood. If you have a lot of patches and bare spots, it'll be faster and easier to just prime the entire surface. Also seal discolored areas or marks left by crayons, pens or markers to prevent them from bleeding through the finish coat of paint.

Add a conditioner to latex paint

Most pros prefer to use oil-based paint on trim for two reasons: Oil-based paint doesn't dry as fast as water-based paint, leaving more time to brush. And oil-based paint levels out better than most water-based paints, leaving a smoother surface with few visible brush marks. But because water-based paint is more environmentally friendly, less stinky and easier to clean up, it's a better choice for DIYers.

You can make water-based paint perform more like oil paint by adding latex paint conditioner. Floetrol is one brand. Conditioners make the paint flow better and slow down the drying time, allowing you more time to spread the paint without leaving brush marks. Check with the manufacturer of the paint you're using to see if it recommends a particular brand of conditioner.

Paint from a separate pail

Pour paint about 1-1/2 in. deep into a separate pail. A metal painter's pail (shown); a specialty pail called a Handy Paint Pail (handypaintpail.com; $10 at paint stores and home centers); and even an empty 5-quart ice cream pail all work great. Placing a small amount of paint in a pail allows you to easily load the bristles of the brush by dipping them about 1 in. into the paint.

Slap, don't wipe

Slap the brush gently against each side of the bucket to remove the excess paint. This method of brush loading is best for laying on paint because it keeps the bristles fully loaded with paint. To use the brush for cutting-in, follow up by wiping each side of the brush gently on the rim to remove a little more paint.

LATEX PAINT CONDITIONER

Lay on, lay off

The biggest mistake beginners make is to work the paint too long after it's applied. Remember, the paint starts to dry as soon as you put it on, and you have to smooth it out before this happens or you'll end up with brushstrokes or worse. So here's the tip. Load your brush. Then quickly unload on the surface with a few back-and-forth brushstrokes. This is called "laying on" the paint. Repeat this until you've covered a few feet of trim with paint. Don't worry about how it looks yet.

Now, without reloading the brush, drag the tips of the bristles over the wet paint in one long stroke to "lay off" the paint. Start in the unpainted area and drag into the previously painted trim. Sweep your brush up off the surface at the end of each stroke. Areas wider than your brush will require several parallel laying-off strokes to finish. When you're done laying off a section, move on and repeat the process, always working quickly to avoid brushing over partially dried paint. Try to complete shorter pieces of trim with a continuous laying-off brushstroke.

LAYING-OFF STROKE

Cut in edges before you fill the center

Cutting-in is a skill that takes practice to master, but it's worth the effort. To cut in, first load the brush. Then wipe most of the excess paint off by gently scraping the bristles on the edge of the can. Start by pulling the brush along the edge, but keep the bristles about 1/4 in. away from the wall or ceiling to deposit some paint on the wood. Now return with another brushstroke, this time a little closer. Sneaking up to the line like this is easier than trying to get it perfect on the first try. At the end of the stroke, arc the brush away from the cut-in line. Cut in a few feet and then fill the middle using the lay-on, lay-off technique shown above.

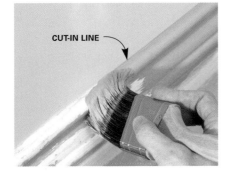

CUT-IN LINE

Don't start a brushstroke on already-smoothed paint

Setting the paintbrush on an area that's already been smoothed out with laying-off strokes will leave an unsightly mark. Try to start laying-off strokes at the end of a trim piece or board, or in an unpainted area. Brush toward the finished area. Then sweep the brush up and off, like an airplane taking off from a runway, to avoid leaving a mark.

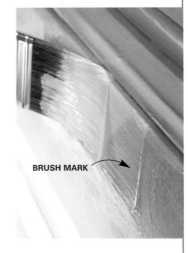

BRUSH MARK

Don't brush across an edge

Brushing across an edge wipes paint from the bristles and creates a heavy buildup of paint that will run or drip. Avoid this by brushing toward edges whenever possible. If you must start a brushstroke at an edge, align the bristles carefully as if you're cutting-in, instead of wiping them against the edge. If you accidentally get a buildup of paint that could cause a run, spread it out right away with a dry paintbrush or wipe it off with a damp rag or your finger.

Painting
PREP **PROBLEM WALLS** FOR PAINTING

It doesn't matter how much abuse your walls have taken; you can repair them and make them perfectly smooth. Most repairs require less than $10 worth of materials and take only a few hours. If you hired a pro to do the work, you'd pay $200 or more. That's because the pro would have to make many trips to your house to complete the job (most fixes require two or three coats of joint compound).

In this article, we'll show you how to fix common wall problems before you paint. Everything you need is available at home centers. For small fixes, pick up spackling compound ($6 for 32 ozs.). For larger repairs, use all-purpose joint compound ($5 for 1 gallon). You may also need mesh tape ($6 per roll).

SEAL TORN PAPER

The back of a chair, a flying video game remote or an aggressive kid with a toy truck can tear the drywall paper face. A coat of paint or joint compound over torn paper will create a fuzzy texture. For a smooth finish, seal the torn paper. Start by cutting away any loose paper. Then seal the exposed drywall with a stain-blocking primer. This keeps the drywall from absorbing moisture from the soon-to-be-applied joint compound. Wait for the primer to dry, then sand the exposed drywall edges to remove paper nubs. Cover the gouge with a thin layer of joint compound, feathering it out along the wall. If necessary, apply a second coat, feathering it as well, then wait for it to dry and sand it smooth.

PRIMER

FILL HOLES THREE TIMES

Fill small holes and indents (less than 1/8 in.) with spackling compound. For larger holes, use joint compound instead.

Apply either compound with a putty knife, spreading it thin on the wall. You'll apply two more coats (the compounds shrink as they dry), so don't worry if the hole isn't filled perfectly the first time. Let each coat of compound dry (read the directions; some dry in just two hours).

Don't believe spackling labels that say you don't have to sand—you do. You'll have to sand between coats if there's any excess compound. After the final coat, use fine-grit paper.

FIX HOLES FAST WITH AN ALUMINUM PATCH

The old method of repairing large holes was to cut out a square in the drywall, attach wood backing and then screw on a new patch of drywall. Aluminum patches ($2 to $4) are a faster, easier solution. Cut the patch so it covers the hole by at least 1 in. on each side, then place it over the hole. One side is sticky to adhere to the wall. Cover the patch with joint compound. Let it dry overnight, then recoat.

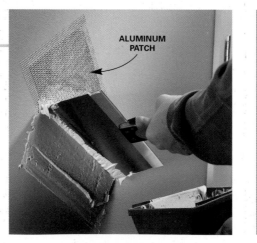

ALUMINUM PATCH

Tip After applying joint compound, be sure to cover it with primer before painting to prevent "flashing." Flashing occurs when joint compound absorbs the paint, dulling the finish.

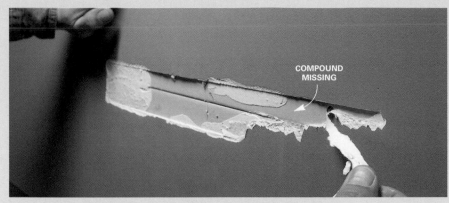

COMPOUND MISSING

1 Cut away loose tape with a utility knife. Be aggressive and cut past where the tape has lifted away from the wall.

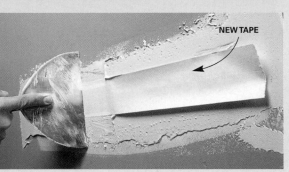

NEW TAPE

2 Place a strip of tape in joint compound a few inches past and directly over the patch. Apply joint compound over the top of the tape.

REPLACE LIFTING TAPE

Tape will lift off the wall if there isn't enough joint compound underneath to adhere it to the drywall. You'll have to cut away the loose tape and replace it. Start by cutting through the paint and joint compound to remove every piece of loose tape. Go beyond the cracked area. Peel away the tape until you see the underlying drywall (**Photo 1**). Then fill the hole with joint compound and wait for it to harden. Embed mesh or paper tape in joint compound over the hole (**Photo 2**). Extend the tape a few inches past the hole on each side. Once it's dry, apply a second coat and feather it to blend the patch with the wall.

FIX NAIL POPS FOREVER

Seasonal expansion and contraction of studs can push nails out of the drywall. You can't just resink the nail and apply joint compound over the top—the nail will pop back out. To permanently fix the problem, drive a drywall screw about 2 in. above or below the popped nail. Use a 1-1/4-in. screw (screws hold better than nails). A longer screw isn't better—it's actually more likely to pop out than a shorter one.

NEW SCREW

POPPED NAIL

Now pull out the nail, holding a wide putty knife under your pry bar to protect the wall. Tap the empty nail hole with the putty knife handle to knock protruding drywall fragments into the wall (or you won't get a smooth coat of filler on the wall). Finally, cover the screw head and fill the nail hole with three coats of joint compound.

BLOCK STAINS WITH SPECIAL PRIMER

Don't expect regular primer or paint to cover marker or crayon marks; they'll bleed through even several coats of paint. The same goes for water stains. First try to wash off the marker or crayon with a Mr. Clean Magic Eraser ($4 for a four-pack) dipped in warm water. If that doesn't work, cover the marks with stain-blocking primer (KILZ and BIN are two brands; $10 for 1 qt.). Apply the primer with a roller so the texture will match the rest of the wall. Buy a cheap disposable roller ($2) and then throw it away when you're done.

HIGHLIGHT HIDDEN FLAWS

Minor wall flaws are often hard to spot—until the afternoon sun hits them and makes them embarrassingly obvious. Find and mark any imperfections in the walls. Start by turning off all the lights in the room and closing the curtains. Then hold a trouble light next to the wall and move it across the surface (a process called "raking").

Wherever the light highlights a problem, even a small one, stick a piece of tape next to it so you can easily find it when you come through with spackling or joint compound. Tape works better than circling the problems with a pencil or pen (which can bleed through the paint).

Painting

TENSION RING   PRONGS   LOCKING CLIP

A PAINT ROLLER THAT WON'T FALL OFF

If you paint like most DIYers—by screwing a broom handle onto a cheap paint roller to cover walls and ceilings—you know how frustrating it is when the roller unscrews from the broom handle as you paint. Purdy's new cageless roller ($15) and QuickFit poles solve that problem. Metal prongs on the roller's handle fit inside receptacles in the pole, and then a clip on the pole locks the handle in place. That keeps the roller from twisting loose—ever!

The cageless roller makes removing used roller covers easier. A tension ring holds the roller cover in place. Just slide the cover over the ring and the cover comes right off. The QuickFit poles, lightweight and comfortable to hold, are available in four lengths (2, 4, 6 and 8 ft.) and extend to twice their length. A lever securely locks the pole at 6-in. intervals. The rollers and QuickFit poles ($37 to $70) are available at Sherwin-Williams stores, some hardware stores and other retailers listed online. **Purdy, (800) 547-0780. purdycorp.com**

HEALTHY SPRAY PAINTING

I bought spray paint to update my lawn furniture, and the clerk recommended a respirator. The cheapest one was $30, but I wonder if I can get by with one of those $5 masks. It seems like overkill to spend $30 on a respirator for a small spray paint job.

Before you pass on the $30 respirator, check out this warning from a typical spray can label: "Repeated or prolonged exposure to these chemicals without the use of a proper respirator can cause permanent brain damage, as well as damage to your lungs." But solvent-based spray paints aren't the only products that present a health hazard. You'll find similar warnings even on water-based spray paints and many insecticides.

The less expensive N95 particulate filtering respirators you mentioned (see p. 25), do a great job of filtering out particulate matter. But they don't adsorb toxic chemical vapors. To do that, you need activated carbon. Most $30 (and up) respirators have a P100 (100 percent efficiency and oil compatible) prefilter and an activated carbon filter for the chemical vapors.

Protect yourself from chemical vapors with a high-quality respirator. Pick one that fits well and feels good, and be sure it's easy to find replacement filters.

However, the $30 carbon filter respirators sold at home centers won't protect you against every single toxic chemical listed on every manufacturer's warning label.

The bottom line is, any carbon filter respirator rated for solvents and paint is better than a $5 particulate respirator.

To save money over the long run, buy a respirator that accepts replaceable filter cartridges. But before you shop online, check out the availability of replacement filters at your local hardware or home center. You don't want to be searching every store in town for the right filter in the middle of a project.

2 Electrical & High-Tech

IN THIS CHAPTER

Question&Comment

EASY FIX FOR WOBBLY OUTLETS

In our kitchen, there's a loose electrical outlet that wobbles every time I plug an appliance into it. Is this dangerous? Can I fix it myself?

The constant movement of loose electrical outlets can loosen the wires connected to the outlet and create dangerous arcing. Luckily, the fix is simple. If the outlet is recessed less than 1/4 in. in noncombustible material, you can fur it out with outlet shims as shown. If it's recessed more than 1/4 in., use a plastic extension ring. You'll find both in the electrical department at home centers.

OUTLET SHIMS

NON-COMBUSTIBLE MATERIAL

LESS THAN 1/4"

<u>CAUTION:</u> **Turn power off before doing this repair.**

1 Turn off the power and check with a voltage tester to make sure there's no power to the outlet. Unscrew the outlet and add enough shims to bring the outlet flush to the wall.

2 Screw the outlet to the box and reinstall the cover plate. Turn the power back on.

CURE RINGING PROBLEMS ON INTERNET PHONE LINES

I chucked my expensive land line and signed up for digital "Voice over Internet Protocol" (VoIP) service. I connected a cable from my old telephone jack to the fancy modem device plugged into my computer. My phones rang just fine before the swap, but now some of them don't ring or the ring is weak and intermittent. What's the deal?

The power required to operate a ringer is referred to as its Ringer Equivalency Number (REN). Old-style desk "gong" phones have a REN value of 1. Land line phone companies provided 5 REN—or five times more power.

But VoIP is in its infancy and there's an "anything goes" attitude when it comes to following the old telephone standards. To keep the modem costs low and power supplies small, some companies skimp on how much REN the modems provide. In your case, your VoIP modem simply isn't providing enough power to ring all the phones in your house. You have a few options, depending on how much you're willing to spend. You can replace all your older REN 1 (and higher) phones and faxes with newer (lower REN) phones (find the REN value on the phone near the line cord jack). Or, you can add a ring generator to your system. We used the Viking Electronics RG-10A Ring Booster ($148; thetwistergroup.com).

A ring generator installs between your VoIP modem

and your wall jack. Some companies call them ring boosters, but they really don't boost the ring signal. Instead, they receive the ring signal from the modem and literally regenerate it at a much higher REN, using power from an AC outlet.

Some models duplicate the ring cadence (really only important if you have distinctive ringing on your VoIP line) and pass all the caller I.D. information through to your phones. Installing a ring generator should solve your ringing problems for good.

Connect the ring generator between your VoIP modem and the house wiring. Plug the new unit into an AC outlet to boost total REN to 12.

HIGH-DEF TV ANTENNA

I'm planning to buy an HDTV this winter. I don't have a satellite dish or cable and am perfectly OK with plain old broadcast TV. Can I get by with my old antenna? If not, how much should I have to spend to get the best picture?

So you either have a set of rabbit ears or a traditional roof- or attic-mounted antenna, right? The truth is that either style might work. But unless you're quite close to the broadcast towers, the rabbit ears can be dicey, and you might have to readjust them every time you change channels. Your reception also depends on the topography and how many tall buildings are in the signal's path. If you have a rooftop antenna, start by attaching it to your new HDTV. If you get a clear picture, great—it means your antenna is aimed properly and you're getting a digital signal. Sit back and enjoy the high-def TV experience. If you're not getting good reception, first try to re-aim your current roof-mounted antenna. Visit antennaweb.org and click on "Choose an antenna." Then enter your street address (you don't have to give them your name, phone or e-mail). The Web site will give you the compass reading pointing toward the broadcast towers in your area. Climb into the attic or up on your roof and use a compass to aim the front of the antenna (shortest prongs are on the front) toward the heading listed on the Web site. Then check your reception.

If you can tune in the channel but get a "pixilated" (choppy) picture, try running a new cable to the antenna. (You'll need a new cable anyway if you have to upgrade to a new digital antenna, so you have nothing to lose.) Use RG-6 quad-shield cable and compression fittings (don't use crimp or screw-on connectors). If you still can't get a good picture, you'll have to swap out your old antenna for a new digital one.

To make shopping for a new antenna easier, antenna manufacturers categorize their antennas by color code. Each color refers to a distance from the broadcast tower. Find the recommended color code for your address from antennaweb.org. Since most broadcast areas will still have TV stations on the VHF band, shop for an antenna that receives both VHF and UHF signals. You'll get the best reception if you mount a directional antenna on the outside of your house at least 4 ft. above the roofline. If you want to pick up additional TV stations from a second transmission tower, either buy an omnidirectional antenna or install a second antenna and aim it toward the other tower. You can install the antenna(s) in your attic, but you'll lose at least 30 percent of the signal strength.

CLEARSTREAM 4 ANTENNA, $150 FROM ANTENNAS-DIRECT.COM

1 Mount a directional VHF/UHF antenna at least 4 ft. above your roofline for best reception. The "Quad-loop" design on this antenna pulls in stations from 65 miles away.

MS2000 METROSTAR OMNIDIRECTIONAL AMPLIFIED TV ANTENNA, $99 FROM WINEGARD-DIRECT.COM

2 Consider an omnidirectional antenna if you want to receive additional TV signals from a second transmission tower. Buy an amplified version for attic installation if you're dead set against outside mounting.

ARE COMPACT FLUORESCENT BULBS REALLY "GREEN"?

Several readers questioned whether CFLs really are "green" since they contribute mercury to the waste stream if they're thrown into the trash or broken.

Each CFL contains about 4 milligrams of mercury, but most of that gets bound to the inside of the bulb as it is used. Only about 11 percent is released into the air and water if the bulb is sent to a landfill. When you consider the amount of mercury released into the environment by coal-fired electrical generating plants, CFLs look even better. Here's an example: If a 13-watt CFL burns out early at 2,000 hours (25 percent of its rated life) and gets

(illegally) buried in a landfill, the total mercury pollution is .7 milligrams. The electricity required to burn a 60-watt incandescent bulb for the same 2,000 hours generates double the mercury (1.45 milligrams). So even when the bulb isn't recycled as the law requires—the worst-case scenario—CFLs are still better for the environment.

To find the nearest recycling center for your CFLs, go to earth911.org and enter "CFL" and your location in the search bars.

Question&Comment

FIX FOR REMOTE CONTROLS

One of the buttons on my TV remote doesn't work anymore. A factory replacement costs a fortune. Is there any way to fix this?

Most remotes have electrically conductive paint on the bottom of each rubber button. The more you use each button, the more the paint wears off. The good news: You can buy a repair kit that includes two-part conductive paint. (We used the Chemtronics CW2605 rubber keypad repair kit, which costs $17 at mcmelectronics.com.) The bad news: You have to figure out how to disassemble the remote, and every one is different. But here are some general disassembly tips:

Start by removing the screws. They're usually hidden in the battery compartment under labels and rubber feet. Next, take a digital photo of the remote with the screws near their holes. Be sure you get a clear shot of all the buttons and any slide switches along the side of the remote. Once you pop open the remote, those slide switches may fly out.

To separate the halves, press a butter knife along the seam and look for "give." Press in at those points and pry the halves apart. Inside you'll find either individual rubber buttons, or a single molded sheet containing all the buttons. If you've spilled anything sticky on your remote, dunk the rubber buttons/sheet, plastic case and any hard plastic buttons in a bowl of warm water and dishwashing liquid. Brush off the debris, rinse all the parts with warm water and let them dry.

Next, following the mixing and application instructions, paint the buttons. Paint all of them as long as you have the case open. The paint dries in about 24 hours, but it needs a full 72 hours to cure completely. That's why we had you take digital photos—so you could remember how to reassemble your remote three days later. Don't rush the curing process or you'll be repeating the repair in a year or so. Reassemble the remote and you're ready to surf.

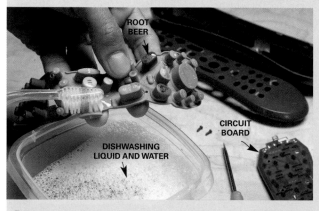

1 Remove the buttons from the circuit board and scrub off any sticky stuff with water and dishwashing liquid.

2 Repaint each button with a new coat of conductive paint. Let it cure for 72 hours before reassembling.

FLIPPING THE SWITCH SHORTENS CFL LIFE

In a recent article, "Switch On to Compact Fluorescents," we told readers not to use CFLs in fixtures that are turned on and off frequently. Some readers have asked, "How frequent is too frequent?" Most experts recommend a minimum burn time of 15 minutes. But the truth is, you can turn them on and off as often as you want without affecting energy use. The energy required to start a CFL is equivalent to about 5 seconds of burn time, so you still save energy even if you have the light on for only a few minutes. However, those frequent on/off cycles shorten the life of the bulb by almost 75 percent. Yet even with that reduced life, CFLs are still cheaper to operate. Here are the numbers: Say a 10,000-hour 13-watt CFL burns out at 2,500 hours. The cost of the CFL plus electricity to run it is $8.01 (at NY electric rates of .1881/kWh). A comparable 60-watt incandescent would cost $29.43. Even at a low electric rate of .0566/kWh, the numbers still favor CFLs—$3.73 vs. $9.71 for the incandescent.

OVERSTUFFED ELECTRICAL BOXES

I need to add a receptacle, and I want to power it from an existing duplex electrical box. That box already has three 14-2 cables. Can I just run a new cable into an unused opening on the existing box, or will the box be too crowded?

As a general rule, a standard 18-cu.-in. box maxes out at three 14-2 cables. (The box size in cubic inches is marked on the inside of the box.) The easiest way to accommodate the fourth cable is to install a larger box. However, you should check with your electrical inspector for a permit and approval.

Stop at a home center and buy a double-gang "old work" box (also called a "remodel box"). You can install a second receptacle in the larger box and cover it with a two-receptacle cover plate. Or you can stick with a single receptacle and use a two-piece "snap together" cover plate (with one receptacle and one blank).

Start by turning off the main breaker. Then remove the existing receptacle and use a tester to make sure none of the wires in the box is "hot." Use a fine-tip marker and tape to label the wires that go to each wire nut so you can keep them straight later.

1 To remove the old box, pry it away from the stud slightly to expose the nail shafts and cut them with a hacksaw. Then work the wires through the box as you pull it free of the hole.

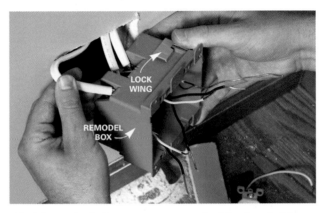

LOCK WING

REMODEL BOX

2 Enlarge the hole to accept a new double electrical box. Fit the wires through the box as you work it into place. Then tighten the lock wings and do the final wiring.

REMODEL GARAGE CONTROLS

My detached garage is equipped with a furnace. When I go out there in the winter, I freeze for an hour while it heats up. I'd like to be able to preheat the garage from inside the house. Is there a way to do that without running wiring?

If your garage gets its power from the house (not from a separate electrical service), use an X10 switch and module. You'll need to mount and power the X10 switch in a new electrical box somewhere in the house. Then install an in-line X10 relay in the electrical box where the furnace gets its power. (We used the Leviton No. 6375 fixture relay 15A, available for $39 from smarthome.com; 800-762-7846.) The X10 switch operates the furnace module by sending a signal throughout the household's electrical system.

If you want the utmost in energy savings, buy an X10 switch with several buttons. (Shown here is the eight-button scene control keypad with dimmer, No. 2486DWH8; $70 from smarthome.com.) Then connect all your garage's electrical devices—heater, small refrigerator, portable tool battery chargers, etc.—to their own X10 modules. Turn on the heater and the fridge an hour before you plan to work out there.

HandyHints®

SOLAR CANDLES

Next time the power goes out and all the flashlights are dead, don't panic—just run out to your garden and grab a few solar lights. They're dim, but they'll cast enough light to help get you through the night.

SOLAR-POWERED "FLASHLIGHT"

MONITOR POWER OUTAGES WITH A PENNY!

Find out if power outages ruined the food in your freezer while you were away on vacation. Freeze a container of water and rest a penny on top of the ice. If the penny is at the bottom when you get back, it means the power was off long enough to melt the water—and thaw (and likely spoil) everything in the freezer.

STOP THAT RINGING

I work nights, so I sleep during the day. But it's really hard to get some z's when a neighbor, the delivery guy or someone else rings the doorbell. Rather than remove the doorbell, I wired a toggle switch ($5) to it and put the switch right on the doorbell cover. When I go to bed each morning, I flip the switch so the doorbell doesn't ring while I'm snoozing. I just have to remember to flip it back when I wake up.

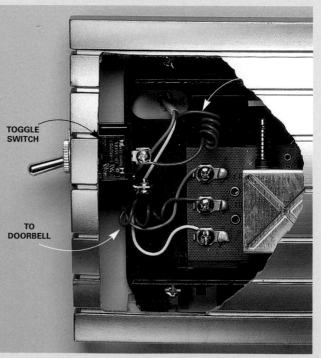

TOGGLE SWITCH

TO DOORBELL

GreatGoofs®

Not the brightest bulb in the pack

I decided to add a photocell sensor to my new porch lights. I installed the sensor and wired the lights, and in all modesty, I must say the workmanship looked great. Then I waited for the sun to go down to admire the results.

Once it was dark, I eagerly ran out to look at my new lights. But they were barely working. The lights kept getting brighter and then dimming. After 10 minutes of waving my hand over the sensor, I realized the problem. I had installed the sensor so it faced the light. When the light got brighter, the sensor closed the circuit, which shut off the light and started the cycle over again. Brilliant!

OVERHEAD ELECTRICAL OUTLETS

Are you always tripping over extension cords that snake all over the floor of your shop? End that hassle by installing ceiling-hung electrical outlets. Place them wherever you frequently need to plug in power tools, vacuum cleaners, steam irons or any other corded tool that you want to plug in right here, right now. The cost per outlet will run about $18.

For each one you'll need:

- A metal electrical box
- A metal box cover with a center knock-out
- A strain-relief cord connector
- Electrical connectors
- A cord receptacle
- A short length of stranded-wire electrical cord (buy 12-3 stranded wire for 20-amp circuits and 14-3 for 15-amp circuits).

Position the receptacles at least an inch above your head so you won't bump your noggin. Turn off the breaker or unscrew the fuse on the circuit you're tying in to. And check for voltage with a voltage sniffer to make sure the power is truly off before you splice into the circuit and wire the new receptacles.

STRAIN-RELIEF CORD CONNECTOR

BETTER CORD CONNECTIONS

I'm always surprised at how many people don't know about this tip. When I plug two extension cords together, I always "tie" them using an easy overhand knot. That way, they don't come unplugged when I'm pulling them across the garage or dragging them around a job site.

New Tools&Gear

FUNKIEST-LOOKING LIGHT EVER

No, this isn't something that fell to Earth from outer space. It's a portable light with 12 rare earth magnets, so you can place it on any steel surface and aim the powerful LED light where you need it. Smaller than a golf ball, Striker's Magnetic LED Light runs on three tiny, nonreplaceable batteries. The downside is the battery life is only about 28 hours. But since the light costs only $8, you could just buy a new one when the batteries run out. It's available at hardware stores and the Web site below.

Striker, (704) 658-9332. strikerhandtools.com

REACHES-ANYWHERE LIGHTER

The Flexible Utility Lighter from BernzOmatic can bend to fit into hard-to-reach areas—such as into a deep vase to light a candle or into a water heater to light a pilot light—with your hand a safe distance away. The flame is both powerful and adjustable, like a miniature blowtorch. A fuel window lets you see when it's time for a refill. To add fuel, just buy a can of butane ($3) at a home center and squirt it through the tiny intake valve in the lighter's handle. No more throwing away empty lighters!

The lighter is priced right too. It costs $7 at home centers (or find retailers on the company's Web site).

BernzOmatic, (800) 654-9011. bernzomatic.com

REMOTE CONTROL POWER OUTLET

Cableorganizer.com has a product that's long over-due: an outlet that lets you control outdoor (or indoor) electricity via a remote control transmitter. Plug the Remote Controlled Power Outlet into an outlet, so you can use the remote control to turn on and off whatever you plug into the power outlet. Or program the outlet to turn off the power after two, four, six or eight hours. It's great for controlling holiday or landscape lights, water features or anything else you don't want to have to plug in or unplug to control.

The remote control runs on a 9-volt battery and sends a signal up to 40 ft. You can use the outlet in damp locations, but it shouldn't be placed on wet ground or in standing water. The three-outlet power strip, priced right at $12, is available at cableorganizer.com (enter "part BL215031").

cableorganizer.com, (866) 222-0030.

EXPANDABLE SURGE PROTECTOR

The sockets on most power strips are so close together that you can't use all of them if you have large plugs, like the ones for charging cell phones. Ideative's Socket Sense ($30) solves that problem. It expands from 13 in. to 18 in., so even with oversized plugs you can still use all six sockets. When you don't need the extra space, just push the surge protector together again.

The outlets are positioned at 45-degree angles to further ensure that bulky plugs won't cover up adjacent sockets. Buy the Socket Sense on the company's Web site.

Ideative, (972) 395-9600. socketsense.com

SUPER-BRIGHT, COMPACT FLASHLIGHT

The new Daylite LED flashlight is the most powerful little flashlight we've seen, and it's small enough to fit in your pocket. It uses both a lens and a reflector (called TrueBeam technology) to project a strong, bright beam. The LEDs last longer and use less battery power than traditional bulbs.

The flashlight runs on three "AAA" batteries and is available for $25 at Ace Hardware and Wal-Mart.

Duracell, (800) 551-2355. duracell.com

DETER BURGLARS WITH A FAKE TV

You know how you can drive by a house at night and tell that someone is watching television by the flickering bluish light the TV casts through the window? The Fake TV from Opto-Electronic Design casts an identical light, fooling burglars into thinking you're home when you're really in Jamaica.

Plug it into a standard outlet. A built-in sensor turns on the Fake TV when the room gets dark and turns it back off in the morning. It's a more convincing deterrent than a light on a timer—which can make it obvious that you're not home. The Fake TV costs $40 on the company's Web site.

Opto-Electronic Design, (888) 621-5800. faketv.com

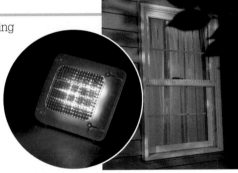

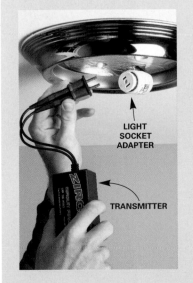

LIGHT SOCKET ADAPTER

TRANSMITTER

NO SHOCKING SURPRISES

Do you identify circuits by flipping breakers and listening for your helper's yell when you've found the right one? Zircon's CF 12 Pro Circuit Breaker Kit has a better way. Plug the transmitter into the circuit, then wave the receiver over the breaker box twice. On the second pass, the receiver identifies the breaker with a green LED light and an alarm. It's handy for tying in to an existing circuit, changing outlets or upgrading light fixtures.

The $120 kit includes an adapter that screws into a light socket for working on fixtures, two adapters with clips for bare wires, and blades that plug into 120- and 240-volt outlets. The CF 12 Circuit Finder ($43) handles outlets only. Available from amazon.com and other retailers.

Zircon, (800) 245-9265. zircon.com

RECEIVER

Cleaning

Faster, easier, smarter ways to keep your whole house clean

TOUGH BUT SAFE HEAVY-DUTY CLEANER

Heavy-duty cleaners like muriatic acid can be dangerous to work with, harmful to the environment and hard to find. Certol's Acid Magic ($7 for 32 ozs.) is a much safer alternative that won't burn your skin. (Check out the cool video on the company's Web site that shows Acid Magic dissolving an eggshell without harming the yolk or the bare hand holding it.) Of course we were skeptical, so we tried it on the rustiest toilet we've ever seen. Acid Magic cleaned it with ease. Then we poured the cleaner in a bucket of water at a 3-to-1 ratio and soaked some rusty tools in it. The tools were clean in a couple of hours without any scrubbing.

You can use Acid Magic wherever you'd use muriatic acid. It cleans masonry surfaces, etches concrete for staining, and maintains the pH and alkalinity in swimming pools. Acid Magic is available at True Value and Ace hardware stores (you may have to special-order it).

Certol, (800) 843-3343. certol.com

CORDLESS SCRUBBER FOR TIGHT SPOTS

Clean out tire rims, small openings and other hard-to-scrub spots quickly with a bottle brush and a cordless drill. Just cut the handle off the brush, put it in a cordless drill and start scrubbing.

GET TOUGH ON GLASS STAINS

If your usual glass cleaner won't remove tough stains, apply a mild abrasive cleaner such as Soft Scrub, Bar Keepers Friend or Bon Ami and scrub with a soft cloth. These abrasives usually won't scratch glass, but test a small area first just to make sure. If elbow grease alone won't do the job or if you have large areas to cover, use a drill and a small buffing wheel ($8 at home centers).

MILD ABRASIVE

BUFFING WHEEL

CLEAN THE AIR WHILE YOU CLEAN HOUSE

With their beater brushes and exhaust, vacuums whip up a dust storm. Later, all that dust settles on the surfaces you just cleaned. But you can use your forced-air heating/cooling system to filter the air while you clean. Just switch the thermostat to "fan" or "fan on." The dust reduction you get depends on your furnace filter. Standard fiberglass filters catch only the largest particles, while a pleated filter with an electrostatic charge will catch almost all the visible dust. Don't forget to switch back to "auto" when you're done.

TURNS FURNACE BLOWER ON

LONG-REACH VACUUM

A PVC pipe connected to a vacuum hose lets you reach up to high spots or into narrow crannies, so you can suck up those cobwebs around skylights or exterminate dust bunnies behind radiators. A 10-ft. piece of PVC pipe costs $5 or less depending on the diameter. In the plumbing aisle, you'll also find PVC and rubber "reducer" couplings that let you connect your vacuum hose to a different-size pipe.

PVC PIPE

MINIMIZE SCUM WITH SYNTHETIC SOAP

In terms of chemistry, some soaps aren't really soap. And these "synthetic" soaps make cleaning your shower or bath easier because they don't contain the ingredients that create tough soap scum. So how do you know if soap is synthetic or the real thing? Any liquid or gel soap is synthetic. Most bar soaps are true soap, but a few, such as Zest and Ivory, are synthetics. Synthetic soaps don't leave tough scum on your sink or tub the way standard soap does.

CLEAN CRUSTY PAINTBRUSHES

After you paint with latex for a few hours, brushes always get a gummy, partially dry ring of paint near the top of the bristles. Instead of getting frustrated trying to rub it away with your fingers, use a fingernail brush. Just wet the paintbrush with warm, soapy water and scrub back and forth to loosen the gunk. Then use downward strokes to comb the paint from the bristles. The brush works great for hands, too.

FINGERNAIL BRUSH

SPEED-CLEAN WITH A PRESSURE WASHER

Once you get your hands on a pressure washer, you'll find endless uses for it: Blast that dingy coat of dirt off your siding and trim, deep-clean embedded grime from your driveway or patio, wash down a deck or fence. While you're at it, don't forget the car, mower, bikes and patio furniture. You may discover so many jobs for a pressure washer that you want to own one. Electric versions usually cost less than $200, but you may want to spend more for a more powerful gas model. Renting first is a good way to find out how much pressure and which features you really need. For about $65, you can rent a pressure washer and do a week's worth of cleaning in one day. Before you rent, gather some tarps to protect plants and make sure your garden hose will reach all the areas you plan to clean. Good preparation lets you get more cleaning done during the rental period.

TARPS PROTECT PLANTS

GAS-POWERED WASHER

Cleaning

EASY-CLEAN CLOSET FLOORS

Household dust consists mostly of tiny fibers shed from clothing and other fabrics. So a closet packed with clothes is a major dust reservoir; every time you open the doors, you whip up a dust cloud. To make matters worse, closet floors are often bypassed by the vacuum because they're cluttered with shoes and other obstacles. The solution is a wire shelf. Install a wire shelf a few inches above the closet floor to clear off the clutter and make vacuuming easy. Get one for about $15 at a home center, install it in a few minutes and you won't be tempted to skip the closet floor next time you vacuum.

BEAT THE DUST OUT OF CUSHIONS

Upholstery absorbs lots of dust—and then sends it airborne every time you sit down. Routine vacuuming reduces the problem, but can't suck out the deep-down dust. So take cushions outside a couple times each year, preferably on a windy day, and spank the dust out of them. An old tennis racket makes a great upholstery beater (and improves your swing!).

CHANGE BAGLESS VACUUM FILTERS EVERY THREE MONTHS

Our vacuum cleaner expert, Russ Battisto, has a repair shop that's brimming with bagless vacuums, and most of them are there for the same reason: filthy clogged air filters and air passages. The repair? Ten minutes of Russ's time and a $30 bill.

It's critical to replace the filters on bagless vacuums every three months. That's because instead of having a big paper bag filtering out the dust and hair, bagless units rely on relatively small filters, which get clogged fast. Clean air filters are critical for air movement on bagless models; even a modestly dirty filter can cut a vacuum cleaner's suction in half.

The tricky part is knowing exactly where the filters are located (**Photo 1**). Some bagless vacuums have two or more filters that need to be washed or replaced (depending on the model) every three months to keep the vacuum in tiptop condition. If you have a washable filter, you can use gentle water pressure from the kitchen sprayer or outside spray nozzle on your hose to clean both sides. To prevent mold or mildew, let the filter dry thoroughly before reusing it.

You can find replacement filters for most models at hardware stores, home centers and vacuum repair shops. For hard-to-find filters, go to the Web site of your vacuum cleaner's manufacturer to get a list of locations.

FILTER NO. 1

FILTER NO. 2

DIRT CUP

1 Depending on the model, a bagless vacuum has two or three filters in various locations that need to be replaced or washed every three months.

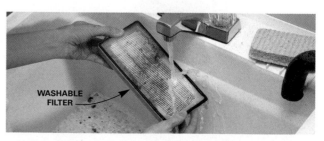

WASHABLE FILTER

2 Use gentle water pressure from a sprayer or faucet to clean both sides of the filter.

GreatGoofs®

Ashes, ashes—they all drift around

We decided to put our house on the market, and one of my jobs was to clean out the fireplace. Armed with my trusty shop vacuum, I went to work sucking up the ashes. Everything was going fine until my wife ran into the room yelling, "Stop!"

I pulled my head out of the firebox to see a huge cloud of ash dust floating across the room. My face turned whiter than the ash as I realized that I'd forgotten to put the filter in the vacuum, and the exhaust vents were blowing the fine particles all over the room. The upside: We were already planning to replace the carpet, and we learned that ash doesn't stick to walls. Now if we can just find a home buyer....

CLEANING SCUMMY SHOWER DOORS

It's not exactly dinner table conversation, but soap- and mineral-covered shower doors are a common, tough to solve problem. Soap and lime scale form a cloudy residue on the glass when the water evaporates. In some cases, the minerals pit and etch the glass, creating a permanent gray or whitish film that you have to live with until you replace the doors.

If your shower doors have a stubborn film, it's tempting to scrub them with steel wool and a strong cleanser. Don't. Steel and Teflon pads, as well as strong ammonia, bleach, acid and vinegar-based cleaners, can damage the shower's anodized aluminum metal track and door frame and even etch the glass. If that happens, the glass will collect deposits even faster after cleaning.

So what can you do besides ditch the doors and hang a curtain instead? There are many products you can try. We had good luck with Bring It On Cleaner, which combines a mild bleach with a mild abrasive in a formula that won't damage glass or aluminum surfaces. All you do is squirt a small amount of the cleaner onto a nonabrasive pad or sponge, rub it on the shower doors and let it sit for 10 minutes. Rub the doors in a circular motion until they're clean and then rinse. Repeat if necessary. For large or really tough to clean surfaces, try using a buffer. Bring It On Cleaner isn't recommended for use on marble, soft plastics, Plexiglas, acrylic tubs, or hardware with a brass or silver finish ($23 for 32 ozs., bringitoncleaner.com; 800-867-2643).

Once the doors are clean, you can prevent the film from forming again by drying the doors after every shower. Also, try applying Aquapel, a glass treatment product typically used for windshields. Aquapel forms a chemical bond with glass and keeps water from beading up and drying on the glass for up to six months. Just squeeze the applicator, rub on the product and then wipe it dry with a paper towel. Aquapel costs $10 for one application to an average-size shower door; large doors may need two. It's available at auto parts stores, aquapel.com (800-861-4999) and other online retailers.

Bring It On Cleaner and Aquapel help clean and protect shower doors from soap scum, mineral deposits and water marks.

MIX YOUR OWN WINDOW CLEANER

You know, most professional window washers don't buy window cleaner. They mix a teaspoon of dishwashing liquid with a few gallons of water. That's it. You can just pour it in a spray bottle for in-house work. For outside windows, get yourself a sponge/squeegee combination window cleaner and dip it right in the bucket.

To see how pros get windows squeaky-clean fast, go to **thefamilyhandyman.com** and search for "wash windows."

Cleaning

STOP COUNTERTOP STAINS

If you have an older plastic laminate countertop, you've probably noticed that it doesn't repel stains like it used to. That's because years of wear have left the surface lightly scratched and porous. The best way to prevent stains is to wipe up spills immediately. But a protective coating of countertop polish ($5) can also help. Plus it will restore the shine to dull countertops. All you have to do is spray it on and wipe it off every few weeks. Most home centers and discount stores carry countertop polish such as Countertop Magic or Hope's Counter Top Polish. If you don't find it in a store, search for "countertop polish" online to find a supplier.

COUNTERTOP POLISH

DISSOLVE RUST WITH ACID

To remove rust stains from a porcelain sink, tub or toilet, skip the standard cleaners and go for a product that contains acid. Don't use any product that contains bleach—that will just make the stains tougher. Look for ingredients like "hydrochloric acid," "hydrogen chloride," "HCL" or "muriatic acid" on the label. Read the whole label to make sure the product won't harm chrome or other finishes. If you're cleaning a toilet, remove as much water as you can to avoid diluting the cleaner. Scrub gently to avoid splatter that can damage your floor, painted surfaces or your skin. Be sure to flush the toilet a few times or rinse the tub thoroughly when you're done so you don't leave any residue behind. For an alternative to acid cleaners, see p. 76.

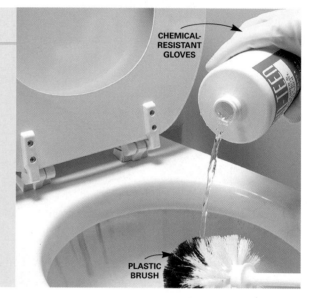

CHEMICAL-RESISTANT GLOVES

PLASTIC BRUSH

RENEW WOOD WITH MINERAL SPIRITS

If the finish on your furniture or woodwork is dull and murky, it may need refinishing. But before you take on that project, take a tip from furniture restorers and clean it with mineral spirits. Mineral spirits—sometimes labeled "paint thinner"—is a gentle solvent that dissolves years of grime and residue from cleaners or polishes without harming wood finishes. Get it at a home center or paint store for $5. Just soak a soft cloth and keep rubbing until the cloth no longer picks up grime. Work in a well-ventilated area and remember that the fumes are flammable. Hang the cloth outdoors to dry before throwing it in the trash.

CLEAN A VACUUM WITH A VACUUM

The typical way to clean the filter of a bagless vacuum is to tap it against the inside of a trash can until most of the dust falls off. But that raises a cloud of dust and doesn't get the filter completely clean. For faster, neater, more effective filter cleaning, use your shop vacuum. Clean prefilter screens and post-filters the same way. Just remember to be gentle with the shop vacuum's nozzle. Some filters have a coating that you can scrape off if you press too hard.

FILTER

3 Plumbing, Heating & Appliances

IN THIS CHAPTER

HomeCare&Repair

FIX A WATER HEATER PILOT LIGHT

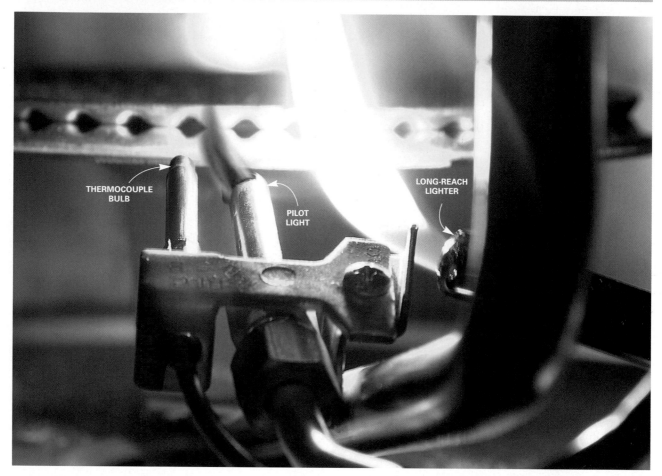

THERMOCOUPLE BULB

PILOT LIGHT

LONG-REACH LIGHTER

No hot water? If you have a natural or propane gas water heater, chances are the pilot has gone out. The pilot is a small flame that ignites the gas burner on your water heater (**photo above**). When it goes out, first try relighting it, following the directions on the water heater label. If the pilot doesn't relight, or if it goes out right after lighting, by far the most common cause is a bad thermocouple (**photo right**). The good news: You can usually replace a thermocouple for about $10 and in less than an hour. You'll get your hot water going without waiting for a pro to show up, and save the $100 to $150 cost of a service call.

To replace the thermocouple, follow the photo series. Be sure to turn off the shutoff valve in the gas line (**Photo 1, inset**); that is, one quarter turn so that the handle is at a right angle to the pipe. Since working room is tight around the burner, we recommend that you simply unscrew the three nuts at the control valve and pull out the entire burner assembly. You'll see either a slot or clips that hold it in place (**Photo 2**). Then either unscrew the thermocouple end or pull it out (depending on the water heater) and take it with you to an appliance parts store to find a match. Position it exactly like the old one.

A thermocouple senses the heat of the pilot and allows gas to flow to the burner. A bad thermocouple will shut off gas to both the pilot and the burner.

When relit, the pilot flame should wrap around the thermocouple bulb.

To reattach the three lines to the gas valve, thread the nuts into place with your fingers and hand-tighten them. Then snug them up with a quarter to half revolution with a wrench. The metals are soft, so don't overtighten.

Be sure to test for gas leaks. You must have the pilot lit and the burner on for this test so that gas is flowing through the large tube. Reopen the shutoff valve, relight the pilot, then turn the control valve to "on." When the gas burner comes on, use a 50/50 dish soap/water mix to test the screw joints for air bubbles that indicate leaks.

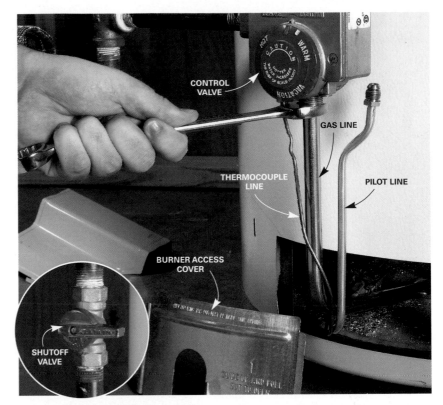

CONTROL VALVE

GAS LINE

THERMOCOUPLE LINE

PILOT LINE

BURNER ACCESS COVER

SHUTOFF VALVE

1 Turn off the control valve and the shutoff. Remove the burner access covers and unscrew the nuts on the gas, pilot and thermocouple lines.

BURNER

SLOT

2 Pull out the burner assembly. Pull out the old thermocouple. Buy a new one that matches the old one in size and length.

Note:

Some gas water heaters have a "closed" burner chamber, which is difficult to access. We recommend that you call a service pro to fix this type. Also, some gas water heaters don't have pilots. Let the pros fix these as well.

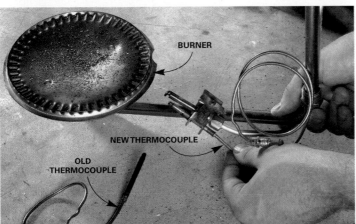

BURNER

NEW THERMOCOUPLE

OLD THERMOCOUPLE

3 Install the new thermocouple exactly like the old, slide the burner assembly back in and reattach the three lines to the control valve.

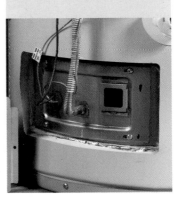

HomeCare&Repair

GET A CLOG OUT OF ANY VACUUM CLEANER

If your vacuum cleaner isn't picking up dirt, and cleaning or replacing the filter or the bag doesn't help, you probably have a clog.

If the attachment hose has no suction, either it or the hose suction port is clogged. Try sucking out the clog with a strong vacuum. If that doesn't work, use the bent hanger technique shown in **Photo 3** to remove the clog. Stubborn clogs in hoses can be forced through with a broom handle (**Photo 2**).

If the machine isn't picking up dirt and the brushes are turning, most likely the suction port at the base of the machine is plugged. Remove the cover on the underside of the machine to access the port. Bend a little barb on the end of a coat hanger or electrical wire and use it to hook the clog to pull it free.

1 Use a shop vacuum to suck clogs out of the suction port or hose.

2 Shove stubborn clogs through the hose with a broom handle.

3 Pull clogs out of the suction port with a bent coat hanger or stiff electrical wire.

TUNE UP A GAS GRILL

Get your gas grill in top cooking condition with this easy yet thorough once-over. These tips will lead to easier starting, more even cooking and better-tasting chow.

According to grill gurus, a smoky buildup on the inside walls and under the cover is good because it imparts flavor during grilling. But food drippings and grease on the grill's exterior and on the grates and burners can attract insects and rodents. They can also clog the burner gas ports, leading to uneven cooking, and plug up the igniter's flame, making lighting a hassle. Here's how to clean your grill's worst spots.

Remove grease from artificial briquettes (if you have them), by flipping them over so the greasy side faces the burners. Replace the grates, light the burners, close the lid and set the flame on high for 15 minutes. Shut off the gas and let the grates cool down to "warm." Scrub them with a brass-bristle brush (not metal, which can scratch them) or wadded up aluminum foil.

Next, service the burner assembly. Unfasten the burner (check your owner's manual for how to do this) and slip the gas tubes off the gas lines. For cleaning (**photo below**), lift out the unit as a whole. Clean the gas tubes and burner unit with a soft cloth and soapy water.

Clean the outside of the grill with a brass-bristle brush and soapy water, then rinse with clear water. Remove and clean the drip pans thoroughly.

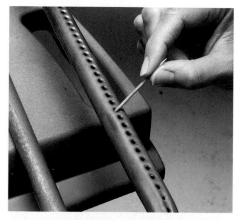

Clear out each gas port on the burner unit with a toothpick. For tougher clogs, use a small drill bit.

REPLACE A
TOILET

Tips for a trouble-free, leak-free installation

by **Gary Wentz**

Whether you're installing a better-flushing toilet or resetting the old one after repairs or remodeling, these tips will help you do it faster and with fewer problems. The job can take less than an hour, but set aside a whole morning in case you run into trouble. Everything you'll need is available at home centers and hardware stores.

Hiring a plumber to replace a toilet typically costs about $100. If there are hidden problems, such as a broken floor flange, that cost can easily double.

Check the "rough-in"

If you're buying a new toilet, you need to know the "rough-in" measurement of the old one. For the vast majority of toilets, the waste pipe is centered about 12 in. from the wall. But with a few models, that measurement is 10 in. or 14 in. To check the rough-in, just measure from the wall to the toilet's hold-down bolts. If that measurement (plus the thickness of the baseboard) isn't approximately 12 in., toilet shopping will be a bit harder. Most home centers carry only one or two 10-in. models and no 14-in. models. If you have to special-order a toilet, be prepared to spend much more.

If there's a door near the toilet, also measure how far the bowl protrudes from the wall. If you replace a standard bowl with an "elongated" model, the door may not close.

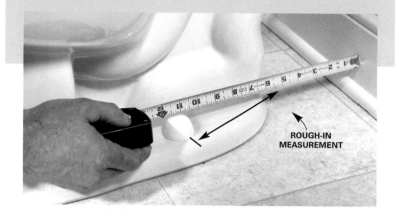

ROUGH-IN MEASUREMENT

Brass bolts are best

Some metal toilet bolts have a yellowish zinc coating that makes them look like brass. So check the label and make sure you're getting brass bolts and nuts ($3). They won't rust away and they're easier to cut off later. If you need to re-anchor the toilet flange, buy stainless steel screws. They won't corrode like steel or break off like brass while you're driving them.

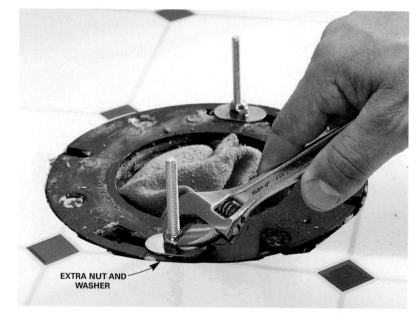

EXTRA NUT AND WASHER

Cut hold-down bolts

Don't be surprised if the old nuts that hold the toilet in place won't budge. Years of corrosion can weld them to their bolts. In that case, a hacksaw blade is the solution. You can buy a "close quarters" blade holder for about $6 at home centers and hardware stores, or just wrap a bare blade with a rag or duct tape. Most toilet bolts and nuts are brass, so they're easy to cut. If the bolt spins, grab it with locking pliers as you cut.

Lock down the bolts

Setting a toilet onto the new bolts can be the most frustrating part of the whole installation. The bolts slip and tip as you're straining to align them with the holes in the toilet. And each time you miss, you risk crushing or shifting the wax ring. The plastic slip-on washers sometimes included with bolts help, but they still allow the bolts to move. The best approach is to buy a second set of nuts and washers so you can lock the bolts in place before you set the toilet. To make sure they're in the correct position, set the toilet and check its height and position. Then lift it off and add the wax ring. To make the bolts easier to find, mark their locations with masking tape.

Eliminate rocking with shims

A toilet that rocks on an uneven floor will eventually break the wax ring seal and leak. So check for wobbles after you've set the toilet in place and loosely tightened the nuts. For slight wobbles, slip coins or stainless steel washers into the gaps under the toilet. Don't use regular steel washers, which might rust and stain the floor. For larger gaps, use shims. There are plastic shims made especially for toilets, but plastic construction shims ($3) like the ones shown here work just as well. When you've eliminated the wobble, tighten the nuts, cut off the shims and caulk around the toilet base. A toilet set on thick vinyl flooring can loosen as the vinyl compresses. In that case, just retighten the nuts a few days after installation.

Cut the bolts last

To make positioning a toilet easier, new toilet bolts are extra long. That means you have to cut off the protruding ends later with a hacksaw. But first connect the water line, flush the toilet a couple of times and check for leaks. Leaving the bolts uncut until you've done these final checks lets you easily remove and reset the toilet if you find any problems.

After cutting, double-check the bolts for tightness. Cutting often loosens the nuts a bit.

Shake your booty to squish the wax

When you set the toilet in place, you have to squish the wax ring until the toilet settles to the floor. DON'T force the toilet down by tightening the nuts on the toilet bolts—that might crack the porcelain base. Instead, sit on the toilet backward with your weight centered over the wax ring. Then wiggle your bottom like a belly dancer until the toilet reaches the floor. But don't go wild. You want to drive the toilet straight down with minimal twisting or shifting of it from side to side. When the toilet reaches the floor, snug down the toilet bolt nuts. Warning: To avoid ridicule, make sure no one is watching while you perform this maneuver!

Don't overtighten the water connections

Do yourself a favor and buy a flexible water supply line. They're a lot easier to install than stiff metal or plastic tubing. Be sure to get one that's covered with stainless steel mesh ($5). For a good seal, hold the hose so it aims straight into the shutoff or fill valve while you're screwing on the connectors. Make them hand-tight, then add another quarter turn with pliers. Connections that are too tight can actually cause leaks or spin the fill valve inside the tank. Check for leaks and tighten them a bit more if needed. ⌂

Question&Comment

SHOWERS AT THE HOSE SPIGOT

Every time I turn on the garden hose, water sprays all over the place right at the spigot. I've replaced the washer several times, but it still happens. I literally have to turn the handle and run. What's going on?

Your water valve is equipped with an "add-on" hose connection vacuum breaker (HCVB), and the rubber gasket inside has failed. The vacuum breaker prevents water from flowing backward into the house. (Vacuum breakers are built into newer frost-proof water valves.) The bottom portion of the breaker unscrews, but it's almost impossible to find replacement gaskets. You can find new HCVBs ($5) near the brass valves in the plumbing section at any home center.

The vacuum breaker screws onto the water valve and locks into place with a tamper-proof setscrew. To remove the faulty vacuum breaker, you'll first have to remove the setscrew(s). Use a small drill bit and drill down next to the setscrew. The brass is soft, so go slowly and be careful not to drill into the valve threads. Then use a larger bit and drill at an angle to demolish the setscrew. Install the new HCVB and you won't have to run away from your water valve.

1 Drill a small "starter" hole next to the setscrew. Switch to a larger drill bit and drill at an angle toward the setscrew. Remove the old vacuum breaker.

SETSCREW

2 Twist the new breaker into position and tighten the setscrew until the head breaks off.

CLOSE HEAT REGISTERS TO SAVE ENERGY?

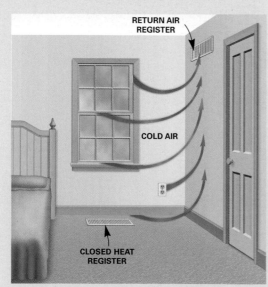

RETURN AIR REGISTER

COLD AIR

CLOSED HEAT REGISTER

Closing the heat register and door without sealing the return air duct can actually increase cold air infiltration and cost you more than you thought you'd save.

I want to save energy by closing off the heat registers and the doors to unused bedrooms. Is there any downside to my idea?

Hold on there. There are three good reasons to get an HVAC contractor involved before you start closing off heat vents, especially with today's high-efficiency furnaces and well-balanced systems. First, it might actually add to your heating bill. That's because with the heat vent closed, the suction from the return air duct can pull in cold air from the outside through any cracks around windows, exterior doors or exterior wall electrical boxes. Second, if the heat duct seams haven't been sealed properly, the extra pressure from closed-off vents will force hot air through the leaks. That can be as much as 15 percent of heated air into basements, crawl spaces and floor cavities instead of into rooms. Finally, if you have a well-designed, finely tuned heating system, closing off too many rooms can damage your furnace because it has to work too hard to distribute the air. So, if you still want to seal off these rooms, consider hiring an HVAC contractor for advice.

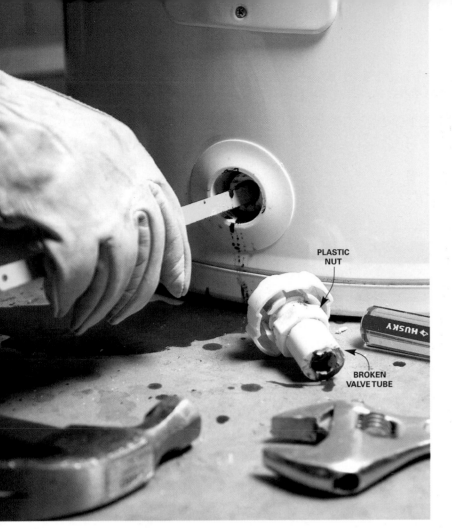

FLUSHING WATER HEATERS

I flushed the sediment out of my water heater and now the drain drips constantly. What's the fix?

Draining sediment several times a year is an effective way to reduce energy costs and increase the life of your water heater. Most water heaters come with crummy valves. And once you open them to drain the sediment, the debris clogs the valve, keeping it from sealing. But you can replace the crummy factory drain valve with a full-port ball valve for about $15. The actual valve replacement takes about an hour, but sediment buildup may slow the draining process. So set aside a full morning for this project.

Start by shutting off the water heater's power or gas supply. Open any hot water faucet until you run out of hot water. Leave the faucet on, close the cold water valve to the tank, and then hook up a garden hose to the valve to drain the tank. After the tank drains completely, unscrew and remove the valve by turning the plastic nut behind the knob. If the valve breaks, don't panic (see **Photo 1**). Stick a wire coat hanger through the opening to break up the sediment. Assemble the new valve (**Photo 2**), shut off the faucet and reopen the cold water supply valve to flush out the tank (**Photo 3**).

> **CAUTION:** Remove the ball valve handle after you flush the water heater, especially if the water heater is located where people could walk by it and accidentally bump the handle. The valve could open and release scalding water, causing serious burns. (Twist-tie the handle to the valve so you don't lose it.)

PLASTIC NUT

BROKEN VALVE TUBE

1 Remove the old valve. If it breaks off, saw the broken portion with a hacksaw blade until you hit metal threads. Then use a hammer and screwdriver to chip out the pieces.

DIELECTRIC NIPPLE

GARDEN HOSE ADAPTER

2" BRASS NIPPLE

2 Remove the handle from the ball valve so you can assemble all the 3/4-in. fittings.

3 Install the new ball valve and flush the sediment into a bucket. Let the water flow until it runs clear.

Question&Comment

PREVENT SCALDING AT HOME

I have young children and am worried that one of them might get scalded in the shower. I can't rip out the tile and install a new temperature-regulating faucet. Is there any other way to tame the hot water?

If your home is plumbed with copper pipe, you can install a mixing valve right at the water heater and set the maximum temperature to 104 degrees F. You may still get some temperature variations due to fast changes in water pressure (such as from a toilet or a washing machine), but there will be no chance of scalding.

But before you break into any pipes or buy a water heater mixing valve, ask your local building inspector if your code requires "point-of-use" tempering valves at each faucet. At about $100 each, these valves may be cheaper than installing temperature-regulating faucets.

DIAL THERMOMETER

MIXING VALVE

HOT WATER IN

COLD WATER IN

MIXED WATER TO HOUSE

1 Cut the copper pipes at your water heater and reroute them through a mixing valve. Install a temperature gauge in a tee fitting near the valve to set the output temperature. We used the Watts MMV-US mixing valve ($120) and the Boshart thermometer, No. TW25-CB2-250-25, $14, which are available at pexsupply.com (888-757-4774).

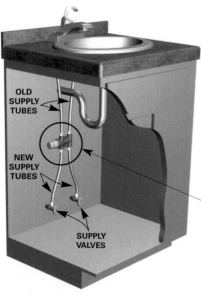

OLD SUPPLY TUBES

NEW SUPPLY TUBES

SUPPLY VALVES

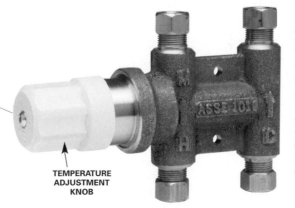

TEMPERATURE ADJUSTMENT KNOB

2 Install a "point-of-use" tempering valve below the sink. (We used the Watts USG-B M1; $92 from plumbersurplus.com; 951-588-0385.) Shut off the supply valves and disconnect the existing supply tubes. Add the tempering valve and two new supply tubes. Then turn on the hot water and adjust the tempering valve to obtain 104 degrees F. or less.

SAVE BIG!
REPLACE YOUR ENERGY GUZZLERS

Don't wait for your energy-hogging appliances to break down. Start saving now!

by **Elisa Bernick**

The furnace (or boiler), water heater and refrigerator are the biggest energy hogs in most homes. It may be hard to believe, but replacing your older but still functioning equipment and appliances with new Energy Star–qualified models can really save you big bucks. In some cases, it can cut your energy bills in half. That's because each of these items has two price tags: the initial cost of the equipment and the cost of operating that equipment over its 10- to 20-year lifetime.

This article will help you decide when it makes economic sense to replace these big-ticket energy guzzlers with new energy-efficient models. And we'll also give you a list of things to look for that can save you hundreds or even thousands of dollars when you do start shopping.

ENERGYGUIDE

Estimated Yearly Operating Cost

$67

630 kWh
Estimated Yearly Electricity Use

Your cost will depend on your utility rates and use.

#1 ENERGY GUZZLER

YOUR REFRIGERATOR

Your refrigerator consumes a whopping 13.7 percent of household energy. Refrigerator efficiency has really improved in the past few years, so if you haven't gotten a new fridge recently, replacing yours probably makes sense. If you have an older second fridge in your garage or basement, you'll save big by replacing it with a newer, more efficient model (or, of course, by getting rid of it!).

Will I save by replacing my existing refrigerator?

—If it's **8 years old or older, yes**. A 2009 model will save 40 percent in energy use over refrigerators manufactured as recently as 2001. It may seem crazy to get rid of a perfectly good 8-year-old fridge, but it's a smart financial move in most cases.

—If it's **5 years old or less, maybe**. Doing a bit of research at energystar.gov can really pay off. Under "Products," choose "appliances," then "refrigerators," and under "For Consumers" use the "Refrigerator Retirement Savings Calculator" to see when it makes sense for you to purchase a new fridge. If your refrigerator needs repairs that cost more than half the price of a new refrigerator, it makes sense to buy a new one—even if yours is only 5 years old.

Refrigerator shopping tips

A new fridge will cost you $800 to $3,000 depending on the size, style and features you choose.

■ Buy an Energy Star–qualified model. It will save you $35 to $70 a year, or between $525 and $1,050 during the 15-year average life of the unit.

■ Buy a 16- to 20-cu.-ft. model with a top or bottom freezer, which are the most energy-efficient sizes and styles. If you can't live without something larger or a side-by-side model, find the most efficient model possible.

■ Buy a model without an automatic icemaker (or don't hook it up) or a through-the-door dispenser. These increase energy use by 14 to 20 percent.

■ Before you buy, get updated efficiency information at aceee.org. The Energy Guide label on a refrigerator will tell you where it falls on a scale of efficiency compared with similar models, but it won't tell you whether it's the most efficient model available.

One great resource is the "Consumer Guide to Home Energy Savings: All New Listings of the Most Efficient Products You Can Buy." It's available for $17.95 plus shipping at aceee.org (202-429-8873).

Don't forget about rebates and recycling

Federal, state and local rebate programs pay you back $30 to $300 for purchasing energy-efficient appliances and equipment as well as for recycling your old equipment. Check out dsireusa.org for a state-by-state list of available rebates.

#2 ENERGY GUZZLER
YOUR HEATING SYSTEM

In a cold climate, two-thirds of your energy budget is spent on heat. Cutting your heating energy use is the single most effective way to cut your utility bills. The information here applies to propane, oil and natural gas systems.

Will I save by replacing my furnace or boiler?

—If it's **15 years old or older, yes**. Furnace and boiler efficiency is measured by annual fuel utilization efficiency (AFUE). Older systems have a 55 to 65 percent AFUE, whereas the least efficient systems today are at least 80 percent efficient.

—If it's **5 years old or less, no**. Replacing your furnace or boiler makes sense only if your system needs serious repair, you're switching fuel types or adding air conditioning.

—If it's **5 to 15 years old, maybe**. Find out how efficient your current unit is at ahrinet.org. Click on "AHRI Directory of Certified Product Performance," choose the equipment type and plug in the specific manufacturer and model number. Then go to energystar.gov and compare the annual operating costs of your current equipment with those of an Energy Star–qualified unit, which uses 6 to 15 percent less energy than a new standard model. Under "Products," click on "heating and cooling," then choose the specific equipment type. On the next page under "For Consumers," use the "Savings Calculator" to determine the

economic benefit of replacing your heating system with a high-efficiency one. You can use the product lists to compare specific Energy Star–qualified equipment by efficiency ratings, brand names and model numbers.

To see whether replacing your current heating equipment makes sense, the final step is to do a simple ROI calculation (see the sidebar on p. 94). It may sound like a lot of work, but an hour of your time could save you thousands of dollars.

When super-efficient heating makes sense

If you live in a cold climate where temperatures remain in subzero territory for a sustained period each winter, it makes sense to spring for a high-efficiency "condensing" furnace or boiler with an AFUE of 90 percent or higher. This will add $500 to $1,000 to the initial price of a furnace and $2,000 to that of a boiler. But over the life span of that equipment (actually the payback period is within three to seven years), you'll recoup those costs and more through lower utility bills. Also, many utilities offer rebates that will cover much of the initial cost difference.

Furnace and boiler shopping tips

A new furnace will cost $3,000 to $3,500, and a new boiler will cost $5,400 to $6,400 depending on the model and difficulty of the installation. Here are some things to keep in mind:

■ Make sure your contractor sizes the furnace or boiler by doing an "ACCA Manual J" (acca.org) or a heat loss analysis. Contractors often oversize equipment "just to make sure," which means you're paying more in usage costs as well as for the unit itself.

■ Buy a unit that's at least 83 percent efficient. Higher efficiency models like these will have vent dampers or an induced draft fan to prevent heated air from escaping up the chimney when the system is off.

■ Choose a furnace with a variable-speed fan motor, which will save you $100 or more each year in electricity costs.

■ Add insulation, seal air leaks, and replace your leaky windows and doors. These energy upgrades might allow you to buy a less expensive heating system and together can cut your fuel bills in half. For how-to information on energy upgrades, search for "save energy" at thefamilyhandyman.com.

What about electric heat?

Even minimum-efficiency electric heating systems (and water heaters) are already 90 to 100 percent efficient, so upgrading to a new system probably won't save you much if you have an electric furnace or boiler, or electric baseboard units. The best way to save on electric heat is to make sure your home is properly insulated and sealed (for how-to information, go to thefamilyhandyman.com and search for "energy audit"). Using off-peak electricity is another great way to save. Contact your power supplier to see if that's an option in your area. If so, you could cut heating costs by 40 percent or more by installing a backup heating system.

#3 ENERGY GUZZLER

YOUR WATER HEATER

Your natural gas or propane water heater uses about 17 percent of the energy in your home and is notoriously inefficient. Even a brand-new, mid-priced conventional tank-style water heater is only 57 to 59 percent efficient because it loses heat through the flue and through the walls of the storage tank. Older water heaters are even worse, wasting more than half the heat. So upgrading your old gas or propane water heater to a high-efficiency model can save big bucks. Electric water heaters are also serious energy guzzlers, but as with electric heat systems, upgrading to a newer electric model probably won't cut your utility bills by much (see sidebar at right).

Will I save by replacing my gas or propane water heater?

—If it's **10 years old or older, yes**. Gas models manufactured before 1998 typically operate at less than 50 percent efficiency.

—If it's **5 years old or less, no**. Replacement only makes sense if your system needs serious repair.

—If it's **between 5 and 10 years old, maybe**. Water heaters last an average of 10 to 15 years. If yours is getting older, it's worth replacing it now before it fails. Check out aceee.org and click on "consumer resources" and then "water heating" to examine your options. Also check out ahrinet.org to find the efficiency ratings of different makes and models. Look at the chart below to calculate the savings from replacing your water heater with a high-efficiency unit, and use the ROI calculation (below, left) to see if replacement makes sense. ⌂

Water heater shopping tips

A new tank-style water heater will cost $900 to $3,000 depending on the model and installation requirements (a power-vented unit that exhausts gases directly outside adds $500 to $1,000 to the price). When you're shopping for a tank-style water heater:

■ **Buy an Energy Star–qualified unit with at least 63 to 67 percent efficiency.**

■ **If you have an electric water heater, call your electric utility and check into off-peak electricity rates.** (You may need a second or larger water heater to take advantage of off-peak rates.) Buy a high-efficiency electric model with an insulation rating of R-22 or better.

■ **Buy the right size for your home.** A water heater that is either too big or too small will be less energy efficient. Use the Peak Water Demand Worksheet at aceee.org.

■ **Examine the efficiency rating (EF) carefully.** Similar water heaters can vary dramatically but with very little price difference. For example, a 64 EF model might cost only $75 more than a 53 EF model.

■ **Look for models with longer warranties (10 to 12 years), which typically mean better insulation and heat transfer, and larger heating elements.**

ROI calculation

To see how much money you'll save each year with more efficient equipment, calculate your return on investment (ROI) using the formula below. (Find your first-year savings at energystar.gov or aceee.org.) Remember, as fuel prices increase, so do your savings.

ROI = first-year savings divided by the installed cost

WATER HEATER TYPE (TANK STYLE)	EFFICIENCY (EF)	INSTALLED COST	YEARLY ENERGY COST	LIFE (YEARS)	TOTAL COST (OVER 13 YEARS)
Conventional gas	0.60	$850	$350	13	$5,394
High-efficiency gas	0.65	$1,025	$323	13	$5,220
Min.-efficiency electric	0.90	$750	$463	13	$6,769
High-efficiency electric	0.95	$820	$439	13	$6,528

HandyHints®

GOLF BALL DRAIN COVER

When I golf, I don't want my ball to be anywhere near water, but at home I use one in the laundry tub. The drain cover on my tub doesn't fit tight anymore, and I find that a golf ball makes a good substitute. This works in most lavatory sink and bathtub drains too.

MARK STRAIGHT LINES ON ROUND PIPES

It's not easy to cut a straight line all the way around a pipe with tin snips or a hacksaw. You can make the job a whole lot easier by marking a perfect cutting line with a square piece of cardboard or stiff paper. Just align the edges of the cardboard and pull it tight around the pipe, then mark the edge all the way around. As long as you follow the line, your cut will be perfectly straight.

HVAC REMINDERS FOR THE FORGETFUL

It's hard for me to keep track of the furnace maintenance schedule. To make it easier, I stuck a small white magnetic board to my furnace duct. I write down the furnace filter size, the brand, the date I last changed the filter, and the date my furnace was last cleaned and checked. When it's time to put in a new filter or have the furnace cleaned, I erase the old date and write down the new one.

SELF-CLEANING BARBECUE

If you're going to do a self-clean cycle on your oven, do double-duty and grab the grease-covered racks out of your barbecue grill and throw those in too. The self-clean cycle will incinerate stubborn deposits with little to no work on your part!

AUGUST '09 RIBFEST DRIPPINGS

Editor's note: Leaving your racks in the oven during the self-cleaning cycle can darken them and make them hard to slide. Rub a few drops of salad oil on the edges afterward for easier sliding.

FIX YOUR DRYER

You can solve most problems youself—
no experience necessary!

by **Rick Muscoplat**

Save at least $80

If your dryer breaks down, here's the first thing to know: You can solve most dryer troubles yourself. There's no need to find a technician, schedule a service call or pay $80 to $200 for repairs.

The fixes we show in this article correct about 90 percent of dryer breakdowns. Most repairs take about an hour, but set aside extra time to locate replacement parts. To find parts, check the yellow pages or search online for "appliance parts." Aside from basic tools like a socket set and screwdrivers, you may need a continuity tester or multimeter to diagnose the problem.

DRYER DISASSEMBLY

Most dryer repairs require some disassembly of the outer cabinet so you can get at the parts inside. If your dryer's lint filter is inside the front door (**Figure A**), disassemble it this way: First, remove the screws at each corner of the control panel. Flip the panel up and back to expose the screws in the top panel. Remove the screws, then pull the top toward you and lift it off. To open the bottom panel, release the spring catches by shoving a putty knife into the slot just above them. With the bottom panel open, you can remove the front panel by removing two screws at the top and two at the bottom.

If your filter slides into the top of the dryer, remove the screws alongside the filter slot. Using a putty knife, release the two spring catches located under the top panel at the front. Tilt the top panel up like a car hood and remove the screws that hold the front panel in place.

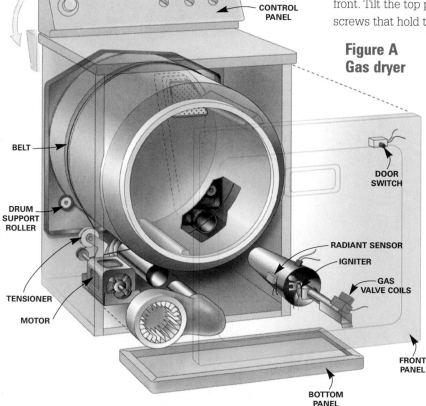

CONTROL PANEL

Figure A
Gas dryer

BELT

DRUM SUPPORT ROLLER

TENSIONER

MOTOR

DOOR SWITCH

RADIANT SENSOR

IGNITER

GAS VALVE COILS

FRONT PANEL

BOTTOM PANEL

Using a continuity tester

Our photos show using a multimeter ($25) to diagnose trouble. But a continuity tester ($5) will also work for all the troubleshooting in this article. To use a continuity tester, simply attach the clamp to one contact point and touch the probe to the other. If the light glows, you've got continuity. If not, you've got trouble.

CAUTION: Don't get shocked! Unplug the dryer before you do any disassembly, diagnostic or repair work. On a gas dryer, also turn off the gas supply shutoff valve.

DRYER WON'T START

If your dryer seems absolutely dead when you turn it on, chances are the door switch is bad or the plunger is broken or bent. Door switches wear out from normal use, but repeatedly slamming the door can speed up their demise. Start by checking the plunger located on the door. If it's missing or bent, replace it. If the plunger checks out, the next step is to remove the top cabinet panel to gain access to the door switch. See the disassembly instructions on p. 96.

Test the switch ($26) for continuity (see p. 96). If the switch is good, test the thermal fuse (see **photo**, p. 98) mounted on the blower housing. If you have a gas dryer with the lint filter in the door, access the thermal fuse by opening the bottom panel. If the filter slides into the top of the machine, remove the entire front panel. On an electric dryer, remove the rear service panel. If you don't get a continuity reading from the thermal fuse, do NOT simply replace it. A blown thermal fuse is a warning that you have other serious problems—either a malfunctioning thermostat or a clogged vent. Fix those before replacing the fuse ($20).

DOOR SWITCH

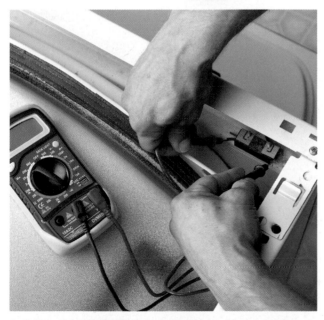

Pull the wires off the door switch. Open and close the door while testing for continuity. If you don't get continuity, replace the switch.

DRYER THUMPS, RUMBLES OR CHIRPS

The drum support rollers are worn. Replace them ($25; shown below). If the noise continues, replace the tensioner roller (p. 99). Since it takes longer to disassemble the machine than to actually replace the rollers and belts, we recommend replacing both of them at the same time—total parts cost is $45.

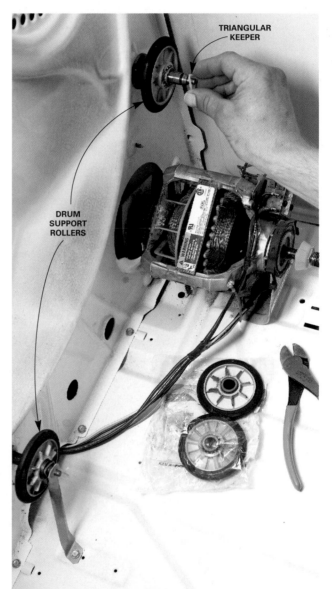

TRIANGULAR KEEPER

DRUM SUPPORT ROLLERS

Clip off the old triangular roller keeper and remove the roller. Wipe the shaft with a rag and rubbing alcohol and install the new roller and keeper. Do NOT lubricate the shaft.

Tip

The first step in any appliance repair is to make sure it's getting electricity. Unplugged cords and tripped breakers are a leading cause of appliance "breakdowns."

NO HEAT

If you have an electric or gas dryer that tumbles but won't heat, check the thermal fuse for continuity. If the thermal fuse checks out, move on to the radiant sensor if you have

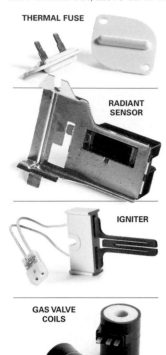

THERMAL FUSE

RADIANT SENSOR

IGNITER

GAS VALVE COILS

a gas dryer. It monitors the igniter and powers up the gas valve coils when the igniter reaches peak temperature. A bum sensor will stop the whole show. Test it for continuity (**Photo 1**) and replace it if it fails ($32). If the sensor is good, disconnect the electrical connector to the igniter and check it for continuity. Again, replace it if it fails the continuity test ($40). If both the radiant sensor and the igniter pass the test, replace the gas valve coils ($30 per set). To replace them, remove the retaining plate, unplug the sensors and pull them off the gas valve.

If the thermal fuse on your electric dryer checks out, test the heater element for continuity. Replace the element ($55) if you don't get continuity (**Photos 2 and 3**).

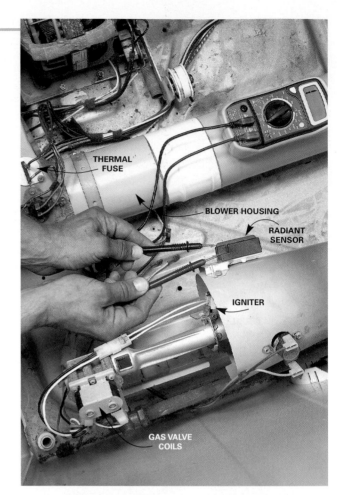

THERMAL FUSE

BLOWER HOUSING

RADIANT SENSOR

IGNITER

GAS VALVE COILS

1 On a gas dryer, test the radiant sensor, igniter and thermal fuse by disconnecting the wires and checking for continuity. Replace them if they fail the continuity test.

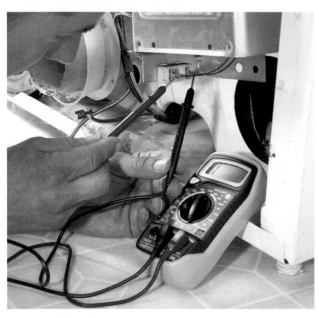

2 Disconnect the wires to the heating element of an electric dryer and test it for continuity. Replace the element if you don't get a continuity reading.

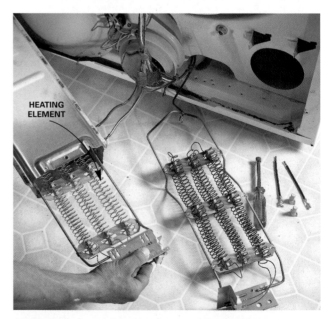

HEATING ELEMENT

3 Replace the bad heating element on an electric dryer by unscrewing the retaining clip at the top of the heater box. Then pull out the box and remove the element retaining screw. Swap the elements and reinstall.

DRUM WON'T ROTATE, BUT THE MOTOR RUNS

You're in luck—it's only a broken belt ($20). Remove the front cabinet panel and lift the entire drum out of the cabinet. Now's the time to fire up your shop vacuum and suck out all the lint. Then spin the tensioner roller by hand to see if it runs smoothly and examine it for cracks. Replace the tensioner ($17) if it fails either test. Reinstall the drum and wrap the new belt around it (ribs facing the drum). Some tensioners are mounted behind the motor, so they're difficult to see from the front access panel. You'll have to do this by feel. Reach your hands around the blower housing and lift the tensioner up while you route the belt around the motor pulley. 🏠

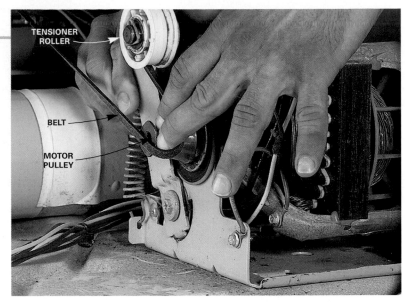

Route the new belt around the drum and toward the motor/tensioner assembly. Reach your hands around the motor and retract the tensioner so you can wrap the belt around the motor pulley.

DollarSavvyHomeowner

Don't slam the lid

If you're in the habit of slamming your washing machine lid shut, your appliance repair person wants to say "Thanks!" Dropping the lid, rather than closing it gently, eventually wrecks the lid switch—and provides easy money for appliance technicians. Our guy charges about $75 to replace the switch. So if you want to avoid a donation to his big screen TV fund, stop slamming the lid.

If your washing machine fills with water, but won't agitate or spin, you've broken the switch. Replacing the switch yourself is a simple job on most machines; just unscrew it, unplug it and install the new one. To find a replacement switch ($20), use the yellow pages or an online search engine to look for "Appliance Parts."

Use less salt—and water

Many water softeners are set to recharge way too often and may not be adjusted for the best salt and water efficiency. That could be costing you $100 or so annually in salt and water costs. How often a water softener recharges is based on two things: water hardness and the number of days or water usage between regenerations. A day timer counts days, and a demand-initiated/metered type measures gallons. Some older softeners don't have meters and can use twice the amount of salt and water used by a metered type. Both types are set up according to the hardness of the water and the number of people living in the house.

Do you have a houseful of kids or an empty nest? Either way, it may be time to tune up your settings.

Start by looking for the utility company's Web site on your water bill. On the site, you can find the Water Quality Report. It will list the range of water hardness in your city's system. You must use the highest number. If you have a well, get a test for hardness and iron from any softener dealer.

Your softener manual may have instructions for changing your hardness and salt dose settings. If not, call the company that sold you the softener or the softener manufacturer. It may tell you how to reset your softener control. If not, have a technician come out to your home to do it and teach you how.

CONNECTING GAS LINES

The right fitting for a safe hookup

by **Jeff Gorton**

Gas connections for your oven or dryer are really pretty simple—it's mostly a matter of screwing stuff together. But knowing which fittings to use where can be tricky, and using the wrong ones can lead to a dangerous leak. This article will show you how to safely connect a gas dryer or gas range.

Kits containing a flexible stainless steel gas line and fittings are available for $20 to $35 at home centers and hardware stores. The kits usually have everything you'll need, but in some cases, you may have to buy a few more fittings. But before you start, check with your local

building inspections department to see if you're allowed to do your own hookup.

On the next pages, we'll show you three common gas piping scenarios. We'll show you one way to make each connection, but there are other equally legitimate ways using common plumbing parts. Don't be confused by the labels FIP and MIP; they simply stand for female pipe threads and male pipe threads, respectively. And when you buy the parts, don't hesitate to ask for help. Then screw all the parts together to make sure they fit.

Reusing a copper coil

It's common for appliances to be connected with a coil of soft copper like the one shown here. The ends of the copper tubing will be flared like the end of a trumpet. A leakproof joint is formed by the perfect fit between the flared end of the tube and the cone-shaped fitting. If the soft copper tubing isn't kinked or damaged, you can reuse it to connect your new appliance. For this dryer connection we purchased a brass elbow with a 1/2-in. flare fitting on one side to match the 1/2-in. flare on the copper tubing, and a 3/8-in. female iron thread fitting on the other to match the 3/8-in. pipe exiting the back of the dryer. Your tubing may be a different size and your appliance may have different threads. Buy fittings to match. Coat threads with pipe thread compound or gas-rated Teflon tape before assembling. Align the copper tubing so the flare fits perfectly before threading on the flare nut. Tighten the nut with an adjustable or open-end wrench.

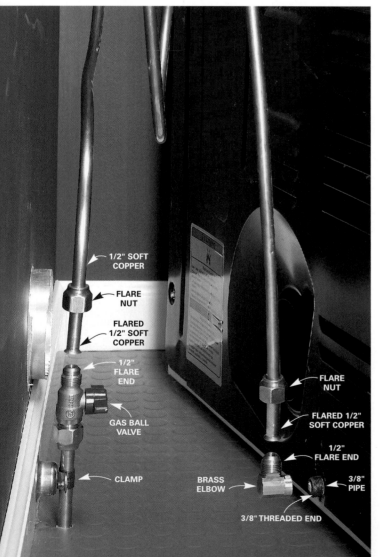

- 1/2" SOFT COPPER
- FLARE NUT
- FLARED 1/2" SOFT COPPER
- 1/2" FLARE END
- GAS BALL VALVE
- CLAMP
- BRASS ELBOW
- 3/8" THREADED END
- FLARE NUT
- FLARED 1/2" SOFT COPPER
- 1/2" FLARE END
- 3/8" PIPE

Test for leaks

Turn the gas back on and swab each joint with a solution of 2 tsp. dishwashing liquid to 1 cup water or with a commercially prepared leak testing solution. Coat each connection and watch for bubbles to form. If you see a bubble, turn off the gas. First try tightening the leaky connection. If this doesn't work, take it apart. Inspect flare connections for debris or damage. Fix leaky threaded connections by reapplying pipe joint compound or gas-rated Teflon tape and reassembling the fitting.

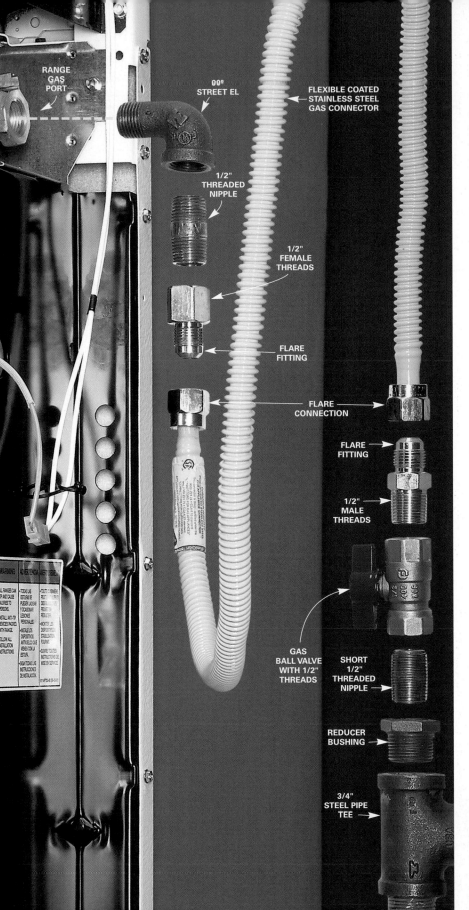

RANGE GAS PORT

00° STREET EL

FLEXIBLE COATED STAINLESS STEEL GAS CONNECTOR

1/2" THREADED NIPPLE

1/2" FEMALE THREADS

FLARE FITTING

FLARE CONNECTION

FLARE FITTING

1/2" MALE THREADS

GAS BALL VALVE WITH 1/2" THREADS

SHORT 1/2" THREADED NIPPLE

REDUCER BUSHING

3/4" STEEL PIPE TEE

WARNING

Connecting to steel pipe

Older houses often have threaded steel gas pipe. If your old appliance is connected with a steel pipe and you're installing a new appliance, buy a gas appliance connecting kit and replace the steel pipe with the flexible stainless steel tube. But remember, you can't connect the flare fitting on the flexible gas line directly to a steel pipe thread. You have to install the flare fitting that's included with the kit.

Also replace old-style gas valves (photo below) with modern ball valves that are labeled for use with gas. Before you replace an old valve, you'll have to find and turn off the main gas valve to the house. It's usually located near where the gas line enters the house. When you turn the gas back on, remember to check all your gas appliances to see if they have pilot lights that need relighting.

The photo shows how to use common plumbing parts to join a new ball valve and a flexible stainless steel connector to steel pipe. Coat all threaded pipe connections with pipe thread compound before assembly. The valve shown has 1/2-in. female pipe threads on both sides. If necessary, use a bushing to reduce the existing 3/4-in. female pipe thread to 1/2 in. Use a 90-degree elbow at the stove to avoid kinking the gas tubing when you push the stove against the wall.

OLD-STYLE GAS VALVE

Old-style gas valves can leak. Replace them with approved ball valves.

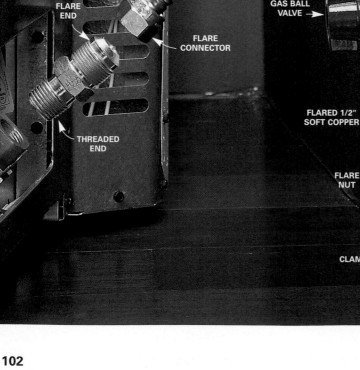

Test for leaks

Turn the gas back on and swab each joint with a solution of 2 tsp. dishwashing liquid to 1 cup water or with a commercially prepared leak testing solution. Coat each connection and watch for bubbles to form. If you see a bubble, turn off the gas. First try tightening the leaky connection. If this doesn't work, take it apart. Inspect flare connections for debris or damage. Fix leaky threaded connections by reapplying pipe joint compound or gas-rated Teflon tape and reassembling the fitting.

FLEXIBLE STAINLESS STEEL GAS CONNECTOR

FLARE CONNECTOR

FLARE END

FEMALE THREADS

GAS BALL VALVE

FLARED 1/2" SOFT COPPER

FLARE NUT

FLARE END

FLARE CONNECTOR

FLARE END

THREADED END

CLAMP

Connecting to soft copper

Connections for flexible "soft" copper are made by flaring the end of the soft copper tubing with a special flaring tool and installing flare fittings that have a matching cone-shaped meeting surface. Common sizes of flare fittings are 3/8 in., 1/2 in. and 5/8 in. Match flare fittings to the outside diameter of the soft copper you're connecting to.

The photo below shows a soft copper line that's kinked and should be replaced. There are two options. You could cut a new length of coiled soft copper, flare the ends and connect it with flare fittings (see p. 100). Or you could replace the damaged tubing with a flexible stainless connector as shown here. If the flare fitting on the flexible stainless gas line matches the size of the flare fitting on the existing gas valve, you can simply screw it on. If the fittings don't match, one solution is to replace the valve with one that has a flare fitting on one side and a 1/2-in. female pipe thread on the other side. Then use the adapter included with your hookup kit to connect the flexible gas line. On the stove end, use another flare-to-pipe-thread fitting.

Remember to apply pipe thread compound or gas-rated Teflon tape to the threads on threaded connections before assembling them. Flare joints rely on a tight fit to seal and don't require additional sealant. ⌂

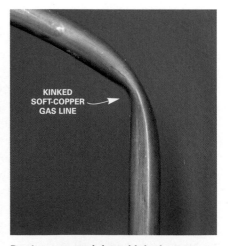

KINKED SOFT-COPPER GAS LINE

Don't try to straighten kinked copper. Replace it instead.

New Tools & Gear

PULL A STRING, SAVE $75 IN HOT WATER

ShowerStart says its Evolve line of showerheads can save up to 2,700 gallons of water a year for an annual savings of $75. They can save you money by conserving hot water. A lot of people let the shower run so the water will warm up while they brush their teeth, talk on the phone or head for a cup of coffee. The problem is that 2-1/2 gallons of water, including hot water, is going down the drain every minute.

Evolve showerheads shut off the water the instant it reaches 95 degrees F. When you're ready to shower, pull the cord or flip a switch (depending on the model) to resume hot water flow. You don't have to keep pulling the cord to keep water flowing.

The rain showerhead shown costs $50; other models start at $40. Buy one at the Web site below or amazon.com.

ShowerStart, (480) 496-2294. evolveshowerheads.com

PLUMBING, HEATING & APPLIANCES

A STYLISH, AFFORDABLE VESSEL SINK

Finding a vessel sink that is simple, elegant and affordable is challenging. Simple and elegant are easy, but the cost of these sinks can be astronomical. Decolav's Classically Redefined Collection bucks the trend. The collection features vessel, drop-in and under-mount sinks that marry classic elegance with contemporary design at reasonable prices. The oval ceramic sink shown costs $233 and is part of a collection that includes many different styles and shapes ranging from $200 to $500. Available at Home Depot, from online retailers and in showrooms around the country. To find a dealer, visit Decolav's Web site.

decolav.com, (561) 274-2110

TWO OVENS IN A SINGLE-OVEN WALL SPACE

Tired of the Thanksgiving shuffle that has you constantly moving dishes in and out of the oven to cook at different temperatures for different lengths of time? Check out the new GE Profile 30-in. single-double wall oven ($2,600), the industry's first oven that cooks dishes at two separate temperatures at the same time. Although it fits into the same wall space as a single standard oven, it provides enough room for a 22-lb. turkey in the 2.8-cu.-ft. lower oven and two 10 x 14-in. casserole dishes in the upper oven. Features include convection settings and slow-cook and pizza modes. Visit GE's Web site for more info (search for "single-double").

ge.appliances.com, (800) 626-2005

Save ON NEW APPLIANCES

Install them yourself!

by **Elisa Bernick**

Nice crisper for veggies!

Lots of room for beer!

SPECIAL SALE
REGULAR PRICE $2,400
SPECIAL PRICE $2,000

When you're buying a new appliance, it's tempting to have the dealer handle the installation hassles. But here are two good reasons to tackle the installation yourself:

Save serious money. Dealers charge anywhere from $100 to $200 to hook up a major appliance. Some dealers may not be able to make gas connections for a gas oven or dryer, which means hiring a plumber and spending even more. For tips on installing gas appliances, see "Connecting Gas Lines," p. 100.

Get it done right. Appliance installation mistakes are a major cause of home catastrophes, from water damage to fires. The quality of dealer installation varies: You might get an experienced perfectionist to install your new appliance or you might get a kid who just started his job last week. By tackling the installation yourself, you can make sure it's safe and reliable.

DIY Success Story

"Last year my wife and I bought all new appliances. The installation fees ($80 to $120) seemed reasonable until I added them up. Then my innate frugality kicked in. It took me two weekends, but in the end I figured I had paid myself about $200 per day. Not bad for a part-time job!"

—Travis Larson, Senior Editor

WHIRLPOOL

Buy a fridge that fits

Most appliances come in standard sizes. But with refrigerators, there's no such thing as "standard." They vary in width, depth and height, and lots of homeowners don't realize this until they try to slide the new fridge into place. Measure before you shop so you're sure your new fridge is going to fit between and under existing cabinets. And make sure its doors and drawers can open fully in your kitchen.

Also measure doorway openings and hallways to be sure the fridge will fit through your front door and into the kitchen. Removing the doors from the refrigerator and freezer will make the unit lighter and easier to carry. This only involves removing a few screws, and will make it easier to fit through doorways without damaging the doorway or the appliance.

Buy "no-burst" stainless steel washer hoses

Yes!
BRAIDED
STAINLESS
STEEL

Many washing machines come without water supply hoses at all or come with poor-quality rubber hoses. Buy quality "no-burst" hoses, which have a braided stainless steel sleeve ($20). Let your homeowner's insurance company know you're using no-burst hoses and you might get a discount on your premium.

Burst washing machine hoses are one of the most common sources of water damage, accounting for more than $150 million in insurance claims each year in the United States.

No
RUBBER

Check your old washer shutoffs

If you have old hose bib–type shutoff valves, don't assume they'll work well after going unused for years. Try the handles a day or two before you plan to install the new washer. If you can't turn them at all, you have two choices: Replace the valves or shut off your main water valve when you replace the washer. If the handles do turn, there's still a good chance the valve won't close completely. So have a bucket handy to catch drips while you replace the washer.

Don't push with your knee

The easiest way to nudge a heavy appliance into place is with your knee—and it's also the easiest way to dent the thin metal. Ease the appliance into position by placing your hands on the sides and pressing firmly with even pressure. Also, take off your rings and other jewelry when you're moving an appliance to avoid scratching it.

Protect the floor

Even the toughest tile floor can be scratched by the metal wheels of a refrigerator. Rolling or pushing them over vinyl or wood flooring can cause dents and gouges. "I learned the hard way how much damage a tiny grain of sand caught beneath the wheel of a refrigerator can cause to a tile floor," says Costas Stavrou, owner of Nicollet Appliance Repair in Minneapolis. "Let's just say the homeowner was not pleased."

Laying down stiff cardboard or a chunk of leftover carpeting usually works fine. If you want the ultimate protection, use a sheet of 1/8-in. hardboard ($7 at home centers). The smooth surface not only protects floors but also allows appliances to move smoothly into and out of place.

WHIRLPOOL

Spend extra for a quiet, energy-efficient dishwasher

Energy Star–qualified dishwashers use about 32 percent less electricity than non–Energy Star models, so they're definitely worth buying, and they're available in every price range. But energy efficiency translates into longer cycle times—up to three hours or more. Keep that in mind when you're pricing dishwashers. You can find Energy Star–qualified dishwashers that clean well at prices from $400 to $1,000. (You probably don't need all the bells and whistles of models priced over $1,000. They don't clean any better than lower-priced dishwashers.)

Often the biggest difference between the cheapest and slightly higher priced models is noise. Dishwashers outfitted with better sound insulation cost more. If your kitchen is open to the rest of the house or near a room you like to use when the dishwasher's running, consider spending an extra $200 to $300 to get a quiet, energy-efficient model.

Beware of plastic fridge tubing

Cheap plastic is unreliable. It can dry, crack and leak as it ages. According to the U.S. insurance industry, leaks from plastic water supply tubing are a primary cause of water damage each year. If your previous icemaker hookup used plastic tubing, replace it with flexible braided stainless line ($15 for 10 ft.). It doesn't kink like copper; the screw-on fittings make it easier to connect than the compression fittings required by plastic or copper; and it provides better water flow than plastic.

If your existing copper tubing is in good shape, reuse it. But if it's kinked, switch to braided stainless. If you have PEX plastic tubing and you've never seen a mouse in your house, you should be fine. Otherwise, stick with the copper or braided stainless steel "gnaw proof" options so you don't encounter a nasty surprise, as TFH editor Travis Larson did. "I came home to a sagging, waterlogged basement ceiling thanks to the leaky plastic line feeding my refrigerator. The telltale signs of a gnawing mouse were all over it!"

A three-hour icemaker supply line leak can be the equivalent of dumping three 55-gal. drums of water on a kitchen floor.

YUMM...

CHEAP PLASTIC TUBING
No

Yes!
BRAIDED STAINLESS STEEL

PEX
OK

WHIRLPOOL

Glass and ceramic cooktops require special care

A new smooth glass or ceramic cooktop adds a sleek, updated look to any kitchen. If you buy one, keep in mind that they can be damaged without proper care. Most require a special cleanser to keep them looking good. If you switch from coiled burners to a glass cooktop, replace your older copper-bottomed pots and pans with a set that won't damage the cooktop surface. Pans with colored bottoms can fuse with the glass top and damage it. Also, lesser-quality pans can warp due to the intense heat of glass cooktops, and rough-bottomed pans can scratch the glass surface.

Induction cooktops and dual-fuel ranges have special requirements as well. Induction cooking requires cookware made of steel, cast iron or some other combination of metals that will react with the magnetic field. And both induction cooktops and dual-fuel ranges with a gas cooktop and electric oven require your kitchen to be wired for 220 volts (which isn't likely if you're currently using gas). Be sure to add these costs to the appliance price tag to get the real cost of your new purchase.

Never, ever use plastic dryer duct

When you replace your dryer, take the opportunity to clean any lint that has built up in your existing dryer duct. If you have to replace any ducting, smooth rigid metal duct is the best choice. If you have to use flexible duct, make sure it's semi-rigid metal duct ($15 for 8 ft. at home centers) rather than thin foil or flexible plastic duct, which are both fire hazards. Avoid using screws to connect the vent pipe sections. They collect lint that can block the vent. Instead, connect all the sections with aluminum foil tape.

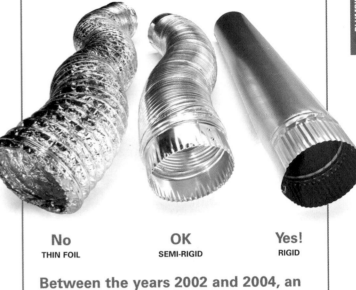

| **No** | **OK** | **Yes!** |
| THIN FOIL | SEMI-RIGID | RIGID |

Between the years 2002 and 2004, an annual average of 12,700 clothes dryer fires occurred...failure to clean out lint buildup is the leading factor.

—U.S. FIRE ADMINISTRATION

Check for leaks

After you've hooked up a water-using appliance, wipe up any water that dripped during the installation and run the appliance through a couple of cycles to be sure there aren't any leaks. Give it some time. A leak may not show up for 20 to 30 minutes. Do this before you reattach the front access panel of your dishwasher. Get down on your hands and knees and check for leaks underneath it with a flashlight.

After hooking up your new icemaker, check that it's filling, and look for leaks behind the fridge before you push it back to the wall. Run a small load in your new washing machine and watch it drain. Make sure the drain hose doesn't leap out of place when the water pours through it. If there's a leak, tightening the connection just a little is usually enough to stop it.

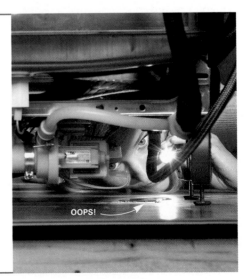

OOPS!

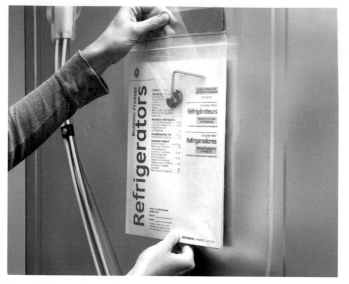

Don't lose the manual

New appliances come with manuals, wrenches, extra washers and accessories. Put it all in a zippered plastic bag and tape or tack it to the appliance, the wall or inside a nearby cabinet so you have everything together when you need it.

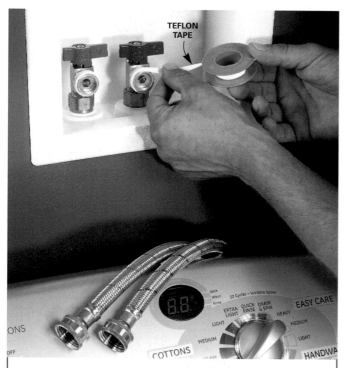

TEFLON TAPE

Make washer hoses easier to remove

Once you screw your new washer hoses to the shutoff valves, there's a good chance you won't unscrew them again for a decade or more. To make the hoses easier to unscrew years from now, use Teflon pipe thread tape or pipe joint compound on the threads. It won't prevent leaks, but it will prevent mineral deposits and corrosion from welding the hose fittings to the valves.

Install leak detectors

Consider installing leak detector units behind or under water-using appliances to prevent water damage from leaky hoses. Battery-operated models ($15 to $25) sound an alarm when they detect water. Other models, like the one shown here ($135), automatically shut off the water when they detect leakage on the floor. Some monitors can be wired to a centrally monitored alarm system or to an automatic shutoff valve on your main water line or at individual shutoffs. ⌂

CONTROL UNIT

AUTOMATIC SHUTOFF

SENSOR

GreatGoofs®

A new toilet to go with that seat

My dad waited until I came home from college to ask me to install the soft-cushion toilet seat he'd just bought. I sprayed the old, rusty toilet seat bolts with a heavy dose of lubricant and then got out the wrench and went to work on them. Unfortunately, the wrench slipped off the lubricated bolt and the handle busted a nice hole in the toilet, sending water all over the floor. With my tail between my legs, I had to tell my dad that he needed a new toilet to go with his new seat.

I replaced the toilet, but haven't had my dad ask me to do anything around the house since. (I guess that means it worked out for the best after all!)

Why, that quiet little drip!

The water dispenser in my refrigerator door wasn't working, so I figured the solenoid valve was shot. After a one-hour trip to the parts store for a new $60 valve, I installed it. Guess what? Still no water! After 30 minutes of troubleshooting and checking the electrical connections and the water hookup, I was as perplexed as ever. That's when my 7-year-old daughter waltzed in and asked me what I was doing. Then she told me that she'd pressed the water lock button on the fridge door after learning about water conservation in school. I felt like a big drip!

Not your mom's home cooking

On a cold night last winter, my wife was in the kitchen using the microwave. From the next room, I heard the timer bell ding, the microwave door open, and then a loud "Oh, shoot!" Since her feet were cold, my wife decided to warm up her slippers in the microwave. Unfortunately, she cooked them on high for three minutes. What came out looked like a scene from "The Blob." Not only had her slippers been nuked, but every time we used the microwave after that, the food came out tasting like burnt slippers. It was a tough call, but I threw out the microwave and kept the wife.

GreatGoofs®

Lesson learned the slimy way

My wife was complaining about the slow-draining sink in our kitchen, so I put my handyman prowess to work. I planned to use the blow feature on my shop vacuum to push the clog through the drain line.

As I inserted the hose into the drain, my wife asked, "Don't you think we should cover the other drain?" But it was too late. I'd already flipped on the vacuum, causing stinky, slimy water to shoot out of the other drain and drench us. Next time I'll let her finish talking before I start working.

Sewer with a secret

We purchased our home six years ago and have had problems with the sewer backing up for the last four. After having the sewer line snaked, jetted and scoped, we learned that the backflow valve cap had broken off and become lodged in the line. We hired someone with a backhoe to dig up the line, but we couldn't find the broken cap. Completely puzzled, we again called the company that scoped it to locate the lodged cap (another charge).

While we waited, the backhoe operator asked my husband if he'd checked the cleanout drain. "Cleanout drain?" my husband repeated as his face turned pale. Sure enough, under a piece of carpet in the basement was the drain, and inside the drain was the broken cap. Then we went upstairs to take a good, long look at our dug-up backyard. It was like buying a price tag with no clothing attached.

Water and ceilings don't mix

The spring and pulley on my dishwasher door broke, so I bought the part to fix it and made the repair in about 30 minutes. As I pushed the dishwasher back into place, I felt pretty good about saving the $100 I would have had to pay a repairman.

Early the next morning, while I was still enjoying a peaceful night's sleep, my wife ran into the bedroom screaming that the basement ceiling was falling down and the basement was flooded. Turns out, when I pushed the dishwasher back in, it pulled the water supply line free. The water ran onto the underlying ceiling all night, ruining everything below. That $100 I saved cost me $1,000 for a new ceiling and flooring.

4 Woodworking & Furniture Projects, Tools & Tips

IN THIS CHAPTER

Do's&Don'ts

PERFECT **ROUTED EDGES**

It's almost magical the way you can transform a square-edged board into a wooden masterpiece with just a router and bit. Modern router bits with carbide cutters and guide bearings make the task almost foolproof. But there are a few tips and tricks that'll simplify the job and give you the best results. In this article, we'll show you these tips, as well as ways to secure small pieces of wood while you rout them.

Edge-forming router bits range from simple round-over or bevel bits to intricate cove, ogee and classical bits. You'll find a selection of common profiles at home centers and hardware stores, but to see the wide range of profiles available, search online for "router bits" or visit the Freud or Bosch Web sites. Carbide edge-forming bits cost about $20 and up depending on the size and shape.

Rout the ends first

If you rout the sides first, the split-out will occur on the previously shaped edge (see **photo** on the right). But if you rout the ends first, you'll cut off any damaged areas when you rout the sides.

ROUT FIRST

CHIP

END-GRAIN CHIPPING

Don't rout the sides before the ends

If you're planning to rout the ends as well as one or both sides of a board, rout the two ends first. Here's why. End grain has a tendency to split out as the bit exits the end of the cut.

Move the router in the right direction

Router bits spin clockwise as you look down on the router, so moving the router counterclockwise tends to pull the pilot bearing tight against the wood and allows easy control of the router. When you're routing the outside perimeter of a board, move the router counterclockwise. However, when you're routing the inside of something like a picture frame, move the router in a clockwise direction.

TABLE SAW

Make moldings with your router

One way to make narrow moldings with your router is to use a router table and featherboards. But if you don't have a setup like this, try the method shown here. Start by routing the desired profile on a wide board. Then make the molding by cutting the shaped edge from the wide board with a table saw. Repeat the process until the board is too narrow to work with.

Router tips

- Insert the router bit fully into the collet. Then pull it back out 1/8 in. before tightening the collet nuts.
- Sand the edge of boards before routing them so the guide bearing will ride on a smooth surface. If you don't, irregularities in the edge on the board will be transferred to the routed shape.

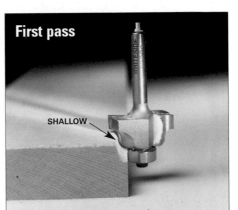

First pass

SHALLOW

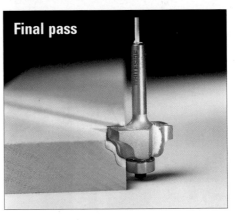

Final pass

- Press the base of the router tight to the wood surface to prevent the router from tipping. A tipped router will cut an irregular profile.
- Make deep-profile cuts in two or three shallow passes to avoid burns and chatter marks. Set the router depth for a shallow cut and rout all sides. Then adjust the router for a deeper cut and repeat the process.
- Replace your old steel bits with modern carbide bits. Carbide lasts longer and makes cleaner cuts with less effort.
- Clean your router bits with a special blade-and-bit cleaning solution to remove wood pitch. You'll find blade-and-bit cleaner at woodworking stores.

Do's&Don'ts

Hold narrow strips with stops

Narrow strips are difficult to rout because clamps get in the way. The solution is to screw blocks to your workbench to corral the strip of wood. If you're routing a thin piece of wood, the bearing on the router bit will most likely extend below the piece of wood you're routing. In this case, hang the piece of wood over the edge of the bench at least 1/4 in. so the bit doesn't hit the workbench. Screw a strip of equal thickness behind the long edge of the narrow strip you're routing. Then screw a thinner stop block at the end to keep the board from sliding.

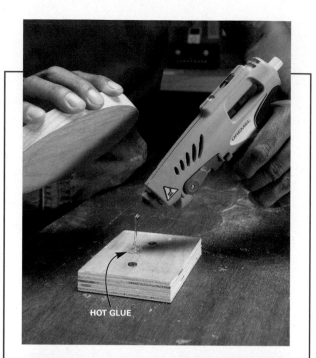

HOT GLUE

OVERHANGING EDGE

EQUAL THICKNESS BOARD

STOP BLOCK

Secure small work with hot-melt glue

Here's a nifty trick for securing small pieces while you rout them. Start by screwing a scrap of wood to the workbench to elevate your project and provide clearance for the bearing. The scrap should be smaller than the piece you're routing. Then apply 1/2 teaspoon of hot-melt glue to the scrap and stick your workpiece to it. Allow it to cool a few minutes before you rout the edge. When you're done, just twist the routed piece to break it free. Then scrape off the hot-melt glue with a chisel or putty knife. Rout gently; don't make an aggressive cut or you could dislodge your work.

IRON-ON **EDGE BANDING**

With a roll of wood veneer edge banding and a few simple tools, you can cover raw plywood edges so the plywood is nearly indistinguishable from solid wood. Iron-on edge banding is wood veneer with hot-melt adhesive preapplied to the back. You simply hold the edge banding in place, run over it with a household iron to heat the adhesive, let it cool and trim the edges flush. We'll show you how to do it and share some tips for getting perfect results every time.

7/8" OAK EDGE BANDING

You'll find edge banding in common species like birch, oak and cherry at home centers and lumberyards. For exotic species and a greater variety of widths, search online or visit a specialty woodworking store like Rockler or Woodcraft. Rolls of edge banding come in lengths of 8 ft. to 250 ft. and widths of 13/16 in. to 2 in. For typical 3/4-in. plywood, buy 13/16- or 7/8-in.-wide edge banding (20¢ to 65¢ per linear ft.).

If you'd rather cover the edges with solid wood nosing, go to thefamilyhandyman.com and search for "wood nosing."

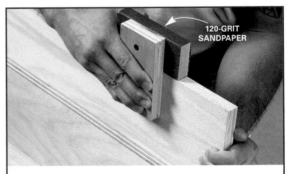

120-GRIT SANDPAPER

Clean up the edges

Saw marks or other roughness will prevent a strong bond between the edge banding and the plywood. To avoid loose edge banding, sand the edges of the plywood smooth before you apply it. To keep from rounding edges while you sand, wrap a quarter sheet of 120-grit sandpaper around a small block of 3/4-in. plywood and screw another scrap to it as a guide. When the sandpaper starts showing signs of wear, remove the screw and reposition the sandpaper. After sanding, vacuum the edge to remove any dust.

Do's&Don'ts

"COTTON" SETTING

ROLL OF EDGE BANDING

Iron on the edge banding

Use your regular clothes iron if you wish, but be aware that you may get adhesive on the soleplate. To be safe, buy a cheap iron from a thrift store or discount retailer. Empty the water out to avoid any steam and move the heat setting to "cotton." Use a scissors to cut a length of edge banding about 1 in. longer than the edge you're covering. Starting at one end, center the edge banding with equal overhangs on each side and set the preheated iron at that end. Move the iron along the surface, keeping the edge banding centered with your other hand. Move the iron along at a rate of about 2 in. per second. The goal is to melt the adhesive without scorching the wood.

Don't sweat it if you scorch or misalign the banding during application. Just run the iron over it again to soften the glue so you can peel the banding away. Cut yourself a new piece and start over.

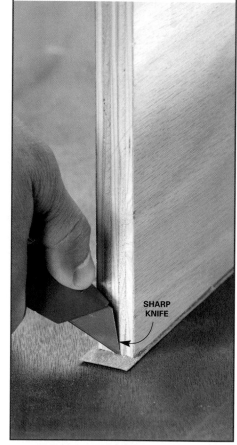

Slice off the ends

The easiest way to remove the overhanging ends is to simply slice them off with a utility knife. Place the edge banding on a work surface and lightly score it a couple of times. Don't worry about cutting all the way through. Just lift the plywood and bend up the banding to snap it off.

SHARP KNIFE

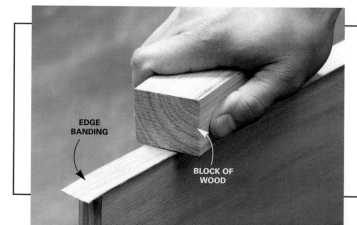

EDGE BANDING

BLOCK OF WOOD

Press it while it's hot

Make sure the edge banding is fully adhered by pressing it down with a block of wood while it's still hot. Go back and forth over the edge a few times while the glue is cooling. Look for any areas that are raised. Heat those spots again and press them again with the block.

Use a trimmer on edges

The quickest and easiest way to trim the edge banding flush to the plywood is with a special edge banding tool, such as the FastCap trimmer shown here (No. 836877; $20 at Woodcraft stores or online at woodcraft.com).

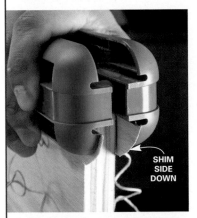

SHIM SIDE DOWN

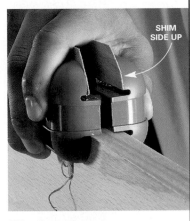

SHIM SIDE UP

Make a shallow pass first

Trim with the shimmed side first. Since less veneer is being removed with this side of the trimmer, the likelihood of runaway splits is greatly reduced. Start at one end and squeeze the trimmer until the shims are against the plywood. Then press down and slide the trimmer along the edge. Thin strips of veneer will peel away from both edges.

Flip the trimmer for the final pass

Flip the trimmer over and use the unshimmed side for a final trimming. When you're through, the edge banding should be almost perfectly flush with the plywood. If you missed any spots, just make another pass or two with the trimmer. The final sanding will remove the sharp edge and any remaining overhang.

Touch up with a sanding block

After you trim them, the edges will be sharp. Ease them with 150-grit sandpaper on a sanding block. Hold the sanding block at a slight angle and smooth out the edge. Sand gently and inspect the edge often to avoid sanding through the thin veneer.

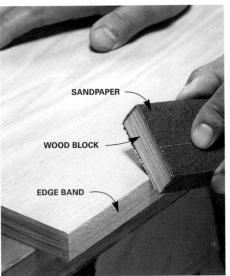

SANDPAPER

WOOD BLOCK

EDGE BAND

Don't leave a splice where it'll show

Splices can be hard to see on raw edge banding, but they may be highly visible after stain is applied. Inspect the edge banding before you cut it to length so you can cut around splices and avoid surprises later. Avoid waste by using spliced pieces in less visible areas.

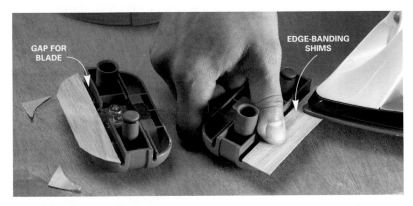

GAP FOR BLADE

EDGE-BANDING SHIMS

Modify your trimmer

Trimming the overhanging edges flush to the plywood without damaging the edge banding can be tricky. If the trimming blade catches in the wood grain, it can split the thin veneer and you'd have to start over. Prevent that headache by shimming one side of the trimmer with strips of edge banding so that it doesn't cut as deep. Just "tack" the shims on with the iron, making sure to leave a gap where the blades are. Since this trimmer has two cutting sides, you can leave the shims on one side to make the initial pass, and then just flip it over to make the final pass.

SPLICE

Do's&Don'ts

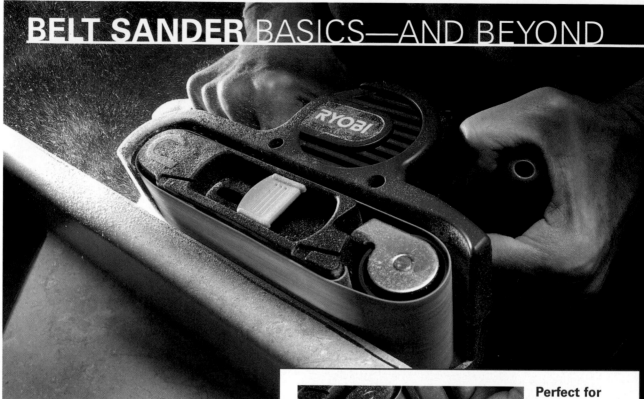

BELT SANDER BASICS—AND BEYOND

Belt sanders are the big, powerful gorillas of the sanding world. Few tools can save you as much time—or wreck your project faster. If you're new to belt sanders or have been frustrated by yours, read on to find out how to keep that big ape under control.

What it'll do for you

Belt sanders are multiuse tools. They are commonly used for trimming to a scribed line (**photo right**), sanding very rough surfaces, leveling surfaces (like a replacement board in a hardwood floor) and freehand rounding and shaping. Because they have a lot of power and can handle coarse grits, they excel at the rapid removal of wood. Also, unlike orbital and vibrating sanders, the sanding action is linear, so even with coarse grits you can sand with the grain and get a good-looking result. Though a belt sander isn't an essential tool in the homeowner's arsenal, you won't find many experienced DIYers or carpenters without one.

Buying a sander and belts

The best multipurpose belt sander takes a 3-in.-wide belt. You'll see machines designed for wider and narrower belts, but they're for specialized tasks. Within the 3-in. class,

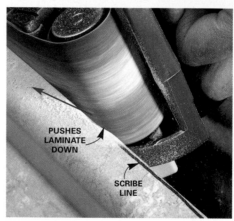

PUSHES LAMINATE DOWN

SCRIBE LINE

Perfect for scribing
A common use for a small belt sander is scribing. You can gradually sneak up on a curved line for a perfect fit. On a laminate countertop, make sure the direction of belt travel pushes the laminate down.

there are smaller tools that take 3 x 18-in. belts, midsize machines that take 3 x 21-in. belts and a couple of large sanders that take 3 x 24-in. belts. The smaller tools are lighter and easier to use one-handed for shaping and scribing. They're good for smaller work and casual use. The larger tools have more surface area and weight for smoothing wide surfaces. They're better for bigger work and shop use. The 3 x 21-in. machines are a good compromise. You'll find 3 x 18-in. sanders for $50 to $150 and 3 x 21-in. sanders for $100 to $250.

ALUMINUM OXIDE

ZIRCONIA

You'll also find smaller belt sanders that take 2-1/2-in.-

GOUGE

Gouging is the enemy

This painted panel shows a common problem: horseshoe-shaped gouges at the end of a board. To prevent gouges, use clean, new belts, avoid grits finer than 120, and keep the plate under the belt (the platen) clean and free of dust.

THEN, WITH GRAIN

GRAIN DIRECTION

FIRST, AT ANGLE TO GRAIN

The top tool for rough flattening

Belt sanders excel at the rapid removal of wood, making them the best handheld power tool for leveling and smoothing rough boards. Start at an angle to the grain for aggressive leveling, then finish with the grain. Eighty-grit is good for starting, then switch to 120-grit.

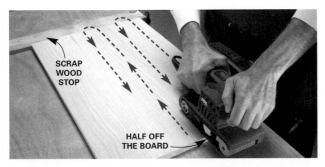

SCRAP WOOD STOP

HALF OFF THE BOARD

Use good technique

Don't push down on the sander; let its weight do the work. Go slowly, overlap passes and allow the tool to go past the end without dipping. Be careful not to tip the sander or change speed or direction. Put the cord over your shoulder so it's out of the way.

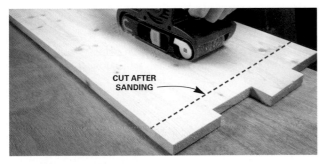

CUT AFTER SANDING

Trim after sanding

It's hard to keep a belt sander from gouging or rounding over the ends of a board. So if you can, belt-sand the board before cutting it to final length. You can then safely move on to a palm sander and finer grits.

wide belts. They're light and very handy for one-handed use. Sanders with 4-in.-wide belts are heavy-duty machines best left to cabinetmakers.

Use your sander safely

Belt sanders are relatively safe tools, but it's still smart to take precautions.

■ Wear hearing protection—these babies are LOUD!

■ Don't breathe dust. It's not just unpleasant; it's bad for you. Wear a dust mask while sanding, unless you rig up a shop vacuum for dust collection (**photo**, p. 120).

■ Unplug the tool before changing belts or emptying the dust bag. I have a scar that attests to the importance of this seemingly grandmotherly precaution.

■ If you use the belt sander to sand metal, you'll create sparks, which can start a fire if they mix with the sawdust in the machine and the dust bag. Blow or vacuum the dust out of the sander before you use it on metal, and remove the dust bag.

■ Make sure the trigger is off before plugging the sander in. Belt sanders have a locking button that holds the switch in the "on" position. Sounds kinda "duh," but trust me, it happens. You don't want the sander to fly across the room when you plug it in, do you?

■ Belt sanders exert a fair amount of force on the work. So if your work isn't securely held, it'll slide away from or right into you. Clamps get in the way, but a simple stop on the appropriate side of the workpiece (**photo at left**) will keep it from sliding. Choose a stop that's a little thinner than the workpiece so the sander will clear it at the edge.

Tuning up your sander

First, make sure the belt is oriented properly. Some belts have a preferred direction, indicated by an arrow on the inside. Nondirectional belts can be installed either way. The only adjustment you'll probably have to make is "tracking" to keep the belt centered on the roller. Hold the sander up, turn it on, and see if the belt either rubs against the housing or starts working its way off the rollers. With the trigger on, adjust the tracking knob until the belt is centered on the rollers. You may have to make a slight adjustment when the sander is on the wood. If your sander has automatic tracking, you don't need to mess with any of that nonsense.

Some sanders have variable speed. You can go at maximum speed most of the time, but you'll want to throttle it back for delicate work.

Pick a belt, but not any belt

Personally, I use 80- and 120-grit belts regularly, and rarely, 50-grit. Grits coarser than 50 leave deep scratches that are difficult to remove. And if you're doing finer sanding, you're better off using a random-orbit sander. Remember one of

Do's&Don'ts

the rules of sanding: You can skip one grade of grit, but it wastes time and you'll just wear out belts skipping two. For example, you can go from 80 to 120, skipping 100 grit, but don't go from 50 to 120.

Aluminum oxide is the traditional grit material. You'll find it in less-expensive khaki-color form, good if you need a disposable belt, and longer-lasting, dark brown premium belts. However, for grits of 80 and coarser, many people now prefer zirconia belts (sometimes called "planer" belts). They have sharper, tougher cutting particles that cut more aggressively, last longer and don't clog as easily. These belts are usually bright blue or purple. Zirconia belts run about $2.50 each, and premium aluminum oxide belts are about $2.

Soup up your sander

Belt sanders are simple tools that don't need many improvements. However, if you use your belt sander in the shop, consider these two upgrades.

Dust collection. Belt sanders always come with a built-in dust bag that collects most of the coarser dust and needs regular emptying. However, plenty of fine dust still gets into the air. If you're doing a lot of belt sanding, it's worth getting a hose that allows you to connect your sander to a shop vacuum.

You can sometimes use the hose that came with your shop vacuum, but it's usually too large or too stiff. The alternative is a super-flexible, small-diameter hose designed for dust collection. You can buy one at a woodworking specialty store or online (search "vacuum hose"). Dust ports vary widely (some are square, which is a challenge), so you may have to fiddle around to get the hose to fit. There are commercial adapters ($10 to $20; pick one up when you buy your hose) or you can cobble something together with—you guessed it—duct tape.

Shop-made stand. A handy accessory if you do much woodworking is a stand that holds your sander on its side, upside down or vertical, allowing you to bring the work to the tool instead of vice versa. The design of the stand is completely dependent on the shape of your sander, so we won't give plans. However, it generally involves several layers of plywood, each with cutouts to accommodate the parts of the sander that protrude, plus a couple of hose clamps or other clamping devices to hold the sander securely. Add another piece of plywood to act as a table, if needed.

Stands like this are particularly useful if you want to sand lots of small parts—for example, if you're making lots of wooden toys. For inspiration, search online for "belt sander stand photo."

Watch out on plywood
Belt sanders take off serious amounts of wood, so they can wreck plywood pretty much instantly. If you have to sand solid-wood edging flush with plywood, draw a pencil line on the plywood to tell you when the sander starts removing veneer. If you have variable speed, dial it down.

Keep the belt clean
Dirty belts make for lousy work. A belt-cleaning stick ($8) removes pitch buildup that happens with all woods, especially pine or sappy woods. Push it against the moving belt, or for larger sanders, clamp the stick in a vise and sand it.

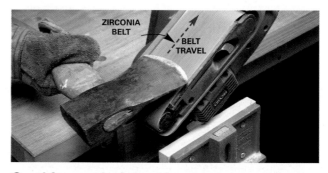

Good for rough sharpening
You can use a belt sander for rough sharpening of tools like axes, shovels, knives and chisels. Remove the dust bag and remove all dust from the sander (sparks and dust are a bad combination), then use a zirconia belt for best results.

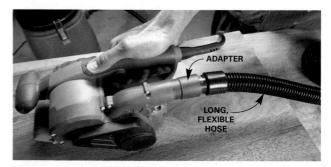

Better dust collection
The bag on a belt sander provides decent dust collection, but with a little fiddling you can attach a long, soft hose and a shop vacuum to your belt sander. The payoff: no bag emptying and almost no dust in the air.

A SMOOTH, FAST
POLYURETHANE FINISH

Even though I've built dozens of cabinets and furniture pieces, I don't consider myself a high-end finisher. But I've developed my own little collection of tips, systems and techniques for applying oil-based polyurethane. It gives me great results, quickly and painlessly. This is a skip-the-brush system. It's all about rolling poly on the big areas, using wipe-on poly on the small ones, and above all, controlling dust. I'll show you the tips I used while I was finishing my latest project, a flat-screen TV stand.

Sand out the pencil marks

Begin by drawing light, squiggly pencil lines on the surface at each grit stage. When the pencil lines disappear, you're ready to move on to the

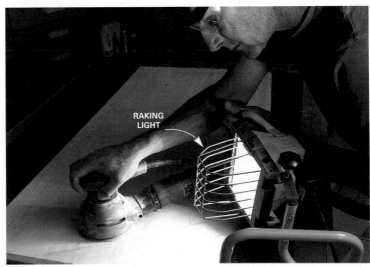

RAKING LIGHT

Use a light held at a low, raking angle to check for scratches, dirt and any other imperfections while you sand and apply finish coats.

next grit. You're wasting your time sanding coarse, open-grained woods like ash or oak baby-butt smooth. I generally start at 80 grit and end with 100 or 120 grit. Sanding through all the grits to 220 grit won't improve the finish one bit. But with closed-grained woods like maple or birch, don't skip any grit steps, and go all the way to 220 grit.

A clean work area is key

The more dust free the project and the surrounding surfaces, the less work you'll have and the more flawless your finish will be. Before the finishing starts, I vacuum the project, the workbench and the floor. Under the piece to be finished, I spread out 6-mil poly to protect the floor from drips and spills and make cleanup easy. I'll reuse these sheets several times, then toss them. Don't finish on the same day you sand; the dust stays in the air for hours. Start finishing with clean clothes and hair.

Wipe down with mineral spirits

Wipe down the project with a tack cloth, or a lint-free cloth saturated with solvent. I like to use an old, clean cotton T-shirt for this and the wipe-on step shown later. This step removes nearly all traces of dust. It only takes a few minutes for the solvent to evaporate so you can get started on finishing. Don't use water; it'll raise the grain and you'll have to sand again.

Use a roller on large flat surfaces

I love these little rollers. You can get the poly on fast and evenly. No brushstrokes, puddles or thin spots. I've had bubble problems with some rollers. I prefer to use 6-in. microfiber rollers ($5 at Lowe's) dampened with mineral spirits. There's always a bit of left-over lint, but only on the first coat. A Teflon baking tray makes a great rolling pan.

Don't freak out when you see the finish right after you lay it down. It'll look like it's full of flaws. Just roll it out and use the raking light to make sure the surface is completely covered. Don't keep working the finish. Let it be, and it will flatten out. I keep a can of spray poly handy in case of bubbles. A light mist knocks them out.

After each coat, redip the roller in mineral spirits and put it into a zippered plastic bag for the next coat and leave the wet tray to dry. In a couple of hours, the dried poly just peels right out of the pan. I'll usually

Lose the dust
Wipe down every square inch of the workpiece with a lint-free cotton cloth dampened with mineral spirits or denatured alcohol.

6" MICROFIBER ROLLER

VARNISH IN BAKING SHEET

Roll on poly fast—then quit
Dampen the roller with mineral spirits and roll the poly on all of the large flat areas and cabinet interiors. Coat the surface and quit. Don't continue to work the finish.

FRESHLY COATED BOTTOM

STANDOFF

Finish both sides at once
Coat the bottom first and then flip over the top, resting it on standoffs while you roll the finish on the top. The Painter's Pyramid shown is available at home centers.

Use wipe-on poly for small or tight areas
Dribble wipe-on poly on the rag and wet the entire area. Sand between coats with extra-fine sanding pads.

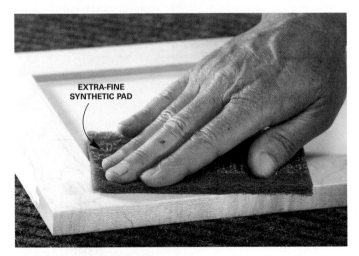

EXTRA-FINE
SYNTHETIC PAD

Lightly sand between coats
Wipe off dust whiskers with extra-fine sanding pads. For larger blemishes, use 280-grit paper. The raking light will show you when the surface is smooth.

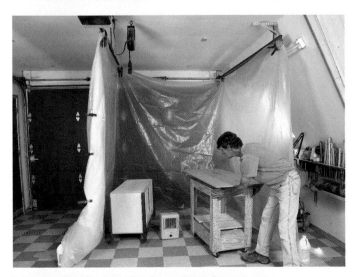

Let the final coat dry in a dust-free area
For big projects, build a temporary drying booth with poly sheeting. If it's cool, use an electric space heater to hasten drying and shorten the time that dust can get embedded in the finish.

put two coats on cabinet interiors and sides, and three coats on tabletops for extra protection.

Finish both sides at once

With a solid wood top like this one, finish both the top and the bottom surfaces, even if the bottom won't show. Skip this step and the top can twist, cup or warp. To save drying time, coat the bottom and then immediately flip it over to finish the top. I just don't care if there are a few fingerprints. Right after the top is rolled out, I roll the edges and then go around them with a dry foam brush to eliminate any drips or thick spots. I skip the final coat on the underside. Being short a single coat on the underside isn't a big deal.

Zero cleanup with wipe-on poly

After the roll-on coats are dry, I use wipe-on oil poly (use the same sheen you chose for the roll-on poly) for the face frames, legs, doors or any other narrow, small or intricate areas. I do this after the large areas are dry so I don't smudge adjacent areas. I like it because only two things get dirty: a glove and a cotton rag, both of which I toss after each coat. (Spread them out to dry first.) I can put on two to four coats in one day depending on the temperature and humidity. There are no drips, sags or runs—ever. And because it dries so fast, there's rarely a dust problem. The downside? Because the coats are so thin, you need lots of them. I'll put on as many as eight coats of wipe-on when two rolled coats would do the trick.

Sand with pads and paper

I lightly sand between coats with extra-fine synthetic sanding pads. The goal is to roughen the surface a bit and rub out dust motes, hairs and drips. If there are stubborn nibs that stand up to the pads, grab 280-grit and be more aggressive. Then just wipe off the dust with mineral spirits and apply another coat.

Final coat gets special treatment

For the final coat, I vacuum the work area again and let the dust settle overnight. In the winter, I warm the room and then turn off the overhead furnace a couple of hours before finishing to settle any dust.

After the finish is on, I immediately roll small workpieces into my shop bathroom, which is nearly dust free. If it's cool in the bathroom, I use an electric space heater to speed up the drying. If it's a big project, I make a drying booth out of 6-mil poly sheeting first, which nearly eliminates dust specks.

SUPER-SIMPLE
WORKBENCH

Got two hours on your hands and 50 bucks in your pocket? Do we have a workbench for you!

by **Travis Larson**

T his sturdy 30-in. x 6-ft.-long workbench is the ultimate in simplicity. It's made from only fifteen 8-ft.-long 2x4s and one sheet of 1/2-in. plywood. Follow the cutting diagrams to cut the parts: **Figure B** to cut the plywood tops, then **Figure C** to cut all the framing. Use the lengths provided in the Cutting List. You can either screw the framing together with 3-in. screws or hand- or power-nail it together with 3-in. nails. Screw the plywood down with 1-5/8-in. screws.

To make these project plans even easier to follow, we tinted the parts that get added at each step.

CUTTING LIST

KEY	QTY.	SIZE & DESCRIPTION
A	9	71-7/8" (backer boards, upper shelf legs and rims)
B	4	68-7/8" (work surface and lower shelf rim)
C	4	35-1/2" (legs)
D	4	27" (end rims)
E	5	24" (work surface joists)
F	5	15" (lower shelf joists)
G	7	9" (upper shelf joists)

Figure A: Main workbench parts

Figure B
Plywood cutting diagram

WASTE

UPPER
SHELF
2' x 12"

UPPER
SHELF
4' x 12"

LOWER
SHELF
18" x 6'

WORK
SURFACE
30" x 6'

G

A

A

A A

WORK
SURFACE

E

D

B

LEGS

C

LOWER
SHELF

F

B

A

D

C

A

Tip Use paint cans to support the lower shelf frame when you're attaching it to the main workbench legs.

1 **Assemble the frames for the work surface and lower shelf**

E

B

D

WORK SURFACE

F

B

D

LOWER SHELF

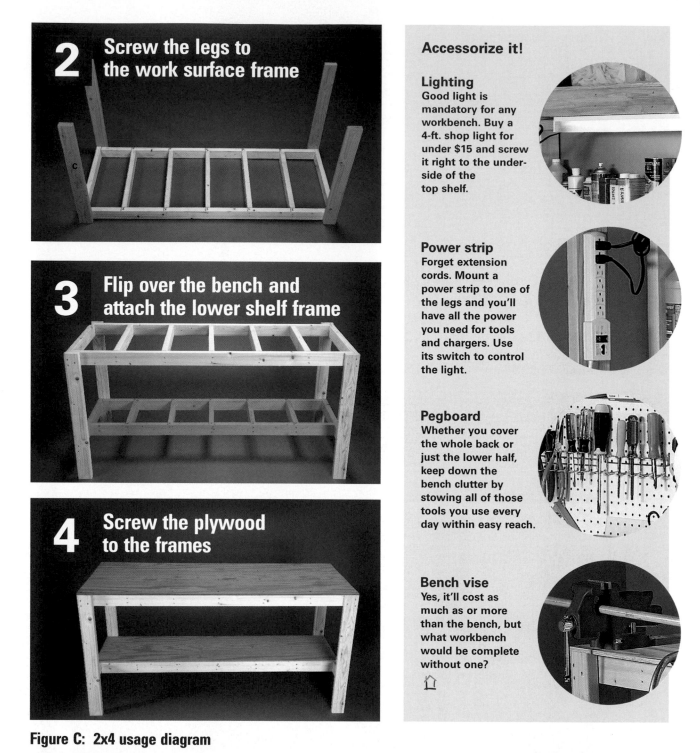

2 Screw the legs to the work surface frame

3 Flip over the bench and attach the lower shelf frame

4 Screw the plywood to the frames

Accessorize it!

Lighting
Good light is mandatory for any workbench. Buy a 4-ft. shop light for under $15 and screw it right to the underside of the top shelf.

Power strip
Forget extension cords. Mount a power strip to one of the legs and you'll have all the power you need for tools and chargers. Use its switch to control the light.

Pegboard
Whether you cover the whole back or just the lower half, keep down the bench clutter by stowing all of those tools you use every day within easy reach.

Bench vise
Yes, it'll cost as much as or more than the bench, but what workbench would be complete without one?

Figure C: 2x4 usage diagram

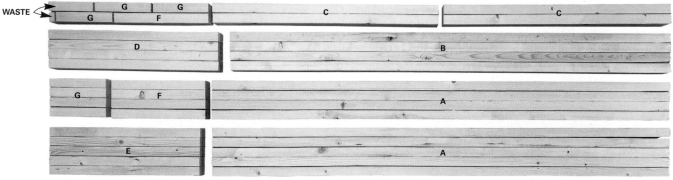

WASTE

DIY success story

Around these parts, everyone knows I'm the least "wood savvy" of all the editors. So when Travis heard I wanted to build a workbench for my son, he handed me his design. My job was to build it and report back on how it went.

Maybe Travis can build this baby in two hours, but it took "Musco Junior" and me about 3-1/2. The most time-consuming part was cutting the studs according to the diagram to get maximum yield from the lumber. Once cut, the pieces flew together (we used a framing nailer). Since he'll be sharing the workbench with his wife and her gardening stuff, we added a replaceable 1/8-in. hardboard workbench top coated with glossy paint to make it easier to clean. Next, we made the pegboard area larger and added two 5-in. shelves to hold plastic parts bins. The hardboard and pegboard added $16 to the cost. Then we spent $85 on a cold-start fluorescent fixture and bulbs, a vise, plastic bins and pegboard tool holders. This was a great father-son project. If we can do it, so can you!

–Rick Muscoplat

5 Assemble the top shelf frame

6 Add the plywood

7 Attach the top shelf legs upside down

8 Screw the legs to the bench and add the backer boards

BACKER BOARDS (A)

WOODWORKING & FURNITURE PROJECTS, TOOLS & TIPS

CAST CONCRETE TABLE

The look and durability of natural stone— the cost and simplicity of concrete

by **Duane Johnson**

If you want a tabletop that's elegant enough for any indoor setting and tough enough to withstand outdoor weather, you've found it. Tables similar to this one sell for hundreds at garden centers and outdoor furniture stores. But you can make one yourself for $50 to $100.

The total materials cost for the table shown here was about $100. Your cost will depend mostly on the wood you choose for the base and the concrete mix you use (see p. 131). You don't need any special skills or tools, though a table saw and an air-powered brad nailer will speed up building the form. Give yourself half a day to build the form and pour the concrete and an hour to build the table base. A few days after casting the top, you'll spend a couple of hours removing the form, chipping the edges and applying a sealer.

Build the form

Melamine-coated particleboard is the perfect form material

Endless possibilities

Most of us think of concrete as a practical material, but it's also one of the most versatile decorative materials around. It can take on just about any color or shape. And surface treatment options are endless. You can cast "fossil" imprints using leaves, ferns or seashells. For a completely different look, you can cast inlays like glass or tile permanently in the surface. To see how, see "Easy inlays" on p. 129.

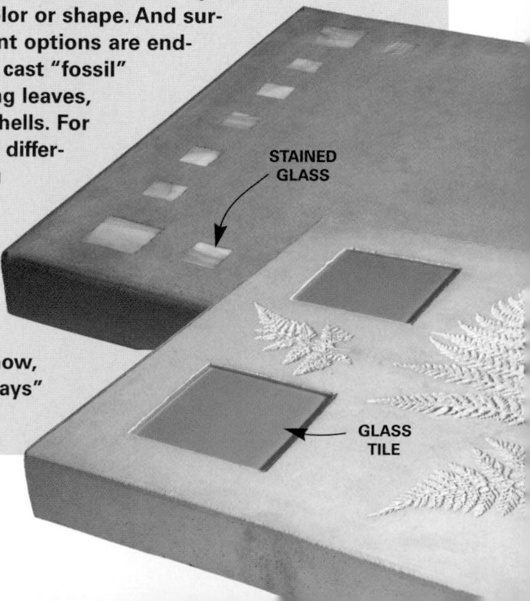

STAINED GLASS

GLASS TILE

Figure A: Cutting diagram for the concrete form

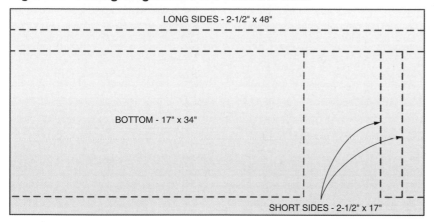

LONG SIDES - 2-1/2" x 48"

BOTTOM - 17" x 34"

SHORT SIDES - 2-1/2" x 17"

Figure B: Table base

Cut the parts to the dimensions shown and join them with metal brackets. We spent $30 on cedar lumber, but any rot-resistant wood in 2x4 and 4x4 dimensions is a good choice. Pressure-treated lumber will cost about $12. Fasten the top to the base with a few dabs of hot-melt glue.

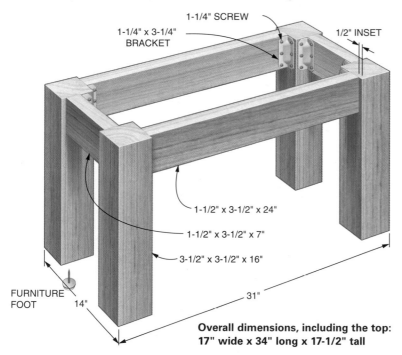

1-1/4" SCREW

1-1/4" x 3-1/4" BRACKET

1/2" INSET

1-1/2" x 3-1/2" x 24"

1-1/2" x 3-1/2" x 7"

3-1/2" x 3-1/2" x 16"

FURNITURE FOOT

14"

31"

Overall dimensions, including the top: 17" wide x 34" long x 17-1/2" tall

MATERIALS LIST

Everything you need—except the concrete mix—is available at home centers.

2' x 4' sheet of 3/4"-thick melamine ($10)

4x4 x 8'

2x4 x 8'

Plastic furniture feet ($2)

Silicone caulk ($4)

Spray adhesive ($5)

Cement colorant ($10 to $25)

1-1/4" screws ($3)

8 metal brackets (we used Simpson GA2 gusset angle brackets, which measure 1-1/4" x 3-1/4" and cost $8)

Acrylic grout and tile sealer ($15)

Countertop mix ($35 to $50)

Easy inlays

It's easy to embed small decorative objects in the concrete top. Unlike the casts of ferns and leaves, which leave only the imprint behind, an inlay stays in place permanently. You can inlay anything that's durable and has crisp edges. Tiles and colored glass are the most common inlays, but you can also use coins or other metal objects. Simply spread a thin coat of silicone caulk over the face you want exposed and press it down on the melamine base. After the concrete mix hardens, carefully scrape away the silicone film left on the inlay with a razor blade.

Glue inlays face down to the form with silicone caulk. Be sure to remove excess caulk that squeezes out around the inlay.

for this project because it's smooth, water-resistant and inexpensive ($10 for a 2 x 4-ft. sheet). Cut the form parts as shown in **Figure A**. The two long sides overhang the form for easier removal later. A brad nailer is the fastest way to assemble the form (**Photo 1**). If you use screws or drive nails by hand, be sure to drill pilot holes to avoid splitting the particleboard. Whatever fastening method you use, space fasteners about 6 in. apart and make sure they don't create humps inside the form.

Next, caulk the inside corners to seal the form and create rounded edges on the tabletop (**Photo 2**). Do this even if you plan to chip off the edges later. Use colored silicone caulk, which will show up well

WOODWORKING & FURNITURE PROJECTS, TOOLS & TIPS

1 Build the form from melamine-coated particleboard to give the concrete a smooth finish and make the form easy to remove.

SMOOTH CAULK BEAD

2 Caulk the corners of the form. Any imperfections in the caulk will show up on the tabletop. So use masking tape to create neat, even edges.

3 Glue down leaves with spray adhesive to cast "fossils" in the tabletop. Press the leaves completely flat so concrete can't seep under them.

against the white melamine. That way, you can easily spot and clean off smudges. *Keep in mind that every tiny imperfection on the form will show up on the finished tabletop.*

For neat caulk lines, run masking tape about 3/16 in. from the corners. Apply the caulk one side at a time, smooth it with your finger and remove the tape quickly before the caulk skins over (**Photo 2**). The tape ridges along the caulk lines will show on the finished top and make a perfect chisel guide for chipping the edges later (**Photo 8**).

If you want to cast leaf or fern "fossils" in the top, first press them for a day or two in a book or between scraps of cardboard. Then lay them out on newspaper and coat them with spray adhesive (such as 3M General Purpose 45). Press them onto the form so they lie perfectly flat (**Photo 3**). Thick stems may not lie flat and can leave imprints that are too deep. To avoid this, we shaved some of our fern stems down with a razor blade.

Mix and pour

We mixed our concrete in a bucket, using a drill and a large paint mixer attachment ($10). This method is fast, but it requires a powerful 1/2-in. drill and won't work well with thicker mixes. Instead, you can use a garden hoe and a plastic cement tub ($6). Be patient and mix thoroughly so you completely wet all the powdered ingredients. Pay attention to the product's mixing instructions, especially the recommended amount of water. An extra cup of water can make the mix too thin.

Set your form on a solid surface and level it both front to back and side to side. Otherwise one side of your top will be thicker than the other. Then pour in the mix around the edges to get an even distribution of material (**Photo 4**). Pouring the entire mix in the middle might concentrate the heavier particles there and weaken the edges. Wear plastic gloves as you work the material into all corners and edges (**Photo 5**). Use a gentle touch, however, if you have fragile objects glued to the bottom. If the mix you use requires

Choosing a mix

The best concrete mix for this project is a countertop mix, which pros use to cast concrete countertops. Ask for one at a local concrete products dealer (under "Concrete Products" in your yellow pages). Prices for a 50- or 70-lb. sack run from $35 to $50. (You'll need about 50 lbs. of mix to make the 17-in. x 34-in. x 1-1/2-in. top shown.) The brands share one key factor—special additives called "super-plasticizers," which allow you to add less water. Less water means a denser, stronger top. Some mixes contain fibers to help prevent cracking. Others require wire reinforcement.

You can buy color additives when you buy the mix, or buy concrete color from a more limited selection at a home center. We added 5 ozs. of Quikrete Liquid Cement Color ("Charcoal") to a 50-lb. sack of mix to get a slate color.

Here are a few mixes worth considering:

■ **LifeTime Floors Quicktops (50-lb. bag, $48), lifetimefloors.biz.**
We chose this product because it's easy to mix, doesn't need reinforcement and hardens in just four hours. It's white, so it can take on any color. The fine consistency allows for detailed imprints, and the edges chip neatly. The version we used (Quicktops One) contains white aggregate that you can expose if you chip the edges or grind the surface. Distribution is regional, but you can mail order it. Go to the Web site for more information.

■ **Quikrete Non-Shrink Precision Grout Mix (50-lb. bag, $13), quikrete.com.**
Although it's not designed for tops, we got good results using this inexpensive mix. It takes imprints well, chips neatly and is available at some home centers. It does require reinforcement, however. Quikrete also makes a countertop mix.

■ **Buddy Rhodes Concrete Counter Mix (70-lb. bag, $45), buddyrhodes.com.**
This white counter mix takes color well, hardens in about 12 hours and requires reinforcement.

■ **Cheng Pro-Formula Mix ($21 to $71 per package), chengconcrete.com.**
This is a package of plasticizers, reinforcing fiber and colorants that you mix into standard high-strength concrete mix. These products are designed for surface grinding, which exposes the aggregate. The excellent Web site is full of design ideas and other useful information.

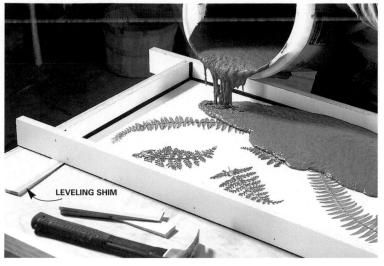

LEVELING SHIM

4 Pour the mix evenly around the perimeter of the form. The form must be level—set a level across it and slip shims under the low end.

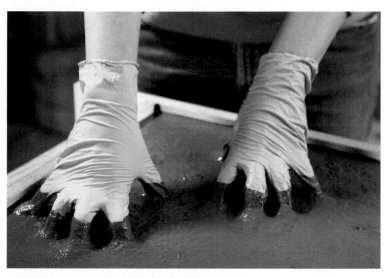

5 Work the mix into corners and around objects cast into the tabletop. Then lightly tap the sides of the form with a hammer to drive out air bubbles.

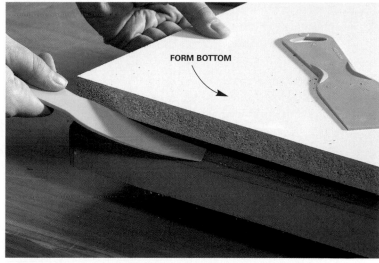

FORM BOTTOM

6 Remove the form, starting with the sides. Then flip the tabletop over and pry off the bottom panel with a plastic putty knife.

7 Scrub the leaves out of their imprints with a stiff plastic brush. Scour the whole surface to remove excess colorant and melamine residue.

8 Create a natural stone look by chipping the edges with a cold chisel. Chip around all four edges, then flip the top over and chip from the other side.

wire reinforcement, pour and work in about two-thirds of the mix. Then add the wire and the remaining mix.

All pours contain trapped air, which will leave holes in the finished top unless you work them out. To drive out bubbles, tap the sides and bottom of the form with a hammer and continue rapping until you don't see any more bubbles coming up. However, if you have pea gravel or other "aggregate" in your mix, limit your tapping. Otherwise, the aggregate will settle to the bottom and weaken or perhaps ruin the appearance of your table. And keep in mind that the tabletop doesn't have to be perfectly smooth. A few holes or imperfections in the surface may simply add more natural character.

When you're finished, cover the top with plastic and let the concrete harden and cure anywhere from four hours to two days, depending on the brand.

Release the form and finish

To remove the form, pry off the long sides and then the short sides. Pry against the form base rather than the concrete. If you have to pry off the form base, use a plastic putty knife; metal will mar the surface (**Photo 6**). If your top has imprints with fine detail, cover it with plastic and let it harden for an extra day. Then scrub with water (**Photo 7**). Use a plastic putty knife to scrape off melamine residue that won't scrub off.

The mix we used chips off neatly for a rough edge look (**Photo 8**). Be sure to set the top on plywood on a solid surface. We used a 3/4-in.-wide cold chisel, but you can use whatever width best produces the effect you want. For safety, hone down any sharp edges with a file or sandpaper.

Your top will withstand outdoor weather, but it's susceptible to stains. To prevent them, and to bring out more color, we recommend that you seal it with an acrylic sealer ($10 in the tile aisle at home centers). The first coat will sink in and the surface will remain dull. After it dries, apply a second coat, and perhaps a third, until the surface retains a shine.

Well done! Chances are that once you complete one top, you'll want to make another. 🏠

InstantProject

SIMPLE **WINDOW PLANTER**

You can put together this simple window planter in less an hour. For each planter, you'll need three 6-in. clay pots, 3 ft. each of 1x10 and 1x3, and 2 ft. of 2x8.

Cut the 1x10 and 1x3 to length (see photos for dimensions). Pot diameters vary, so size the holes by scribing and cutting out a 6-in. circle from cardboard to ensure that the pot will rest on its rim (**Photo 1**). Keep testing until you

find the size. Then lay out and cut the openings.

Use a 5-gallon pail lid to scribe the bracket curves (**Photo 2**). Make sure the grain runs parallel to the shelf for strength. Smooth off the rough edges and paint the parts before assembly—especially if you want the two-tone look. Then screw the parts together with 2-in. exterior screws.

Mount the shelf to the wall by screwing through the hanging strip into the wall framing.

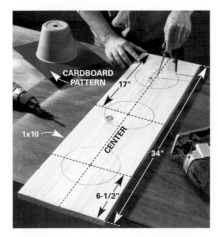

1 Mark the 6-in.-diameter holes with a compass. Then drill 1/2-in. starter holes and cut out the openings with a jigsaw.

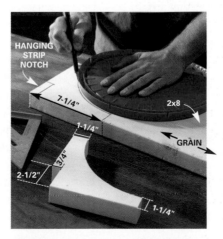

2 Mark the notch for the hanging strip and both 1-1/4-in. ends on the brackets. Draw the curve and cut the openings with a jigsaw.

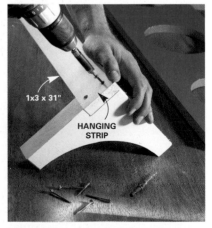

3 Predrill and screw the hanging strip to the brackets. Then center and screw the shelf to the brackets and to the hanging strip.

TOOL SAFETY: DON'T BE A DUMMY!

Best ways to avoid the most common injuries from tools

What's the best way to demonstrate really dangerous tool practices without taking the risk of hurting someone? With a crash test dummy, of course. It's just not easy to explain stupid techniques using words alone. That's where our dummy, Nigel, comes in!

Every year, emergency rooms report 120,000 visits for injuries caused by four tools: table saws, circular saws, nail guns and utility knives. Add to this the 200,000 ER visits for eye injuries—a large percentage of which occur during work around the house—and it's easy to see how we came up with this list of the most dangerous don'ts.

Our dummy, Nigel, is making some common mistakes that can result in severe injuries. But these are only a few examples of things not to do. Don't you be a dummy! When you start on your next project, keep these don'ts in mind so you don't become the next statistic.

Don't crosscut against the table saw fence

Nigel the dummy is demonstrating one of the most dangerous table saw practices: cutting a board to length using the fence as a guide. There's a good chance the board will get pinched between the blade and the fence and get thrown back into his body with lots of force. That nasty incident is called "kickback." Broken thumbs, cracked ribs, ruptured spleens and punctured eyes are only a few of the resultant injuries you can suffer. About 35,000 people end up in the emergency room every year with table saw injuries, with 10 percent of them hospitalized. Industry experts estimate that about half of table saw injuries are caused either directly or indirectly by kickback.

In addition to avoiding the dangerous technique Nigel is using to crosscut a board, here are a few other ways to prevent kickback injuries:

- Don't cut anything that's longer than it is wide with the shorter side against the fence. If you want to crosscut with a table saw, use the miter gauge or a crosscutting sled. To learn how to build one, go to **thefamilyhandyman.com** and search for "crosscutting sled."
- Avoid ripping wet, bowed or twisted lumber.
- Position your body to the right or left of the miter saw slots, not directly behind the blade.
- Don't let anyone walk behind you when you're operating the saw.

CAUTION: Don't use the fence as a guide for crosscutting. Instead, use the miter gauge or build a crosscutting sled.

NIGEL

DANGEROUS CROSSCUT

BLADE IS TOO HIGH

WOODWORKING & FURNITURE PROJECTS, TOOLS & TIPS

NOTE: NO CRASH TEST DUMMIES WERE HARMED IN THE MAKING OF THIS STORY

Don't remove that blade guard!

Every table saw sold includes a blade guard, which has a splitter attached. The guard covers the blade, preventing you from accidentally touching it, and the splitter keeps wood from pinching on the blade and kicking back. Don't take them off! Sure, the guard may be a nuisance at times, but it's better to be inconvenienced than to lose one or more fingers. Of the 35,000 emergency room visits we talked about earlier, 83 percent involve contact with the blade.

RED ALERT: Even a dummy should have enough common sense to avoid this technique. Nigel's finger is so close to the blade that a split second of inattention or a kickback could send him to the crash-test dummy hospital.

NO PUSH STICK

NO BLADE GUARD

If you're buying a table saw, consider spending extra for the SawStop brand. It's the only saw on the market that stops the blade when skin touches it. If your blade guard is missing, contact the manufacturer for a replacement (see p. 154). An add-on guard like the HTC Brett-Guard ($200 to $375) is a good option if your original guard is missing or doesn't work well. If $200 sounds like too much money, ask yourself what a finger is worth.

Even with a blade guard installed, you should keep your fingers away from the blade. Always use a push stick for rips less than 4 in. wide. If you're using your thumb to push the piece and the piece kicks back, you risk torn ligaments, tendons and broken bones. Push the cut piece past the blade, turn off the saw and wait for the blade to stop before retrieving the ripped piece. Don't reach near a spinning blade to remove a cutoff.

Don't put your hand directly behind a circular saw

There are an estimated 14,000 visits to the emergency room every year as a result of circular saw injuries. Many of these injuries result in lost or severely damaged fingers. When you're using a circular saw, remember that if the blade binds, the saw can shoot backward a lot faster than you can move your hand out of the way. Anything in the blade's path, including fingers, hands, legs or feet, is in danger of getting cut. Avoid the risk by clamping your work and keeping both hands on the saw whenever possible. Also keep your body to the side of the saw rather than directly behind it.

CAUTION: Don't hold a board like this. Use a temporary nail or clamp instead. Nigel risks losing a finger or two if the saw binds.

DANGEROUS HAND POSITION

Don't put your hands near a nail gun

Even if you're a nail gun expert, nails don't always go straight. Wood grain or knots can deflect the nail and cause it to shoot out the side of the board. If you're driving the nail at an angle to toenail a board, there's a good chance the nail can glance off and go shooting into space. If you must hold a board with your free hand, keep it well away from the nail gun muzzle. If you're reaching over a board to hold it down, move your hand out of the nail's path. Also avoid shooting into large knots that can deflect the nail. And, of course, always wear eye protection when you're using a nail gun.

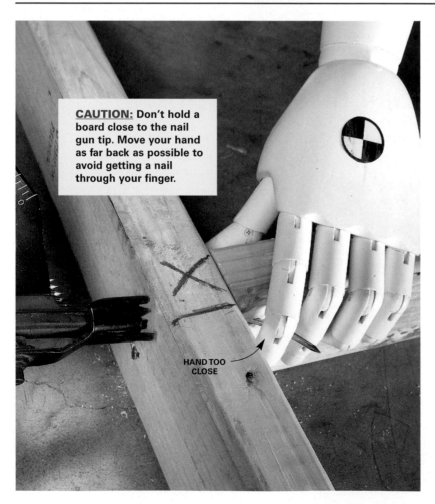

CAUTION: Don't hold a board close to the nail gun tip. Move your hand as far back as possible to avoid getting a nail through your finger.

HAND TOO CLOSE

Don't be sloppy with nail guns

You've all seen the news stories. X-rays of big nails embedded in someone's head, lodged in a spine or stuck in a foot. Ask any carpenter and you're sure to hear a story about a nail that went through a finger or hand. A tool that's powerful enough to shoot a 3-in.-long nail into wood can easily penetrate skin and bone. Depending on the type, some nail guns can be set to "bump-trip." In this mode, the operator can simply hold down the trigger and bump the nail gun nose against the surface to shoot a nail. This is great for speeding up jobs like nailing down plywood sheathing, but it creates a risk if you hold the trigger while carrying the nail gun. Bump your leg and you'll be heading to the emergency room. In incidents where accidental contact caused an injury, more than 80 percent of the time the operator had a finger on the trigger.

There are two ways to avoid this. First, get out your owner's manual and see if you can set your nail gun to sequential mode. This requires you to push down the muzzle and then pull the trigger for each nail. Second, keep your hand off the trigger when you're carrying a nail gun, or better yet, unplug the hose. Then there's no chance of accidental firing.

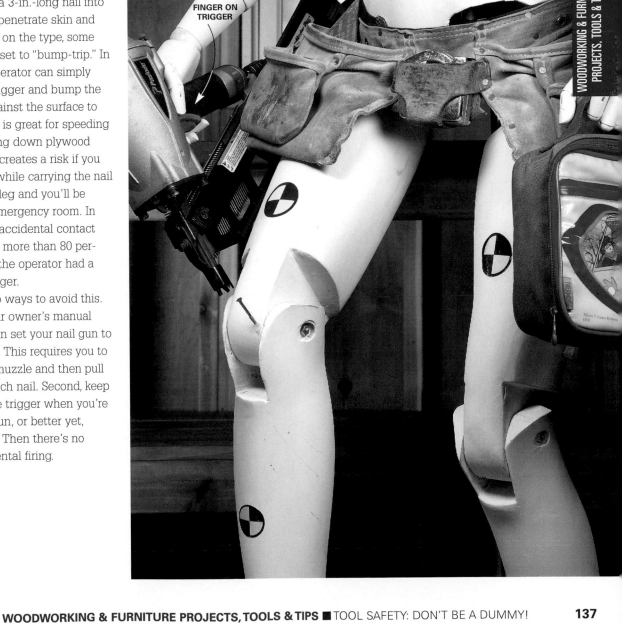

RED ALERT: Nigel should have disconnected the hose and kept his finger off the trigger while he went for his lunch break. You can reduce the chance of a nail gun injury by taking these two steps.

FINGER ON TRIGGER

WOODWORKING & FURNITURE PROJECTS, TOOLS & TIPS

Don't get careless with a knife

Power tools are one thing, but did you know that utility knives are one of the most dangerous tools, accounting for a whopping 60,000 estimated emergency room visits a year? One slip is all it takes to put a deep cut in any body part that's in the way. And while most cuts are superficial and may only require a few stitches, permanent tendon and nerve damage is common.

The best way to avoid an injury is to clamp materials whenever possible to avoid having to hand-hold them. If you do have to hold something while you're cutting, imagine a line at right angles to the cutting line and keep your hand behind it (on the dull side of the blade).

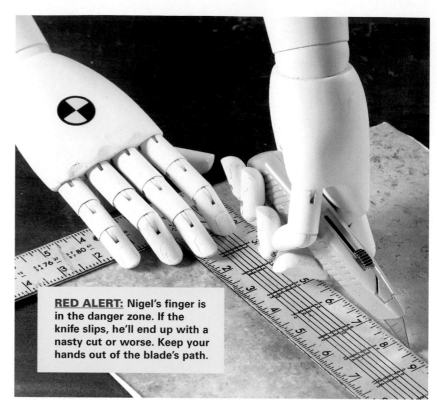

RED ALERT: Nigel's finger is in the danger zone. If the knife slips, he'll end up with a nasty cut or worse. Keep your hands out of the blade's path.

NO EYE PROTECTION

RED ALERT: Nigel is a dummy! He's got eye protection readily available and isn't using it. Keep eye protection handy and don't forget to wear it.

Don't risk your eyes

It's hard to think of a good reason not to wear safety glasses, goggles or a face shield when you're working around the house. It's obvious that Nigel should be wearing his face shield. Of the more than 200,000 emergency room visits a year for eye injuries, at least 10,000 of them involve grinders. Browsing accident reports on the Internet will convince you of the risk. Wood chips, metal shards, bits of tile, household chemicals, paint, solvents and sticks are some of the things that injure eyes. The good news is that it's easy to protect your vision. Just choose the right eye protection for the task at hand. For general work around the house, wear ANSI-approved safety glasses or goggles. Look on the frame for the "Z87+" marking, which indicates that the glasses are rated for high impact. Wear a face shield for grinding operations. Buy several pairs of safety glasses and keep them in convenient locations so you'll always have them on hand. ⌂

DollarSavvyHomeowner

RESTORE A SAW BLADE

High-quality blades for miter saws and table saws are expensive—and worth every penny. But before you buy a new blade, take a close look at the old one. If the teeth are caked with resin, a quick cleaning may make it cut (almost) like new again. Just spray on a heavy coat of oven cleaner and let it soak in for 10 minutes. Then scrub with an old toothbrush. If the gunk doesn't come off easily, wait a few more minutes. When you're done, wipe the blade dry. Remember that oven cleaner is nasty stuff. Wear rubber gloves and goggles and keep it off nearby surfaces.

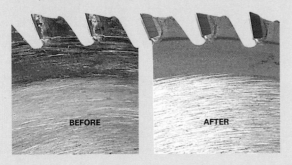

BEFORE   AFTER

BUY LUMBER WITH CUT LENGTHS IN MIND

Whether you're buying wood to frame a garage or build an Adirondack chair, select lengths so you'll have as little waste as possible. Sounds simple, but you do have to think it through before trucking off to the lumberyard. Bring a list of cut lengths and quantities with you. The lengths you're after, in the quality you need, may not be available. For example, if you were planning to cut 12-ft. boards into a bunch of 4-ft. lengths, you may have to settle for 8-ft. stock. So be smart when choosing lengths.

BENCH
TREATED LENGTHS
(4) 2x4 x 42" (2) 8'
(2) 2x6 x 36" (1) 6'
CEDAR
(4) 2x4 x 26" (4) 6'
(4) 2x4 x 24" (4) 6'
(2) 2x10 x 54" (1) 10'
(4) 2x6 x 54" (2) 10'

HOMEMADE CLAMPS

If you're serious about woodworking, spending serious money on long clamps is smart. But if you're a once-in-a-while woodworker like reader Gus Anderson, you can get by with 2x4s and blocks. To apply pressure, just wedge shims against the blocks. Be sure to use straight 2x4s so your work can lie perfectly flat. He suggests slipping wax paper or aluminum foil under the joints so you don't glue your project to the 2x4s. And as with any clamping job, test the assembly before you apply any glue. That way, you can be sure that all the parts squeeze together just right.

ShopTips

ADJUSTABLE DUST CONTROL

Trust us—this shop vacuum hose holder will serve you well. Use it to hold the orbital sander dust hose at workbench height and you won't have to constantly drag the hose over the bench edge while you sand. Or connect an attachment to the hose and position it next to just about any dust-producing power tool.

The project, which will take you a few hours to build, costs less than $25. Rip and cut to size any 3/4-in. plywood or solid wood for the parts. All the materials are available at home centers except the T-Track parts. Get those at rockler.com.

MENDING PLATE

Figure A: Hose holder

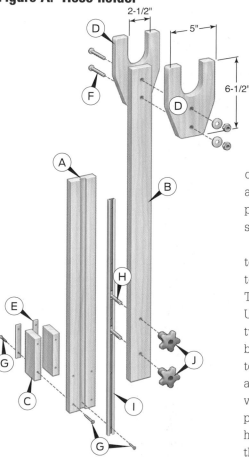

2-1/2"
5"
6-1/2"

The trickiest part of building this is cutting the lower brackets and fitting them to your vacuum. Modify our bracket design as necessary. We cut the 2 x 5-in. bracket pieces with a compound 5-degree angle and a 10-degree bevel to fit the curve of the canister. A band saw or scroll saw will cut both these angles in one pass. Experiment until the pieces fit tight and the upper board rises vertically.

Saw or rout a 3/4-in.-wide dado for the T-Track, centering it on the T-Track board; mount the T-Track with screws; then screw and glue on the angled bracket pieces. Mark and drill holes through the canister and attach the assembly with mending plates and 1-1/2-in. No. 10 sheet metal screws.

To make the yoke for the top board, temporarily screw together the yoke pieces. Then cut a 3-in.-deep U-shape in one end with two widths—2-1/8 in. at the bottom for the vacuum hose to fit in snug, and 2-1/2 in. at the top for the pipes. The varying widths allow you to press-fit either the narrower hose or the wider pipe in the yoke.

MATERIALS LIST

KEY	DESCRIPTION
A	One 3" x 24" x 3/4" lower T-Track board
B	One 2-1/2" x 30" x 3/4" upper board
C	Two 2" x 5" x 3/4" bracket boards
D	Two 5" x 7" x 3/4" boards for the yoke
E	Two 4" x 1/2" mending plates
F	Two 2-1/2" x 1/4" carriage bolts, nuts and washers
G	Four 1-1/2" No. 10 sheet metal screws
	T-Track hardware:
H	Two 5/16" x 1-1/2" T-bolts
I	One 24" mini aluminum T-Track
J	Two 5/16" styrene knobs

HOMEMADE LATHE CALIPERS

When you're turning spindles and you need to check the diameter, does it bug you to have to stop and adjust those antiquated metal calipers?

End the frustration by creating wood calipers for any sizes you frequently check. Here's how: Clamp 7-in.-long pieces of 1/2-in. plywood edge-to-edge on a drill press and drill holes with the desired diameters centered at the seam. Cut the pieces into a comfortable shape, hinge them at the narrow end with a strip of leather or plastic, label them and keep them handy for your next turning adventure!

LEATHER HINGE

SEPARATE PIECES

FOOLPROOF TOOL SHARPENING

The Work Sharp system gives you precise results quickly and easily when you sharpen nearly any cutting edge. And the edge is visible as it gets sharpened, so you can actually see what you're doing.

The WS2000 model costs $100. The larger WS3000 with adjustable chisel port and slower wheel speed (for better control) costs $200. They're available online and at Rockler.

SHARPENING PORT

DIGITAL ANGLE GAUGE

Woodworkers are forever looking for an angle—preferably a perfect one. But you can't count on a tool's angle-setting indicators when true precision is called for. This digital angle gauge ($40 at rockler.com) changes all that—it magnetically attaches to a tool's blade, fence or table, so you can set perfectly accurate angles in seconds.

EASY-PEEL LABELS

Here's a slick way to remove those pesky labels from boards and plywood. Heat the label with a hair dryer and peel it off with a putty knife or sharp chisel. Go slow and tug gently and it'll come off in one piece and leave no scraps behind to tease away. Even though the spot will look clean, there will be a little adhesive left on the wood, and the label footprint will reappear the second you put a finish over it. So rub the spot with acetone and sand lightly to remove it completely.

ShopTips™

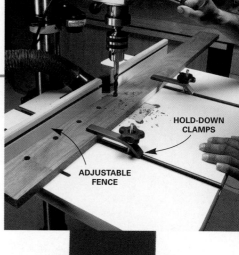

HOLD-DOWN CLAMPS

ADJUSTABLE FENCE

DRILL PRESS TABLE

If you have a conventional drill press with the standard dinky metal table, this well-designed accessory will transform it into a woodworker's dream. The 4-sq.-ft. surface supports large boards for any drilling or drum-sanding task. The fence splits to varying widths—great for picking up chips with the vacuum port or drilling scalloped edges with a hole saw poking partway out. After using the Rockler table ($100 at rockler.com), we wondered why special woodworkers' tables weren't options on all drill presses.

REPAIR FOR STRIPPED SCREWS

Sometimes the wood surrounding a screw becomes so torn up that it no longer holds the screw securely. Here's a rock-solid remedy. Drill a 1/4-in. hole to clear the torn fibers, then glue a short piece of 1/4-in. dowel in the hole. When the glue is dry, saw or sand the dowel flush with the board surface, then drill a pilot hole in the dowel and drive in the screw.

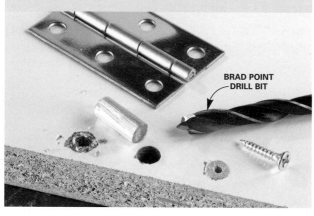

BRAD POINT DRILL BIT

BENCH BRUSH AND DUSTPAN

Here's a classic accompaniment to any shop. Run down to Lowe's and pick up the Quickie Bench Brush ($8) and Cleanco Jumbo Metal Dust Pan ($10). No explanation needed. No Lowe's near you? You can get something similar at any home center or woodworking store.

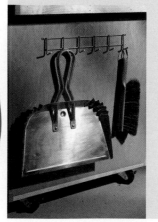

RETRACTABLE AIR HOSE REEL

If you have an air compressor, do yourself a favor and get a retractable hose reel (not one of those cheesy crank models). It prevents trips and tangles when you're using air tools like nailers, sanders and sprayers, and then reels up in seconds when the job's done. Trust us—you will love the convenience. If your shop is in the garage, you can fill the car tires more easily too!

A retractable hose reel like the one shown costs about $80 at home centers.

RETRACTABLE EXTENSION CORD

With a retractable extension cord in the shop, there's no more searching for the extension cord, no more tripping over cords on the floor, and no more constantly bending over to plug in whatever you need. But stay away from wimpy 16- to 18-gauge corded models. They don't carry enough current for many tools. The Husky 14-3, 50-ft. model ($60 at Home Depot) works great, but any 14-3 model with a 13-amp rating will do fine. But as you know, the more you spend....

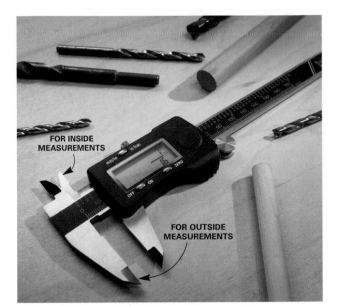

FOR INSIDE MEASUREMENTS

FOR OUTSIDE MEASUREMENTS

DIGITAL CALIPERS

This 6-in. digital caliper guarantees accuracy when you need to measure and fit joints, check board thicknesses while planing, or set cutting depths. Regular metal calipers with etched-on hash marks are inaccurate and hard to read. And dial calipers are spendy. This one, which has a large, easy-to-read display, is not only incredibly accurate (to 1/1,000th of an inch), but also cheap! Call up either fractions of inches or decimals or metric with the push of a button. The 6-in. caliper costs $30 at rockler.com; the 4-in. model, $25.

CAULK TUBE SPOUT SURGERY

Don't discard half-used caulk tubes just because the nozzle is plugged up with dried caulk. Slit the nozzle on both sides and pry out the plug. Then tape the nozzle halves back together with electrical tape and get back to work.

WORKSHOP FILE CRATE

Organize all your tool manuals, sandpaper, receipts, project plans and more in a plastic file box ($5 at an office supply store) loaded with hanging files. If you neatly label the files, the next time you want to take apart the chain saw, or need a piece of 220-grit sandpaper, you won't waste a second rummaging around for the manual or sandpaper.

ShopTips™

PREDRILLED SEAT PATTERNS

Ever wonder how woodworkers drill those odd-angled, perfectly placed leg holes on the underside of chairs and stools and some tables? The answer is a custom drilling template that can be used over and over for dozens of identical furniture pieces. It doesn't take long to make a drilling pattern. And once it's finished, you just clamp it on the seat-to-be, drill through the holes, trace the pattern onto the stock, cut it out and glue in the legs.

To make a pattern, screw and glue together two pieces of 3/4-in. MDF with 1-1/4-in. screws. Set a drill press to the desired leg angle, and drill guide holes so they come out at the proper hole locations on the seat top. Cut the shape you want and clamp it to the seat stock and drill the holes (use a piece of plywood underneath to avoid tear-out). Then trace around the pattern and saw out the seat.

Use a 1-in.-diameter Forstner bit to drill holes in the pattern on the drill press, then switch to a 1-in. Irwin Speedbor bit to drill the seat holes; the guide hole will

keep it perfectly angled while you're drilling. (Speedbor kits are sold at 7corners.com.) These Irwin auger-style bits are very aggressive, so set the drill at a slow speed and practice on a scrap board so you don't wreck your workpiece.

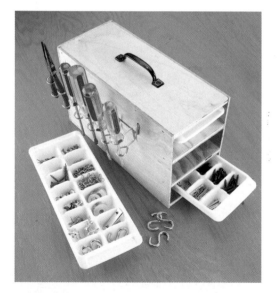

SUPER-COOL HARDWARE TRAYS

Forget the old coffee can filled with your lifetime collection of screws, washers and other hardware. Take 10 minutes to organize the miscellany in ice cube trays. Nail together a case from scrap plywood and carry it right to the job at hand.

MAGNIFYING LAMP

We put this magnifying lamp to work in our shop and immediately saw what we'd been missing. We could gauge how sharp chisels really were and actually read faint drill size etchings and the tiny print on spray cans. But most important, this lamp made quick work of splinter removal. It sports a 60-watt bulb and a 3-3/4-in.-diameter glass lens that triple-powers your peepers. Mounted on a spring-balanced arm with a 36-in. reach, it clamps onto any shelf or workbench. The lamp costs $31 at woodcraft.com.

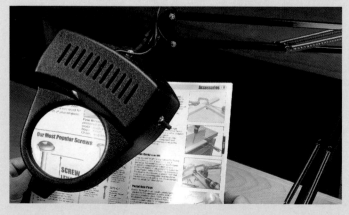

DISPOSABLE
STRAINER

AMBER
SHELLAC

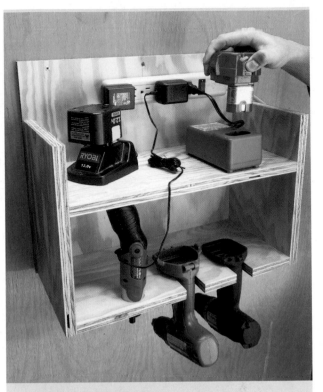

STRAIN AND STOW YOUR FINISH

The first step to a perfect, dust-free finish using previously opened cans of varnish or polyurethane is to filter the liquid. The finish in a can you opened last week or last year is bound to have a little debris floating in it.

After you pry open that crusty lid, be sure to stir the contents thoroughly. It's important to get all of the solids off the bottom and dissolved completely for the finish to perform properly.

To filter out impurities, pour the finish through a disposable paint strainer—suspended in a strainer holder—and into a clean glass jar. Salsa jars are great for this because the brush fits in the opening and the lid seals much better for storage than the lid on the original can. Pick up strainers and a holder at a home center or online at mcfeelys.com.

CORDLESS DRILL-DRIVER STATION

Here's a useful hangout for cordless drill-drivers. It stores them near their chargers so you won't forget to charge them, and keeps them close at hand and ready to go. Best of all, with their own little eagle's nest, your drill-drivers will always be where you can find them.

To make one, rip 3/4-in. plywood into 8-1/2-in.-wide strips. Make your drill-driver station wide enough to hold all your drivers. Cut slots in the lower shelf to fit the driver handles, then glue and nail the station together. Screw the station to a wall near an electrical outlet.

READABLE RULER

If you have metal rulers and squares that are hard to read because rust and grime have filled the indentations, brush correction fluid across the engraved marks. Let it dry, then clean off the dried fluid with fine sandpaper. The tiny marks will now show clearly, and you can skip buying a more powerful pair of cheaters.

UNTREATED

TREATED

ShopTips™

CUSHIONED CONTOUR SANDING

The pad of my random-orbital sander was a tad too firm for refining chair seats. It flattened out areas instead of creating the soft, subtle contours I was after. So I bought an extra pad base for the sander and softened the base by sticking a piece of 3/8-in.-thick closed-cell foam to the bottom with contact cement. My sander uses adhesive-backed sandpaper, which I just stuck right to the foam. (If your sander uses hook-and-loop sandpaper, just glue the foam to the extra base with contact cement and then buy some adhesive-backed discs.) I also unscrew the base and use it as a freehand sander to shape and sand legs, spindles and bowls I'm turning on the lathe. You can buy closed-cell foam at fabric stores or order it online from foamorder.com.

PAD BASE

PAD BASE

CLOSED-CELL FOAM

GAUGE BLOCKS FROM SCRAPS

Go through your collection of scrap plywood and cut a few little squares of each thickness. Every time you work with a new plywood thickness, cut a few squares of it, too. Label each square with its thickness and keep them handy. They're great for measuring depths of grooves and gauging saw blade and router bit cutting depths. Pile up various squares to get just about any thickness you want. For many small measuring tasks, it's easier to use gauge blocks than to use a tape measure.

VENTILATED SHOP VACUUM ATTACHMENT

Floor attachments on new shop vacuums have little risers on the bottom edge so the attachment doesn't get glued to the floor by suction, making serious debris pick-up next to impossible. For older attachments without risers, there's an easy fix: Cut 1/4-in.-deep notches every inch or so along the rim with a hacksaw. Now the attachment will slide around without sticking to the floor and clean much more effectively.

EXHAUST FAN

FURNACE FILTER FABRIC

LOW-BUDGET VENTILATION

In his finishing room, professional woodworker Dave Munkittrick uses a ventilation system that's economical, simple and effective. He stuck a plywood insert with a hole for a fan in one window, and in the other window he taped a piece of furnace filter material. When he turns on the fan, air is pulled through the fabric, filtered of dust and exhausted through the fan. But even with the good ventilation, he still wears a respirator for extra protection.

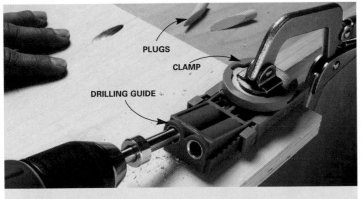

PLUGS

CLAMP

DRILLING GUIDE

POCKET HOLE JIG

OK, here's a secret weapon. This Kreg pocket hole jig ($40 at home centers) makes joinery simple for anyone who has an electric drill. It creates strong joints fast with no glue or mess. Just clamp the jig to the parts you're joining, drill a couple of holes, then screw the parts together. Tight and strong joints every time. It works great for joining wood of nearly any size, type or dimension. Kreg offers a wide variety of accessories as well as more expensive rigs, but the Model R3 is all a home woodworker needs to build professional-grade furniture or cabinets.

BIFOCAL SAFETY GLASSES

Any farsighted woodsmith would love a pair of bifocal safety glasses—no more constantly switching between safety glasses and cheaters. These glasses ($7 at woodcraft.com) are so comfortable that you can put them on when you enter the shop and leave them on until you're done! They come with adjustable frames and shatter-proof, anti-fog lenses. Choose from a range of bifocal powers.

ShopTips™

TIPS FROM A FURNITURE MAESTRO

Our latest search for tips from professional woodworkers led us to Dave Munkittrick's shop in Wisconsin.

"Years ago we left the big city and bought this old farmstead," Dave said. "With a little bit of remodeling, the hog barn became my woodworking shop, and it's been a great place to build, repair and finish furniture for the last 20 years."

Dave's repair and finishing tips are the fruit of careful thought blended with ingenious thriftiness. Translation: Let Dave help you get the job done well—and cheap!

CLEAN CAN RIMS PRESERVE FINISHES

If you force the lids of your finish cans closed when there's finish filling the rim, the can won't seal and the contents will dry out.

"It only takes a few seconds after you're done to rub the can rim with a cotton cloth, which guarantees a clean and tight seal, and makes it easier to open the can next time."

ALWAYS CHECK FOR LOOSE BRISTLES

"Loose bristles coming out of the brush and drying on your project are a headache you can prevent," Dave said. Just smack a clean, dry brush several times against the palm of your hand. Loose bristles stick out from the end of the brush and are easily plucked before you dip the brush in the can.

BIG BOX OF PLASTIC GLOVES

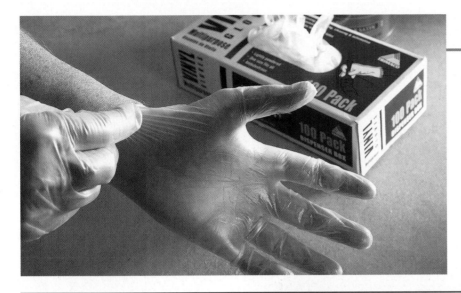

"This may seem like an obvious idea," Dave said while slipping on a pair of plastic gloves. "But if you apply finishes bare-handed and then clean your hands with solvents, they go through your skin and into your system. So I keep a jumbo box of gloves handy and always pull on a new pair when finishing furniture, cleaning brushes or working with any kind of adhesive."

A box of 100 vinyl gloves costs about $14 at home centers.

MINI MALLET FOR TIGHT SPOTS

Dave's mallet for tapping furniture parts together—and apart—is pretty simple. "My rubber mallet was too big to get into small spaces, so I slipped a 1-in. rubber foot from the hardware store onto a ball peen hammer. It fits in tight spots and focuses the hammer blow more accurately during disassembly and glue-ups."

The rubber feet are inexpensive ($3 for a four-pack) and come in various diameters (3/4 in. to 1-1/2 in.). Take your hammer to the store to be sure you get one that fits.

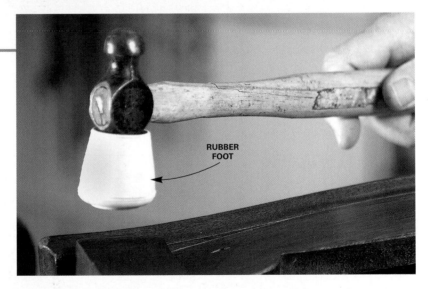

RUBBER FOOT

SPENDY BRUSH— A GREAT INVESTMENT

Dave showed us how to tell a quality paintbrush from a cheap one—good to know when you're at the hardware store. First, he stroked a cheap plastic-bristle brush against a table edge; the bristles split apart. When he stroked an expensive ox-hair brush on the edge, the bristles wrapped around and covered the corner.

Dave's advice: "If you're serious about finishing, invest in high-quality brushes. If you clean them well, they'll last a lifetime, minimize brush marks and hold more finish, so you don't have to reload the brush as often. I'll spend up to $50 for a good brush."

SPENDY BRUSH

CHEAP BRUSH

SIMPLE **BOX SHELVES**

Custom-size and finish these super-simple box shelves for any room in the house

by **Travis Larson**

We've designed these wooden box shelves for heavyweight storage and incredibly easy construction. Use them for hats and gloves, books, games and toys, or even laundry supplies. Custom-size them for whatever space you have available and for whatever it is that needs a home. You'll be able to build one large box from a $45 sheet of plywood and have a bit left over for another box. We'll show you the basics, and you can take it from there. Here's how.

Get these materials

Any veneered 1/2-in. plywood will work, but we suggest birch because the grain doesn't show through paint. Buy a quart of woodworker's glue, and 3/4-in. and 1-in. brads for your nail gun. If you don't have a nailer, you can hand-nail, but it will be a bit of a struggle. You'll also need fast-drying wood filler. Buy a quart of BIN or KILZ primer ($10) and a quart of latex enamel paint in the color of your choice. If you choose a gloss finish, be aware that if you don't pay attention to filling and sanding, every single imperfection will proudly display itself. Also pick up some mini rollers (Photo 6) for applying the finishes. And finally, a flush-trim

Super-strong construction

These box shelves are amazingly sturdy, thanks to the two-layer, 1/2-in. plywood design. The thickness and the overlapping joints make them strong enough to display or store anything. You can even park yourself on one if you need to!

router bit ($20) will speed up the final trimming (Photo 4). That way you can cut the outer panels a little long and achieve perfectly flush ends without the hassle of precise cutting.

Cutting the parts

It's easiest to rip the parts on a table saw, but you can use a circular saw and a ripping guide. If that's your plan, use a crosscutting jig (Photo 1) when you cut the lengths. Use fine-tooth crosscutting blades for both types of saws. After deciding on the size of your box, you'll need to rip two different widths for the box panels. Rip the four inner panels 1/2 in. narrower than the final box depths, and rip the four outer panels to match the final depth. Be sure to rip enough material to get all of the parts made. If you like adjustable shelves, drill the peg holes before assembly. Measure the inner box after assembly to get the dimensions for the back panel. Cut the back 1/8 in. overlong in both directions and rout off the excess as we show in Photo 4. As you glue and nail on the back, bend out any bows in the sides (Photo 2).

Cut the top and bottom outer panels to length, 1/8 in. longer than the box. Apply a bead of glue about 1/4 in. in from the edges and a second bead in a zigzag pattern in the middle (Photo 3). Align the panels flush with the front and with equal overhangs at the ends. Nail the parts together with 3/4-in. nails. Be careful. It's tough to fix the damage from nails that miss the mark. If you have clamps, use them to squeeze closed any gaps. A tight joint will

Figure A: Simple box

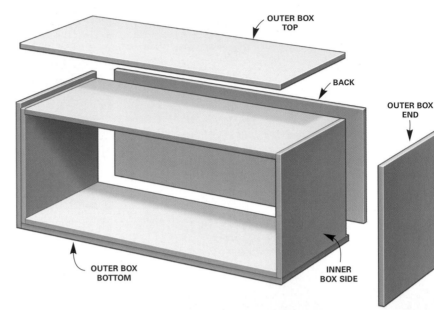

OUTER BOX TOP

BACK

OUTER BOX END

OUTER BOX BOTTOM

INNER BOX SIDE

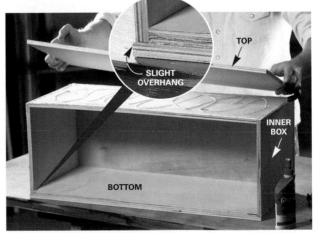

CROSS-CUTTING JIG

1 Cut the box parts to length. A simple homemade crosscutting jig lets you make perfect cuts with a circular saw.

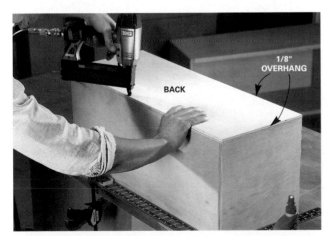

1/8" OVERHANG

BACK

2 Glue and nail the box together, using a framing square to hold it square. Make the back 1/8 in. larger than the box, then glue and nail it in place and rout any overhangs (Photo 4).

TOP

SLIGHT OVERHANG

INNER BOX

BOTTOM

3 Add a second layer of plywood to the top and bottom of the box. To avoid fussy measuring and cutting, oversize each panel by 1/8 in. and cut off the excess later.

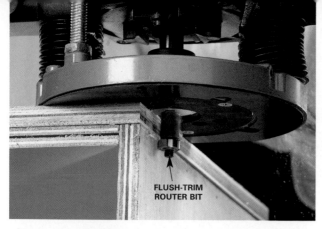

4 Trim the overhanging plywood with a flush-trim router bit. The bit leaves a straight, smooth cut that's perfectly flush at the ends. Install the end panels using the same method.

FLUSH-TRIM ROUTER BIT

5 Fill the plywood edges as well as nail holes and dents. Use a fast-drying filler so you can sand the patches right away.

FAST-DRYING FILLER

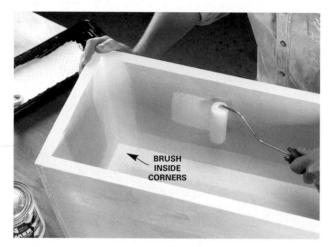

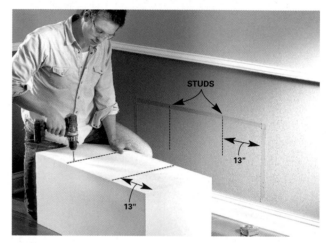

6 Prime the box, brushing the inside corners first. For a fast, smooth finish on the rest of the box, use a small roller. Then sand the primer, and paint using the same method.

BRUSH INSIDE CORNERS

7 Outline the box location on the wall and mark the wall studs. Use the outline to mark the pilot holes and then drill them through the back of the box.

STUDS

13"

13"

reduce the amount of sanding and filling you have to do later. For a perfect edge, shave the overhangs with a flush-trim router bit (**Photo 4**). As before, cut the side panels 1/8 in. longer than the box sides, and then apply and trim them as you did with the top and the bottom.

Finish the box

Sand the exposed plywood edges until they're smooth, first with 80-grit paper and then 120-grit. Then work wood filler into all of the edge grain, nail holes and dents (**Photo 5**). After the filler sets, sand everything flat with 120-grit paper.

Brush primer into the inside corners and then roll primer onto the rest of the box (**Photo 6**). After it dries, voids that didn't get filled will be very apparent. So fill anything you missed, and then sand and prime those spots again. Brush and roll on two coats of paint, lightly sanding between the coats with 220-grit paper.

Wall mounting

It's imperative that you screw these boxes to at least two wall studs; no wall anchors of any kind will pass muster. Use at least two 3-in. deck screws near the top and two

8 Align the box with the outline and screw it to the wall studs with 3-in. deck screws.

3" DECK SCREWS

more at the bottom into separate studs. If more studs are available, use those, too. In **Photos 7 and 8**, we show you an easy way to position and drill pilot holes so the screws will hit the studs when you mount the boxes. ⬆

InstantProject

STAIR-STEP PLANT STAND

If you're looking for a fun, simple project, maybe this plant stand will fit the bill. You build it from boards that are cut into just two lengths, stacked into squares and nailed together. You'll only need seven 8-ft.-long 1x2s, exterior wood glue and a few dozen galvanized 4d finish nails. We used cedar for its looks and its longevity outside, but any wood will do. Cut the 1x2s into sixteen 20-in. pieces and twenty-seven 10-3/4-in. pieces.

Don't fret over the assembly; it's really very simple. Just follow the photos for the proper positioning of the two lengths and the number of layers. Adjust the gap spacing with scrap 1x2s, and make sure everything is square as you stack up each layer. When it looks good, nail the pieces together using one nail and a dab of glue at every intersection. Keep the nails 3/4 in. away from the ends of the boards to prevent splitting. When your plant stand is complete, sand all the outside edges and apply an exterior stain or preservative. Then start moving in the blooms.

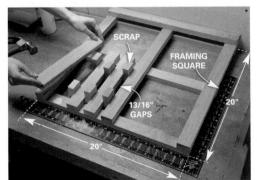

1 Dry-fit the first two layers (without glue or nails) using a square to get the spacing right, and make sure everything fits well.

2 Then glue and nail the boards at each intersection.

New Tools&Gear

SAFEST TABLE SAW EVER

Of the dozens of carpenters and woodworkers I've worked with over the years, a large number have had close calls—or worse—with table saws. The SawStop table saw is the best way to make sure that a binding board or a moment's lapse in concentration doesn't change your life forever. Even with the blade guard off—a bad habit that many people just can't break—the SawStop instantly retracts the blade (within five milliseconds) if any part of the body comes in contact with the blade. The blade might nick the skin, but it won't cut off a finger. The manufacturer estimates a table saw injury happens every nine minutes.

SawStop makes a 10-in. cabinet saw (starting at $2,800) and a 10-in. contractor's saw (starting at $1,600), and thus far, is the only manufacturer offering this safety feature. Either saw is expensive—several hundred dollars more than other table saws—but severed fingers cost even more! Both SawStop saws are high-quality table saws that match the performance of the top-of-the-line saws, so you can do great work without worrying about losing a finger. A replacement blade cartridge (if you touch the spinning blade and it retracts, you'll need a new one) costs $70. Find retailers on the company's Web site. **SawStop, (503) 570-3200. sawstop.com**

PHOTOGRAPHY SAWSTOP

**REAL NICK
AFTER SAWSTOP
INCIDENT**

A GREAT READ FOR DIYERS

In his engaging, informative new book, *A Splintered History of Wood: Belt Sander Races, Blind Woodworkers & Baseball Bats*, Spike Carlsen has collected amazing stories about wood, the people who work it, and the role of wood in our lives and our history. You won't find complex tables of elasticity, but you'll get a chuckle out of the Wild Man of the West, the world's greatest chain saw artist, who carves wooden belt buckles—while customers are wearing them! You'll also marvel at 50,000-year-old wood dug from swamps, the making of a Steinway grand piano, and the factory in Maine that produces 50 billion toothpicks.

Spike's wide-eyed enthusiasm is catching, and his curiosity takes him way beyond the ordinary. Unlike most books on wood, *Splintered History* isn't written for woodworkers. It's for anybody interested in how this humble material, and the people who work it, have made us who we are. It's available at bookstores, including amazon.com, for less than $25.

Recognize Spike's name? He's the former executive editor at *The Family Handyman* and masterminded many of your favorite projects.

FOOT
PEDAL

SAWHORSE WITH HANDS-FREE CLAMP

Rockwell's heavy-duty Jawhorse is a sawhorse with a built-in clamp that you tighten with your foot. It's the perfect solution if you often work alone and need an extra set of hands for clamping tools, projects or lumber. The substantial 37-in. jaw width makes clamping wide projects a snap. Or clamp on a piece of plywood for an instant workbench or a platform for any portable tool.

The awesome clamping power eliminates the need for a second sawhorse (in most cases). The tripod bases keep the Jawhorse stable during use. When you're through, the Jawhorse folds up like a collapsible sawhorse. But at $180, the Jawhorse costs a lot more than a set of traditional sawhorses. Buy it on the company's Web site or amazon.com.
Rockwell, (866) 514-7625. rockwelltools.com

HYBRID DUST COLLECTOR

If you use your shop vacuum as a dust collector for power tools, you know it's a hassle to constantly empty the canister and clean the filter. The Dust Deputy from Oneida Air Systems converts any shop vacuum into an ad hoc version of more serious—and more expensive—dedicated dust collectors. The bucket collects most of the dust and chips so they don't fill the shop vacuum's canister and clog the filter. Emptying the bucket is a breeze (check out the video on the company's Web site).

The complete kit (including bucket and hose) costs $100. If you want to supply a bucket and fasteners, the cyclone alone costs $60, but then you'll have to figure out how to hook everything up. Both options are available on the Web site.
Oneida Air Systems, (800) 732-4065.
dustdeputy.com

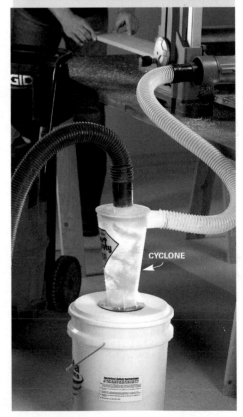

CYCLONE

SHAKER
BOOKCASE

Build this heirloom with modern tools and materials

by **Eric Smith**

Making high-end furniture like this bookcase can seem intimidating, but once you get started, all you really need are a few key tools and the patience to get your measurements right. The basic structure of this bookcase is just two plywood boxes with a cherry face frame that has doors attached to it. Although there are quite a few

High-end doors with biscuits

The frame-and-panel doors for this project look difficult to build, but the only special tools you need to make them are a biscuit joiner and a router, and the only skill required is the ability to measure accurately. Just assemble the door frame with biscuits, then cut the rabbets with a self-piloting router bit. Set a plywood or glass panel in and the door is done.

PLYWOOD PANEL

ROUND-OVER

BISCUIT

RABBET

parts to cut, there's nothing complicated about how they go together.

This project will take two to three weekends to build, and the wood will cost roughly $1,200 if you use top-quality cherry. You can reduce the cost by as much as half if you use a less expensive wood like oak and if you plane and rip the boards yourself.

To build the bookcase, you'll need a table saw, a biscuit joiner, a router, and a compressor and pneumatic brad nailer, in addition to standard tools like a drill and a random orbit sander. Cherry and maple plywood and hardwood are available in a wide variety of sizes from full-service lumberyards, woodworking and cabinetmaking suppliers, and online distributors.

Build the plywood boxes

Rip the plywood parts for the tops, bottoms and sides (see **Figure A**), then cut them to length. Whenever possible, stack up same-length parts and cut them together—or use a stop—so the sizes match exactly. Use less expensive maple plywood for the base, which is covered by the cherry face frame; use cherry plywood for the open upper unit. Mark the position of the box sides on the box tops and bottoms, then predrill and screw the pieces together with 1-5/8-in. screws. Attach the nailers at the bottoms with glue and 1-1/4-in. finish nails. Glue and screw the brace for the center leg to the back of the bottom nailer.

Nail the plywood backs to the boxes, carefully nailing along centerlines (**Photo 1**). You can use a single sheet of maple for the base, but cut the cherry plywood back for the top unit in three sections so the grain pattern will be vertical (see Cutting List).

We installed a hidden base for the lower part of the bookcase, for both support and ease of cleaning underneath it. When painted flat black, this hidden base almost disappears. (If you don't wish to add this base, add another leg in the back.)

Attach the shelf supports to the upper unit with glue and brad nails, then fit the bottom shelf piece between the supports. Set the drawer dividers and blocking in

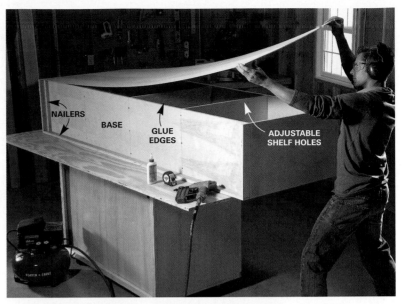

NAILERS BASE GLUE EDGES ADJUSTABLE SHELF HOLES

1 Assemble the plywood boxes that make the base and upper unit, then square them as you install the 1/4-in. plywood backs.

BLOCKING
BLOCKING
SHELF SUPPORTS

2 Fasten the drawer dividers and shelf supports inside the upper cabinet. Position the dividers carefully so the drawers fit perfectly.

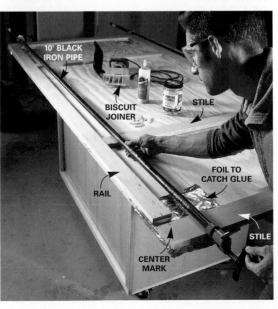

10' BLACK IRON PIPE
BISCUIT JOINER
STILE
FOIL TO CATCH GLUE
RAIL
STILE
CENTER MARK

3 Glue and clamp the face frame with long pipe clamps. Use slow-setting glue so you have time to square it.

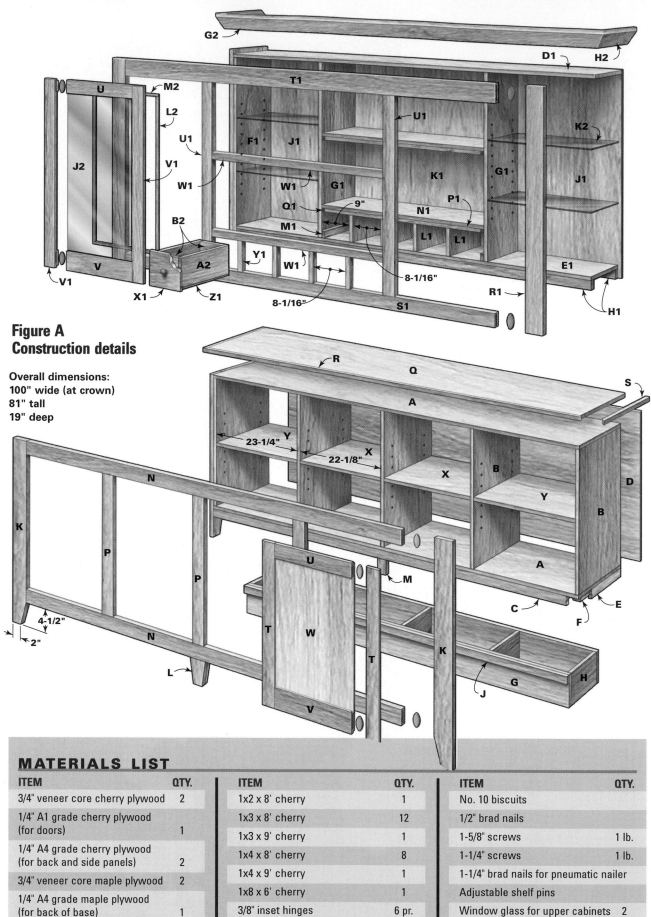

Figure A
Construction details

Overall dimensions:
100" wide (at crown)
81" tall
19" deep

MATERIALS LIST

ITEM	QTY.
3/4" veneer core cherry plywood	2
1/4" A1 grade cherry plywood (for doors)	1
1/4" A4 grade cherry plywood (for back and side panels)	2
3/4" veneer core maple plywood	2
1/4" A4 grade maple plywood (for back of base)	1
1/2" maple plywood (1/2 sheet)	1

ITEM	QTY.
1x2 x 8' cherry	1
1x3 x 8' cherry	12
1x3 x 9' cherry	1
1x4 x 8' cherry	8
1x4 x 9' cherry	1
1x8 x 6' cherry	1
3/8" inset hinges	6 pr.
Black ceramic knobs ($2 at home centers)	11

ITEM	QTY.
No. 10 biscuits	
1/2" brad nails	
1-5/8" screws	1 lb.
1-1/4" screws	1 lb.
1-1/4" brad nails for pneumatic nailer	
Adjustable shelf pins	
Window glass for upper cabinets	2
1/4" polished-edge glass shelves	4

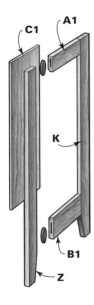

CUTTING LIST: BASE

KEY QTY. SIZE & DESCRIPTION

(A – J are maple plywood)

KEY	QTY.	SIZE & DESCRIPTION
A	2	94-1/2" x 17" x 3/4" top and bottom
B	5	27-1/2" x 17" x 3/4" sides
C	1	94-1/2" x 1-11/16" x 3/4" nailer
D	1	94-1/2" x 30-3/4" x 1/4" back
E	2	16-1/4" x 1-11/16" x 3/4" nailers
F	2	16-1/4" x 1-1/2" x 3/4" nailers
G	2	84" x 6-1/4" x 3/4" base support
H	5	10-1/2" x 6-1/4" x 3/4" base support
J	1	84" x 3/4" x 3/4" nailer

(K – C1 are solid cherry unless noted)

KEY	QTY.	SIZE & DESCRIPTION
K	4	35-1/4" x 3-1/2" x 3/4" legs (front and rear)
L	1	4-1/2" x 3-1/2" x 1-1/2" center leg (glue two 3/4" pieces)
M	1	4" x 3/4" x 3/4" center leg brace
N	2	89-1/16" x 2-1/2" x 3/4" face frame rails
P	3	25-3/4" x 2-1/2" x 3/4" face frame stiles
Q	1	96" x 18-1/16" x 3/4" top (cherry plywood)
R	1	97-1/2" x 3/4" x 3/4" top edge
S	2	18-3/4" x 3/4" x 3/4" top edge
T	8	26-1/4" x 2-1/2" x 3/4" door stiles
U	6	16" x 2-1/2" x 3/4" door rails
V	6	16" x 3-1/2" x 3/4" door rails
W	4	21" x 16-5/8" x 1/4" door panels (cherry plywood)
X	2	22" x 16-1/2" x 3/4" shelves (maple plywood)
Y	2	23-1/8" x 16-1/2" x 3/4" shelves (maple plywood)
Z	2	35-1/4" x 2-3/4" x 3/4" side panel legs
A1	2	11" x 2-1/2" x 3/4" side panel rails
B1	2	11" x 3-1/2" x 3/4" side panel rails
C1	2	25-1/2" x 11-3/4" x 1/4" side panels (cherry plywood)

CUTTING LIST: UPPER UNIT

KEY QTY. SIZE & DESCRIPTION

(D1 – P1 are cherry plywood)

KEY	QTY.	SIZE & DESCRIPTION
D1	1	94-1/2" x 11" x 3/4" top
E1	1	93-1/16" x 11" x 3/4" bottom
F1	2	41-1/4" x 11" x 3/4" sides
G1	2	38-13/16" x 11" x 3/4" sides
H1	2	93-1/16" x 1-3/4" x 3/4" nailers
J1	2	42" x 24-5/16" x 1/4" back side panels (cut so grain is vertical)
K1	1	42" x 45-3/4" x 1/4" back (center panel)
L1	4	11" x 5-3/4" x 3/4" drawer dividers (maple plywood)
M1	2	11" x 1-1/2" x 3/4" blocking
N1	2	45" x 11" x 3/4" shelves
P1	2	43-1/2" x 11" x 3/4" shelves

(All remaining pieces are solid cherry unless noted)

KEY	QTY.	SIZE & DESCRIPTION
Q1	4	11" x 3/4" x 3/4" shelf supports
R1	2	43" x 3-1/2" x 3/4" face frame stiles
S1	1	89-1/8" x 2-1/2" x 3/4" face frame rail
T1	1	89-1/8" x 3-1/2" x 3/4" upper face frame rail
U1	2	37" x 2-1/2" x 3/4" center face frame stiles
V1	4	37-1/2" x 2-1/2" x 3/4" door stiles
W1	2	43-1/4" x 1-1/2" x 3/4" shelf edge
X1	5	8-3/4" (cut down to 8-1/2" after rabbeting) x 6-1/4" x 3/4" drawer faces
Y1	4	5-3/4" x 3/4" x 3/4" drawer divider edges
Z1	5	11-1/4" x 7-15/16" x 1/4" plywood drawer bottoms
A2	10	11-1/4" x 5-3/8" x 1/2" maple plywood drawer sides
B2	10	7" x 5-3/8" x 1/2" maple plywood drawer fronts and backs
C2	2	43" x 2-1/2" x 3/4" side panel stiles
D2	2	43" x 1-3/4" x 3/4" side panel stiles
E2	4	7" x 3-1/2" x 3/4" side panel rails
F2	2	7-3/4" x 36-3/4" x 1/4" cherry plywood side panels
G2	1	99-7/8" x 3-1/8" x 3/4" crown molding
H2	2	13-7/8" x 3-1/8" x 3/4" crown molding
J2	2	32-1/8" x 16-1/2" x 1/16" glass doors (window glass, $10 per pane from glass supplier or hardware store)
K2	4	10-3/4" x 23-1/8" x 1/4" glass shelves (polished edges—special order from glass supplier, $20 per shelf)
L2	4	32-1/4" x 1/4" x 1/4" stop (for glass door)
M2	4	16-1/8" x 1/4" x 1/4" stop (for glass door)

CENTER LEG SUPPORT

TOP

SIDE PANEL

HIDDEN BASE

FIRST PASS

SECOND PASS

4 Align the face frame with the side panels as you lay it in place. Apply glue generously, then nail the pieces together. Use as few nails as possible.

5 Cut rabbets in the inside and outside of the completed door frames with a rabbeting bit. Cut two passes for a clean cut with minimal splintering.

place, making sure they're perpendicular to the face before screwing them in (**Photo 2**). Glue and nail the two plywood shelves together, then nail the upper shelf to the shelf supports. Also screw the back to the top shelf to keep the shelf from sagging.

Assemble the drawer boxes with glue and 1-1/4-in. nails. We used 1/2-in. maple plywood with 1/4-in. bottoms (instead of 3/4-in.) so the drawers would have more inside space.

Build the face frames

Lay the plywood boxes flat and, before you cut anything, carefully check the rail and stile sizes in the Cutting List against the boxes you've made. The face frame for the base unit must be perfectly flush with the top, but 1/16 in. to 1/8 in. longer than the plywood box plus the side panels to compensate for slight variations in the sides. The bottom rails must be even with or slightly above the plywood bottoms to hide the plywood edge. Take your time with this. The difference between amateur and professional results comes down to getting these 1/16-in. measurements right.

Before starting, test your biscuit joiner on the end of a scrap 1x3. We used No. 10 biscuits, but we had to adjust the depth of cut of the biscuit joiner so it wouldn't cut through the sides of the 1x3, and even then the biscuits were exposed (though hidden on the inside of the door) by the 3/8-in. rabbet cut. You can use a No. 0

biscuit for the wood doors, but the heavy glass doors require a No. 10 (or else two No. 0 biscuits).

Mark and cut all the biscuit slots, then assemble the entire face frame dry, without glue, to make sure everything will fit correctly.

Glue the biscuits for the center stiles first. After you clamp them, measure diagonally from corner to corner to make sure the frame is square. (The two measurements should match.) Apply enough glue to the biscuit slots so a little oozes out when you clamp the joint—too much just means more cleanup, but too little makes a weak joint. Use

Figure B
Shaker-style crown molding

To make flat crown molding that matches the Shaker style better than the profiles sold at lumberyards do, set the table saw blade at 35 degrees, then make four edge cuts in the order shown here (remember to use the blade guard—we removed it for clarity). Use tape to mark 1 in. down from the top of the upper rail, and hold the crown against the tape as you nail it. Use test pieces to get the exact angle for the miter cuts at the corner.

UPPER RAIL

TAPE

1"

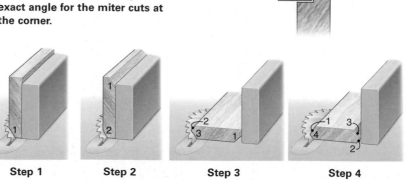

Step 1　　Step 2　　Step 3　　Step 4

6 Square the rounded inside corners left by the rabbeting bit. Make shallow cuts with a sharp chisel to avoid splitting the wood.

CHISEL

7 Make your own edge molding for the base's plywood top. Round the edges of a board with a router and then cut off strips on the table saw.

1/4" ROUND-OVER

8 Attach the hinges to the doors before putting in the panels or glass, then reach inside and mark the hinge screw locations.

HIDDEN SCREW HOLE

a slower-setting glue so you don't have to rush. Place a piece of foil or plastic under the joints so you don't accidentally glue the frame to the worktable. (For more on biscuit joiners, search "biscuit" at **thefamilyhandyman.com**.)

After the center stiles have dried enough to stay in place—about 15 minutes—glue the end stiles to the rails (**Photo 3**) with pipe clamps ($56 for two pipe clamps and 3/4-in. x 10-ft. black iron pipe). Cut the tapers on the legs for the base with a circular saw before gluing.

Cut and assemble the side panels, also using biscuits. After the glue dries, sand the panel until the joints are flat, then cut a 3/8-in. rabbet around the inside of the panel with a router and self-piloting rabbet bit (the same bit will be used to make the doors; see **Photo 5**). Nail in the 1/4-in. panel with 1/2-in. brad nails (**Photo 9**).

Attach the face frames

Screw the top to the base, overhanging it 3/4 in. on the sides and front. Only the front 6 in. will be visible, so place the best side of the cherry plywood there (and don't put screws there).

Set the face frame and side panels into place and line up all the edges (**Photo 4**). Glue and nail the pieces to the framework and to one another with 1-1/4-in. brad nails. To ensure a tight fit, clamp the face frame to the side panels before nailing them together.

Cut and nail the edging for the plywood shelves and drawer dividers on the upper unit separately after the face frames are attached, with glue but without biscuits. Sand the corners and joints flush, then sand all the surfaces smooth with 150- or 180-grit sandpaper.

Assemble the doors

Mark centers on all the rails and corresponding marks on the stiles, then join the doors with biscuits and clamps, just as with the face frames.

Give the doors several hours to dry after assembling them, then sand both sides until all the joints are perfectly flat and even.

Set the router to a depth of 3/16 in. for the first pass—or less if the wood you use seems to splinter easily (**Photo 5**).

Square the inside corners (**Photo 6**), then turn the doors over and round the outside edges with a 3/16-in. self-piloting round-over bit.

Add edging to the top

Cut four edges in a 9-ft. piece of cherry 1x3 with a 1/4-in. self-piloting round-over bit. Rip two 3/4-in.-wide strips (**Photo 7**), then cut and temporarily clamp the front edge piece in place. Use the leftover piece from the cut as a test piece to get the angle and fit of the side pieces exactly right.

Cut the side pieces, then mark and cut both the front and side pieces for biscuits—two on each side and six across the front. The biscuits keep the edging from breaking off when the base is lifted by the edges (as we learned by experience). Spread glue along the whole edge, then insert the biscuits and nail the edging into place. Wipe away glue drips, then sand smooth with 150-grit sandpaper after the glue dries so the top feels like one piece of wood.

Hang the doors

Attach the hinges to the doors, then drill holes for the hinges in the door frames (**Photo 8**). We used 3/8-in.-inset snap-closing chrome hinges (available for $3 a pair from rockler.com, item No. 32142). Other styles of 3/8-in.-inset hinges that are surface mounted are available at home centers.

Set the plywood door panels into the frames with a light bead of glue and 1/2-in. brad nails (**Photo 9**), then hang the doors. Wait until the doors are finished to set the glass panels in—both for easier finishing and to avoid raw wood edges under the glass.

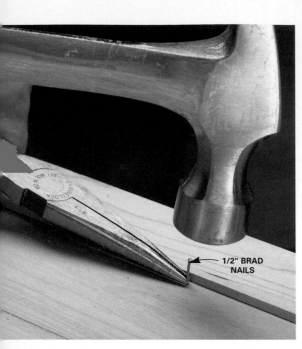

9 Set the panels into the frames on a narrow bead of glue, then tack the panels in place with 1/2-in. brad nails.

Attach the drawer fronts

Rip the 1x8 piece of cherry to the width in the Cutting List, then cut a 3/8-in. rabbet in both sides. Cut the cherry into 8-3/4-in. pieces, numbering them in order so the grain on the finished drawers will match. Cut the same rabbets on the sides, then cut 1/8 in. off each side (but not the top or the bottom) to create a 1/4-in. gap between drawer faces. (Note: Or you can cut the pieces 8-1/2-in. wide, then use a 1/4-in. rabbet bit on the sides.)

Round the drawer edges with the 3/16-in. round-over bit, then drill center holes for the drawer pulls with a 3/16-in. bit. That will leave a hole just sloppy enough for fine adjustments, enabling you to get all the drawer faces aligned with each other. Clamp the faces to the boxes, then fasten them together with 1-1/4-in. screws and set them in the openings (**Photo 10**). Align the drawers, tighten the screws, then open the drawers and predrill and screw the boxes to the faces from the inside with two screws. Remove the screw from the drawer face. Drill holes for the knobs in the drawers and doors.

Cut and attach the crown molding to the upper cabinet (see **Figure B**). Sand the entire bookcase smooth with 150- or

10 Screw the drawer faces to the drawer boxes through the knob hole and set them in the opening against the bottom edge. Align them with each other and with the doors.

11 Fasten the window stop through predrilled holes using a tack hammer and brads. Slide the hammer back and forth on a piece of heavy paper or cardboard.

180-grit sandpaper, then apply a coat of sanding sealer followed by stain (optional) and two coats of urethane. Paint the hidden base black to make it less obvious. After the first coat of urethane, fill nail holes with colored wood putty, mixing the colors to match different wood tones. Once the finishing is done, install the adjustable shelf pins and shelves.

Finally, secure the glass in the upper doors with wood stop and 1/2-in. brad nails (**Photo 11**). Predrill nail holes in the stop before you set it against the glass.

Set the upper unit on top of the base, using two metal angles at the back to tie the two pieces together. Shim as needed under the legs and base to keep the bookcase from rocking and to make it parallel to the wall. ⌂

Question&Comment

CAN THIS POLY BE SAVED?

I opened a can of polyurethane and it was skinned over. Can I peel off the skin and use the rest?

Probably. Check the remaining material to make sure it's clear and particle-free. If the polyurethane has crud in it, try filtering it through cheesecloth. Then try brushing it on scrap wood. If it goes on fine, use it.

If the poly is water-based and too thick, thin it by adding water (no more than 10 percent). You can also thin solvent-based poly by adding up to 10 percent mineral spirits, but only if you live in a state that allows it. Some East Coast states and California prohibit users from adding solvents after the can is opened. In that case, you'll have to recycle the old stuff and buy a fresh can.

Always test thinned polyurethane on scrap wood before applying it to your project. Chances are it will work just fine. But if it doesn't look right, buy fresh material.

HandyHints

EASY I.D. SYSTEM FOR FASTENERS

I keep a lot of different size screws and doodads in a plastic storage bin. I got sick and tired of pulling out 15 drawers to find what I needed, so I came up with this easy system. I take one of the doodads from each drawer and hot-glue it to the drawer front. Now I can instantly find exactly what I need.

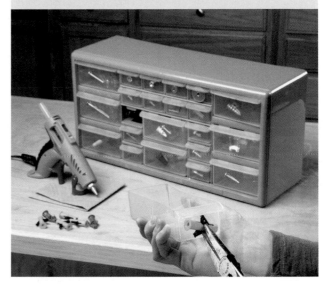

GreatGoofs

New desk, big hole

My father, a university professor, just treated himself to a beautiful solid oak roll-down desk. He mounted a surge protector to the back of the desk to plug in his computer, printer and phone, then drilled a 2-in. hole through the back to run the electrical lines.

He was very pleased with his handiwork since all of the cords were now hidden. But his smile quickly disappeared when he rolled the top closed and noticed the 2-in. hole he'd drilled through the upper right-hand corner of the cover when it was rolled up and hidden in the desk back. He claims the hole was intentional so light would charge his solar calculator. But we all know the truth.

FUN AND FUNCTIONAL STORAGE

The folks at Blu Dot have an excellent sense of humor (check out their Web site for some laughs). They also manufacture affordable and well-designed furniture, storage products and accessories. Their 2D3D line features a variety of useful items that come flat-packed. You simply fold the item along the perforated lines and hang it on the wall. Blu Dot's Web site calls these products "functional origami without the paper cuts." Each piece is made of powder-coated steel and comes in gray, white and red. Along with the magazine rack (pictured, $99) the 2D3D line includes a hanging CD rack, coatrack and more.
bludot.com, (612) 782-1844

1 The box arrives looking like this.

2 The magazine rack has perforated fold lines.

3 Voilà – the finished product!

BUDGET-MINDED LUXURY

Myson's new Pearl portable towel warmer ($225) is a surprisingly affordable and practical luxury. Unlike hydronic towel warmers, which must be plumbed into a hot-water heating system, this electric towel warmer simply plugs into any standard 120-volt outlet. It uses less energy than a 150-watt lightbulb. The Pearl line includes two wall-mounted units ($225 for the 10-rail and $200 for the 8-rail), which are perfect for bath towels. And who could resist moving the portable model (shown) from the mudroom to the laundry to the kitchen for drying mittens, socks and dish towels?

To locate a dealer, visit
mysoninc.com, (800) 698-9690

FREE PAINT AND SOLVENT STORAGE

Liquid laundry detergent containers are simply too well designed and useful to just toss in the recycling bin. Fill the wide-neck bottles with leftover paint. They'll seal much better than the can, so the paint will last forever, and it's easy to pour out the paint when you need it. And if you're a serious woodworker, the faucet-style bottles are great for storing and dispensing varnish and thinner. Just push on the valve button and fill a container with however much you need for the project.

COAT HOOKS THAT REALLY ROCK

If you love the look of natural materials, check out this sturdy coatrack featuring handmade stones collected along New England's beaches. Tumbled smooth from years in the ocean, each stone is drilled and attached to a copper standoff and then mounted to a solid hardwood backplate. The stones come in a variety of sizes and colors. Cabinet knobs and drawer pulls are also available; the stones for these are permanently bonded to a stainless steel stem. The knobs and pulls cost $14, and the hooks range in price from $50 to $200 depending on the style. See the Web site for purchase information.

sea-stones.com, (206) 202-1092

BOTTLE STOPPERS, TOO!

SEE-THROUGH FASTENER DISPENSER

Little nails and other household fasteners have a way of mysteriously vanishing whenever you need them. To make them easier to find when you need to hang a picture or make a repair, store them in a clear, magnetized paper clip holder. Buy the holder at any office supply store.

MAGNETIC RING

BETTER EXTENSION CORD STORAGE

Here's how to wind up extension cords so they hang easily and don't get tangled. If you're one of those people who wraps cords around your hand and elbow, knock it off! It permanently twists the cords and makes for a tightly wound pile of spaghetti that's bound to be tangled when you go to unwind it.

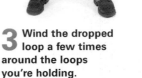

1 Wind the cord in big loops and plug the ends together.

2 Drop one of the outside loops.

3 Wind the dropped loop a few times around the loops you're holding.

4 Stick the rest of that loop through the middle of the coil, give it a tug and hang the cord by its built-in hanging loop.

Don't let all this space go to waste

To gain storage space, you usually have to give up space somewhere else. Not in this case. Hidden under almost every kitchen cabinet, there's a cavity containing nothing but air. This low, shallow cavity isn't prime storage space for everyday items, but it's perfect for bakeware, cleaning supplies, pet dishes and more.

UNDER-CABINET **DRAWERS**

Get more kitchen storage in one weekend

by **Elisa Bernick**

Installing drawers under cabinets sounds like a tough job, requiring fussy planning, the skills of a cabinet-maker and child-size hands to work in that cramped space. But this project is amazingly easy. To simplify the whole process, we designed self-contained drawer units that you can assemble in your shop and then slip into place. To simplify planning, we'll show you three basic measurements that let you size these drawers to fit under any cabinet. Even if you've never built or installed a drawer before, you can do it. This project is economical, too. Our total materials cost for these three drawers was about $100. A cabinetmaker would have charged at least $350 to build and install them. The number of drawers is up to you; install them under all your cabinets or just one.

Will it work with my cabinets?

The vast majority of kitchen cabinets are similar to the ones we show here, with sides that extend to the floor (see **Photo 1**). But there are a few rare exceptions. Some cabinets, for example, stand on legs rather than the cabinet sides. Open the cabinet doors and take a look at the bot-

tom of the cabinet box. If you see screw heads or holes near the corners, your cabinets probably stand on legs rather than the cabinet sides (the screws or holes allow for height adjustment). In that case, installing drawers will require different steps than we show here.

If your cabinets are constructed like ours, you can install drawers just as we did. There are just a few things to keep in mind:

■ If the cabinet is more than 30 in. wide, consider installing two drawers rather than one. Wider drawers tend to bind as you slide them in or out.

■ Your drawers will be shallow; don't expect to store kettles in them. A 4-in.-high toe space will give you storage space that's about 3 in. deep.

■ You can install drawers under a sink cabinet (or a bathroom vanity). But if the sink's plumbing runs through the bottom of the cabinet, the drawers will have to be shorter.

Tools and materials

You could build the drawers with nothing but hand tools and a circular saw, but a table saw and miter saw will give you

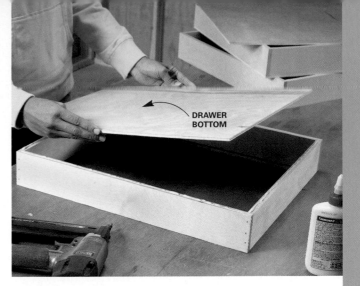

1 Break out the toe-kick backing to open up the spaces under the cabinets. Just drill a hole near the center, cut the backing in half and pull it out.

BACKING

DRYWALL SAW

2 Build super-simple drawer boxes. Just glue and nail the sides, front and back together, then glue and nail on the plywood bottom.

DRAWER BOTTOM

faster, better results. A nail gun is another big time-saver, though you can hammer everything together with 1-1/4-in. finish nails instead.

All the materials are available at most home centers. In the hardware aisle, choose "full-extension" side-mount drawer slides ($12 to $16 per pair; see **Photo 3**). That way, only 3 to 5 in. of the opened drawer will be covered by the overhanging cabinet front. With cheaper "3/4-extension" slides, only about half the drawer will be accessible. If you can't find full-extension slides, or if you want "overtravel" slides that extend even farther, shop the Web. Search for "drawer slides" to find online suppliers. Slides are available in 2-in.-length increments. Most cabinets accept 18- or 20-in. slides.

Choose hardwood plywood like birch or oak for your drawers. Construction-grade tends to warp. Most home centers carry plywood in 2 x 4-ft. and/or 4 x 4-ft. sheets, so you don't have to buy a full 4 x 8 sheet. Pick out straight pine 1x4s for the cradle sides. For the drawer faces, you'll need hardwood that matches your cabinets. If your toe-space height is 4 in. or less, a 1x4 board will do. For a taller toe space, you'll need a 1x6. Most home centers carry only a few types of wood such as oak, cherry, and birch or maple. If your cabinets are made from a less common species, look for a lumberyard that carries a wider selection (check the yellow pages under "Hardwood"). Or improvise—with the right stain, you can make birch or maple approximately match the color of just about any wood. The grain may look different, but that difference usually isn't noticeable in the dark toe space. We used maple faces, even though our cabinets are made from cherry.

Figure A: Drawer unit

The drawer, cradle and slides form a complete unit that's simple to build and easy to install under a cabinet.

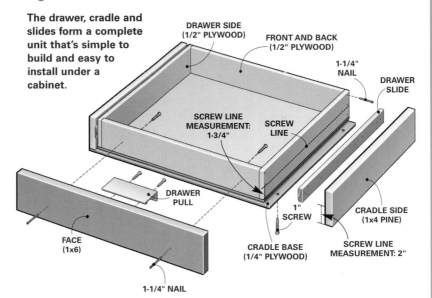

DRAWER SIDE (1/2" PLYWOOD)

FRONT AND BACK (1/2" PLYWOOD)

1-1/4" NAIL

DRAWER SLIDE

SCREW LINE MEASUREMENT: 1-3/4"

SCREW LINE

DRAWER PULL

FACE (1x6)

1" SCREW

CRADLE SIDE (1x4 PINE)

SCREW LINE MEASUREMENT: 2"

CRADLE BASE (1/4" PLYWOOD)

1-1/4" NAIL

MATERIALS LIST

Here's what we used to build drawers to fit under three 24-in.-wide cabinets. Your quantities may differ.

One 4' x 8' sheet of 1/4" birch plywood

One 2' x 4' sheet of 1/2" birch plywood

12' of 1x4 pine

6' of 1x6 maple

3 pairs of drawer slides

Drawer pulls, wood glue, stain, polyurethane, 1-1/4" brads or nails, 1" and 1-5/8" screws.

Remove the toe-kick and measure

Before you buy materials, open up the cavity under the cabinets so you can take measurements. First, pull off the "toe-kick," the strip of plywood or particleboard in the toe space. Usually, the toe-kick is held by just a few small nails

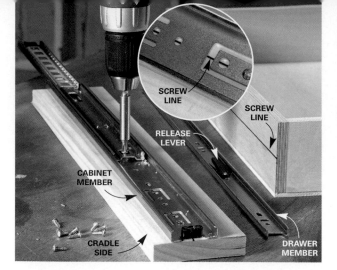

3 Mount the slides, centering the screw holes on the screw lines. Press the release lever to separate the drawer member from the cabinet member.

4 Add the cradle base to create a self-contained drawer unit. Fasten the base with screws only; glue could drip down and gum up the slides.

and is easy to pry off. If you don't plan to cover the entire toe space with drawers, be gentle so you can later cut the toe-kick to length and reinstall a section. If layers of flooring have been added since the cabinets were installed, you'll have to pull the top edge of the toe-kick outward and then pry it up to clear the built-up floor.

Next, remove the toe-kick backing under the cabinets (**Photo 1**). Simply drill a 1-in. hole and cut the backing with a drywall saw. Then grab a flashlight and check for obstructions. Break out any blocking with a chisel or pry bar. Pull out or cut off any nails. Now you'll determine the sizes of the drawers. There's no need for complex calculations—it's all reduced to simple subtraction in **Figure B**.

Build drawers and cradles

If you've ever installed drawer slides similar to the ones we used, you already know how fussy they are. They

require a precise 1/2-in. space on both sides of the drawer—build a drawer that's a hair too wide or narrow and you've got a drawer that won't budge. To sidestep that precision work, build each drawer first and then build a "cradle" around it. If you want to install two drawers under one wide cabinet, build a single cradle with both drawers sharing one of the cradle sides and the cradle base.

Our drawers are as easy as they get: Just nail them together (**Photo 2**). If you're using finish nails rather than a nail gun, predrill so you don't split the plywood parts. Remember to place the front and back between the sides. Then measure and cut the drawer bottoms. As you install each bottom, be sure the drawer box is square using a large carpenter's square or by using the plywood bottom as a guide (this only works if you've cut the bottoms perfectly square). Cut the 1x4 cradle sides to the same length as the drawer sides. In most cases, you can use 1x4s at full

---

Figure B: Drawer sizing simplified

Measurement "A"
- Subtract 1-1/2 in. from "A" to determine the width of drawer sides, front and back.
- Subtract 1/2 in. from "A" to determine the width of drawer faces. The length of each face depends on the width of the cabinet.

Measurement "B"
- Subtract 3-3/4 in. from "B" to determine the length of the drawer front and back. This will make the entire drawer/cradle assembly 1/4 in. smaller than the width of the cavity.

Measurement "C"
- Subtract 1/4 in. from "C" to determine the length of the cradle and drawer sides.
- This is also the maximum length of the drawer slides you can use.

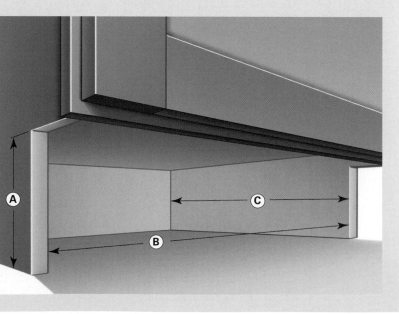

CRADLE

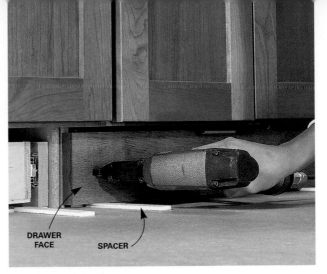

DRAWER FACE   SPACER

5 Slip the cradle under the cabinet and drive screws through the cradle sides just below the slides. Small hands and a small drill make this part easier.

6 Rest the drawer faces on 1/4-in. spacers. Tack the face in place with two nails, then open the drawer and drive screws into the face from the inside of the drawer box.

width (3-1/2 in.). But if your toe-space height (measurement "A" in **Figure B**) is less than 4 in., cut the cradle sides to a width 1/2 in. less than the toe-space height.

Next, mark screw lines on the drawer and cradle sides (see **Figure A** for measurements). Pull each slide apart to separate the drawer member from the cabinet member. Then screw them on (**Photo 3**). Our drawer and cradle sides were the same length as the drawer slides—yours may not be. So be sure to position the *front* ends of each drawer member and cabinet member flush with the *fronts* of the drawer and cradle sides. Slip the slides back together, lay the drawer upside down and screw on the cradle base (**Photo 4**). Then flip the whole unit over and inspect your work. Make sure the drawer opens smoothly. When the drawer is closed, the front of it should be flush with the cradle sides, give or take 1/16 in. Any problems are easy to fix by removing screws and repositioning the slides. **Note:** With our drawer units assembled, the cradle sides are exactly the same height as the drawers. Your drawers may come out a bit higher or lower.

Install the drawers

Before you remove the drawers from their cradles, number them to avoid mix-ups later. Each drawer will slide smoothest in the cradle that was built for it. Slip each cradle into place and fasten it to the cabinet with four 1-5/8-in. screws. If you have flooring that's more than 1/4 in. thick, first set scraps of 1/4- or 1/2-in. plywood under the cabinet to support the cradle. The cradle base can be higher than or flush with the flooring, but not lower than the flooring. Position the cradle sides flush with the cabinet sides and tight against one side (**Photo 5**). Screw the cradle to the cabinet, starting with the tight side. On the other side, don't drive in the screws so hard that you distort the cradle. If the drawer doesn't glide smoothly, slightly loosen those screws. Also be sure the drawer doesn't drag on the floor when opened. Load a few heavy objects into the

drawer and open it. If it drags, remove the front screws from the cradle and slip washers under it. That will give the drawer a slight upward tilt to clear the floor.

Next, cut the drawer faces to width. When you cut them to length, avoid measuring mistakes by marking them while they're in place. Leave a 1/8- to 1/4-in. gap between neighboring faces. At the end of a row of cabinets, make the face flush with the outer side of the cabinet. The method we used to attach the faces works best with a nail gun (**Photo 6**). Driving nails with a hammer can knock the drawer or cradle out of position. If you don't have a nail gun, stick the faces in place with double-face carpet tape. Then pull out each drawer and attach the face by driving two 1-in. screws from inside the drawer. With the faces attached, be sure they don't drag on the floor. If necessary, raise them with washers as described earlier.

Finishing up

Remove the drawers from their cradles for finishing. Unscrew the slides from the drawers and sand the drawer faces with 120-grit sandpaper. Also prepare a few stain-testing blocks, using leftover scraps from the faces and sanding them. We removed one cabinet door and took it to a paint store to have matching stain custom-mixed. If you have the patience to experiment, you could buy a couple of cans of stain and mix them to create your own. Either way, apply the stain to your test blocks before you stain the faces. The match doesn't have to be perfect, since the faces will be shaded by the overhanging cabinet fronts. After staining the faces, we finished our drawers—faces and boxes—with two coats of water-based polyurethane. Before reinstalling the drawers, add the drawer pulls or knobs. We couldn't find pulls that closely matched our existing cabinet hardware, so we chose pulls that fit over the tops of the drawer faces and are hidden under the cabinets ($3 to $8 each; see photo, p. 166). To find similar pulls online, search for "EPCO architectural pull." ⌂

Storage

STORAGE SOLUTIONS **from our readers**

COVERED THE GAP—AND GOT A SHELF

Some projects turn out even better than planned. When Jerry Cameron dreamed up this laundry room shelf, he wasn't really trying to provide a shelf at all. His goal was to hide the ugly dryer duct and washer hoses in his otherwise pristine laundry room. The enclosure he built couldn't be much simpler: It's just two 1x10 pine boards supporting a 1x12 top and a couple of L-brackets fastening the sides to the floor. But with a little router work and a coat of paint, the project looks as good as the rest of the room. And as a practical bonus, the Camerons got a convenient parking space for laundry detergent and other supplies.

"I just wanted to hide the dryer duct and washer hoses, but the shelf turned out to be a handy bonus."

Jerry Cameron

NOT A SHED **!**

Like most of us, Paul Hurwitz has too much stuff. A standard storage shed would be the perfect solution, but his local homeowners' association doesn't allow sheds. So Paul built a non-shed under his deck. The ceiling is made from corrugated plastic panels, which carry away water that drips through the deck boards above. The 8 x 8-ft. space holds lawn equipment and other outdoor gear. Sounds a lot like a shed. But it's not, according to the association rules.

"I can use my 'storage room' just like a shed— as long as I don't call it a shed."

Paul Hurwitz

A HIDDEN SCRAPBOOKING CENTER

If you have a closet you can spare, Jason Kimbel has a clever idea for you: A closet is the perfect space for a compact office, a gift-wrapping center or hobbies like scrapbooking or sewing. Whatever the use, it will be out of the way, and—best of all—you don't have to keep it tidy. Just close the doors to hide the mess. Jason built a desk and cabinets from melamine-coated particleboard.

"The closet doors don't just hide clutter; they keep curious kids away from Mom's projects."

Jason Kimbel

A PLAYHOUSE—AND A TOY SHED!

The area under exterior stairs usually turns into a parking space for miscellaneous junk. So remodeler Dave Upton enclosed the space under those stairs. But he didn't just build a storage space. Using leftover materials from other jobs, he created a playhouse that doubles as toy storage.

"This playhouse is one of my favorite projects ever—it made me the hero of the cutest little girls you ever saw."

Dave Upton

Storage

RECYCLING BIN HANGERS

Here's a simple, no-nonsense way to prevent your recycling bins from hogging precious floor space or getting kicked around the garage: Hang them on the wall.

For a standard 20-in.-long bin, all you need is an 18-in.-long 2x4 at the bottom of the column of bins, and a 1x4 and a 2x4, both 18 in. long, for the top lip of each bin. Level and screw the bottom 2x4 cleat to studs wherever you want the column to start. Then screw the top cleat pieces together with 1-5/8-in. screws (**Photo 1**). Use the bin as a spacer to position the top cleat for each bin. Draw a line to mark the top of the cleat (**Photo 1**) and then screw it to the wall with 3-in. screws (**Photo 2**). Repeat the process for each bin, hang them on the wall and then you can stop kicking those cans!

1 Assemble the top cleats and use a bin to mark their positions. Draw a line to mark the top of the cleat. Keep the pencil flush with the cleat to add an extra 1/4 in. or so to the height. That will make it easier to get the bin in and out.

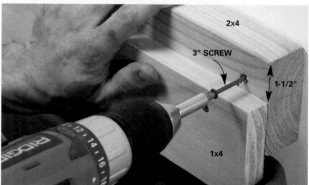

2 Position the cleat on the line and screw it to studs with 3-in. screws. It's much easier if you predrill all the screw holes.

CORD AND HOSE HOOKS

Hanging electrical cords and hoses on thin hooks or nails can cause kinks and damage the sheathing and wires. I had some leftover pieces of 3-in. ABS plastic plumbing pipe from a bathroom remodel, and I realized they'd make perfect hangers.

I screwed 3-in. end caps to a 2x6 with two 1-5/8-in. screws. Fender washers under the screw heads keep them from pulling through the plastic. Then I cemented on 8-in. lengths of end-capped pipe. These "hooks" are so strong that I can actually chin myself on two of them. (And that's 185 lbs. of handymanliness!)

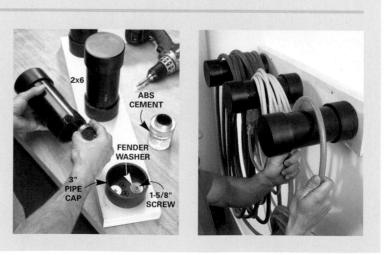

SLEEK AND SIMPLE COAT AND HAT RACK

Organize your hallway or mudroom with this simple, attractive coat and hat rack. You just cut the boards to fit your space, paint them, outfit them with different kinds of hooks to suit your needs and then screw them to the wall. We used 6-ft.-long 1x4s, but use whatever length works for you and the space available. We chose poplar, which is the best choice if you want a painted finish. If you're after a natural wood look, choose any species you want.

Finish the boards first and then attach your hooks. We used drawer pulls down the middle and a robe hook near the top to hold backpacks and larger items. You'll find hooks in a tremendous range of styles, colors and prices at hardware stores and online retailers.

Attach the boards to studs, or to the drywall with screw-in drywall anchors (E-Z Ancor is one brand). Drive three screws in each board: one at the top, one in the middle and one at the bottom. Now you have a great place to hang your hat.

MASKING TAPE FOR LAYOUT

FINISH WASHER

PROTRUDING TIP

2-1/2" SCREW

1 Drive your screws partway into each board so the screw tips poke out the back. Place the boards where you want them, and press hard to mark the spots for your drywall anchors.

SCREW-IN DRYWALL ANCHOR

2 Screw your anchors into each marked spot and then attach the boards.

STORAGE? IN THE FENDER?

We seldom write about vehicle accessories, but we were impressed by Dodge's cool new fender lockers on its 2009 1500 pickups. They're dry, lockable and hold 8.6 cu. ft. of whatever! The Ram Box option also gets you bed options, cargo rails with tie-down cleats and a 2-ft. bed extender. The downside: The Ram Box will set you back $1,895.

GLUE "PRESERVES"

It's frustrating to reach for a previously opened can of PVC cement or tube of silicone sealer only to find that the products have solidified or become an unusable gooey mess. To preserve the life of opened products, store them in a glass jar with a good seal (like a mason jar). I've stored things for five years that are as good as new!

GRANDMA'S PICKLE JAR

Storage

SHOE LADDER

Without constant vigilance, shoes tend to pile up into a mess next to entry doors. Untangle the mess with a simple, attractive shoe ladder that keeps everything from boots to slippers organized and off the floor.

Cut and drill the dowel supports (**Photo 1**), then screw them to 1x4s (**Photo 2**). Cut the 1x4s to fit your shoes and the available space—an average pair of adult shoes needs 10 in. of space. Nail or glue the dowels into the dowel supports, leaving 2 in. (or more) extending beyond the supports at the end to hang sandals or slippers.

Apply finish before you mount the shoe ladder to the wall. Screw the shoe ladder to studs or use heavy-duty toggle-bolt style anchors to hold it in place.

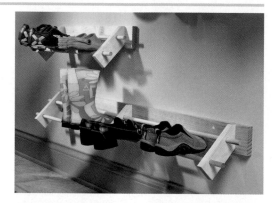

1 Clamp the 1x3 support to a piece of scrap wood as you drill the holes to prevent the wood from splintering.

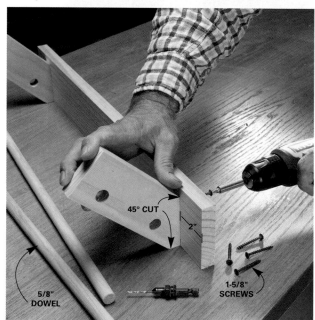

2 Predrill through the back of the 1x4 into the 1x3 supports, then glue and screw the pieces together.

KEEP GLUE FRESH

Tired of having your glue harden before you get a chance to use it all? Store it upside down. Glue, especially polyurethane glue, hardens when exposed to air. But when the bottle is upside down, no air can get in, so the glue stays fresh.

To build a glue bottle rack, drill a hole the size of the spout into a piece of wood, make sure the cap is on tight, then set the glue bottle in. Leave some wood on the bottom of the hole, so any drips will be confined to the rack and not run all over your workbench. But here's the best part: The glue will be ready to squeeze out when you need it. No more shaking glue down from the bottom!

5 Exterior Maintenance & Repairs

IN THIS CHAPTER

HomeCare&Repair

TIPS, FIXES & GEAR FOR A TROUBLE-FREE HOME

FIX YOUR LEAKY FROST-PROOF FAUCET

Leaky, dripping exterior faucets not only waste water but also dump it next to the foundation, right where you don't want it. Luckily, they're easy to fix. If you have a frost-proof faucet like the one we show here, check out these fixes for the most common problems.

If the faucet leaks from around the handle just when the water is turned on, the stem packing may be leaking. In some cases, you can fix this by simply tightening the retaining nut that's under the handle. Remove the screw in the center of the handle and pull the handle off. Try tightening the nut slightly (**Photo 1**). You'll have to experiment to see which direction to turn the nut, since some faucets have reversed threads that tighten counterclockwise.

If simple tightening doesn't solve the problem, you'll have to remove the faucet stem (**Photo 2**) and replace the

RETAINING NUT

1 If you're lucky, you can fix your leaking faucet by simply tightening the nut under the handle. Don't crank it hard, though. If snugging it up doesn't solve the problem, turn off the water and remove the nut to repair the faucet.

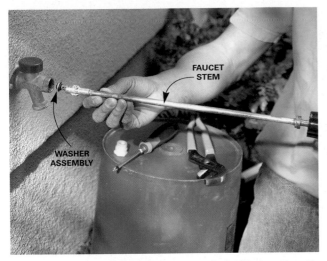

2 Next, remove the faucet stem. It's easier if you reinstall the handle temporarily so you'll have something to grip. You may have to turn the handle to unscrew the faucet stem to get it to come out.

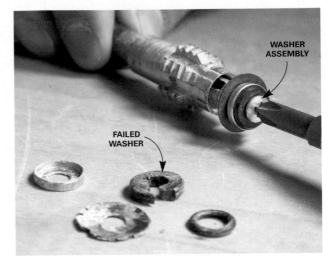

3 Keep track of the parts as you disassemble the faucet so you can install the new ones in the same order.

4 Pop off the vacuum breaker cap to access the parts underneath. Pry from both sides with a pair of screwdrivers.

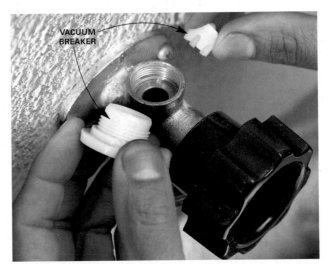

5 Unscrew the retainer and pull out the vacuum breaker. You may be able to fix the leak by simply cleaning the parts and reinstalling them. If this doesn't work, take the parts to the store to find replacement parts.

packing gasket. Turn off the water to the exterior faucet by locating the valve inside the house and closing it (or the main water valve). Buy a repair kit that matches your faucet brand and use the packing from the kit. If your faucet still leaks, the stem may be leaking and you should replace the faucet.

If your faucet leaks out of the spout when it's turned off, the washer is bad. On frost-proof faucets, the washer is located on the end of the long faucet stem. Remove the handle and nut (**Photo 1**) and pull the stem from the faucet (**Photo 2**). You may have to turn the stem to "unscrew" it before it'll come out. Getting the faucet apart is the hard part. After that, you simply replace the old parts with new ones. Pay close attention when you take the parts off (or snap a photo) so you can put the new ones back the same way. Snap off or unscrew the washer assembly and replace it (**Photo 3**). Then reassemble the faucet in the reverse order. If you find that the faucet starts leaking again after a short time, the valve seat is worn and you should replace the entire frost-proof faucet. If the faucet is attached with threads, you can simply turn off the water, unscrew the faucet and replace it with one that's the same length. If it's soldered on, you'll have to break out your torch and soldering tools.

Most frost-proof faucets have a built-in vacuum breaker located on top of the faucet (**Photo 4**). If you see water dribbling out from under the cap when the water is running, it's leaking. **Photos 4 and 5** show how to replace a leaking vacuum breaker. Some repair kits include the parts for this. If not, you'll have to purchase them separately.

Question&Comment

QUIET A NOISY GARAGE DOOR

My garage door makes a horrible racket when it opens and closes. I've disconnected it from the opener to isolate the noise. It's definitely coming from the garage door itself. How do I quiet it down?

The fixes are fairly easy and will take less than an hour. Start by tightening all the door and track hardware (**Photo 1**). Use a deep socket and a ratchet on all the nuts to snug them up. But don't overtighten—that can pull the carriage bolt heads right through the door skin or strip the lag screw holes.

Next, check for worn rollers and hinges (**Photo 2**). Many track rollers have unsealed bearings that self-destruct after years of rolling around in a dirty environment. The wear can be so severe that the rollers actually wobble as the door operates. If your rollers are worn, consider replacing them with nylon rollers with sealed bearings. One source is garage-doors-and-parts.com. Nylon rollers are quieter and don't require periodic oiling. But they are more expensive ($10 vs. $4).

Replace track rollers one at a time (**Photo 2**). If your door uses torsion springs mounted on the header above the door, do NOT attempt to replace the rollers in the bottom brackets. Those brackets are under constant spring tension and can cause serious injury if you unbolt them. That's a job for a pro.

Worn hinges are less common than worn rollers. But sloppy hinges make a lot of noise and can cause the door to bind and wear out the tongue-and-groove joints at the door sections. Some play at the hinge is normal. But if you see an oblong hole where the tubular hinge pin mates with the hinge bracket, replace the hinge. Gray dust and metal filings around the hinge pin are early signs of wear.

Once you've replaced the worn door components, spray the hinges, roller bearings (unsealed style), and springs with garage door lube (such as Multi-Purpose Spray Lube; $9 from garage-doors-and-parts.com). Also hit the torsion bar bearings, the opener track and any other pivot points. The special lube penetrates the parts as a liquid and dries to form a non-tacky grease that won't attract dirt and dust, which can gum things up. Lubricate all moving parts every six months to reduce wear and keep the door quiet. Avoid other lubricants such as oil, grease, or spray lithium grease. They're cheaper, but they don't penetrate as well and tend to pick up dust and grit—just what you don't want on moving parts.

GARAGE DOOR LUBE

NYLON ROLLER

WORN STEEL ROLLER

SEALED BEARINGS

HINGE NUMBER

1 Snug up all the nuts and bolts on your garage door and check for worn parts and replace where needed. Then spray all the moving components with garage door lubricant.

2 Replace the roller by unbolting the hinge and tilting the roller out of the track. Swap out the rollers and reinstall the hinge.

3 Write down the number that's stamped into the hinge and pick up the same number replacement hinge (less than $5 each) at the hardware store. Or take the old hinge with you to match it up.

178

A SIMPLE FIX FOR SLIPPERY STEPS

My steps get really slick when it rains, so I applied traction tape. It came up in less than a week. How can I get it to stick?

Traction tape is a quick and easy solution for slippery steps, whether they're wood or concrete, but you have to seal the pores so the adhesive will hold. Sealing the pores prevents water from getting under the tape and breaking the adhesive bond.

If the steps are painted and the paint is in good shape, just clean it well and apply the tape. If the paint is chipped or peeling or you have raw wood or concrete, clean the surface with lacquer thinner. Then seal it with the recommended primer or contact adhesive, let it dry and apply the tape.

 TRACTION TAPE

1 Cover the steps with masking tape. Then hold down the traction tape (with the paper liner still on) while you cut around the edges with a utility knife.

2 Remove the tape in the cutout area and apply the primer or contact adhesive with a brush. Let it dry before applying the tape.

3 Peel the paper liner off one end and secure the tape to the step. Then position the opposite side and square it up. Pull the liner off at a 90-degree angle to the tape, smoothing the tape as you peel.

PAINTABLE SIDING—OR NOT?

Can aluminum, vinyl and steel siding be painted? I say yes; my dad says no.

You're right, but there are a few rules you must follow. First, scrub the siding with cleaners to remove all the dirt, chalk and mildew. Rinse with clear water. Prime rusted areas on steel siding with an exterior rust-inhibiting primer. Aluminum and steel siding can be painted with any color paint. But vinyl siding can only be painted with a light color. Darker colors will cause the vinyl siding to warp or deform from heat absorption.

HandyHints®

SECURE HAND SAWING

I was trying to cut new downspouts with a hacksaw, and the darn things kept slipping around, making them almost impossible to cut. I clamped a 2x4 to my workbench, pressed the downspout up against it and attempted the cut again. This time the wood kept the downspout in place. You can use this tip to help you cut lots of slippery stuff—gutters, metal pipe, you name it.

"HOT" HOSE TIP

If you're trying to repair a hose by installing a new fitting, you may find it pretty tough to wrestle the barbed end into a stiff rubber hose. Make it easier by softening the end of the hose in a bucket or tea kettle of hot water.

PUDDLE-FREE LAWN CHAIRS

After a rainstorm, plastic lawn chairs always seem to have a puddle of water in the low spot on the seat and inevitably, someone sits down on it. Even newer plastic lawn chairs that come with a predrilled hole in the bottom still collect water. To solve the soggy bottom problem, pour some water onto the seat to find the puddles and then drill small drain holes in the low spots.

DRAINAGE HOLES

SMALL-ENGINE OIL DISPENSER

Want a handy, no-mess way to add oil to small engines? Use a dishwashing detergent squeeze bottle with a push-pull plastic top. Rinse and dry the bottle thoroughly and fill it with oil. You can hold the bottle at any angle and aim the spout into those hard-to-reach oil filler holes. Just pull open the top and give the bottle a squeeze to add just what you need.

RemodelResources

WINDOW SCREENS FOR ALLERGY SUFFERERS

If you've been keeping your windows shut to prevent allergy attacks, PollenTec window screens might help you let the summer breeze in without running for a tissue. The screens look similar to normal screens, but the company says they're designed with a special filter that lets air in while keeping airborne pollens out. The PollenTec screens aren't cheap. The screening material alone costs $10 per sq. ft., or you can order complete screen frames for about $75 for a normal-size window. But if you're shelling out $400 a month for AC bills, being able to open the windows for a cooling breeze might be worth it. Visit the Web site for more information.

pollentec.com, (623) 780-2400

SYNTHETIC SLATE ROOFING SHINGLES

Synthetic slate roofing tiles from DaVinci Roofscapes have the authentic look and durability of natural quarried slate, but at half the installed cost and with faster and easier installation. The lightweight polymer tiles eliminate the need for and cost of the extra roof supports required by natural slate. The tiles have a Class A fire rating (the best), can withstand high-velocity hurricane winds and are backed by a 50-year warranty. Available in nine color blends with color variances that mimic natural slate, the tiles can only be installed by certified roofing contractors. For prices and dealer information, call or check the Web site.

davinciroofscapes.com, (800) 328-4624

6X CLOSE-UP OF POLLENTEC ALLERGY SCREEN

GreatGoofs®

A job well done—and then undone

One of my husband's first jobs when we moved into our house was to replace the torn screen on our patio door. He replaced the screen while I was gone, and I'm sure it must have looked nice. But after putting away his tools in the garage, he realized he'd locked himself out. So what does my handyman husband do? He slits the new screen to reach the screen door lock.

My husband learned two things that day: how to replace a screen and to always leave a door unlocked when you're working around the house.

Gallery of Ideas

Do it yourself
Save $$$

RENEW YOUR CONCRETE PATIO

Concrete stain is a fast, simple way to turn your dull gray patio into a lively, colorful surface that will make your outdoor space more inviting. The stain is nearly foolproof to apply—just wet the concrete and spray on the stain. If you're not happy with the result, you can go back and apply a second or third coat to enhance the color.

The stains are available at home centers in the paint section—the color is added just as with paint. One gallon ($24) covers 200 to 400 sq. ft. A gallon of sealer also costs $24 and covers 200 to 400 sq. ft. A pro would charge $500 or more to do this project, but you can do it yourself for less than $100. You won't need any special tools—just basic painting tools and rain-free weather. If you're cutting kerfs into the concrete, you'll need a masonry blade ($16 at home centers) for your circular saw.

Project Facts
Cost: $48 and up
Skill level: Beginner
Time: 2 days

FROM APRIL, 2009, p. 54

182

FIND AND FIX ROOF LEAKS

FROM JULY/AUGUST, 2009, p. 25

If you have water stains that extend across ceilings or run down walls, the cause is probably a roof leak. Over time, even small leaks can lead to big problems, such as mold, rotted framing and sheathing, destroyed insulation and damaged ceilings. Tracking down the leak is the hard part; the fixes are usually pretty easy.

Project Facts

Cost: $25 and up
Skill level: Intermediate
Time: 4 hours and up

DRIVEWAY MAKEOVER

Most driveways are big and conspicuous. And a long stretch of gray, cracking asphalt can give a home a scruffy look, no matter how handsome the rest of the property is. So a fresh coat of shiny black sealer isn't just protection against expensive driveway damage—it's a face-lift for your home and yard. And you can do it yourself for about half of what a pro would charge.

Project Facts

Cost: $100–$150 (for 750 sq. ft.)
Skill level: Beginner
Time: 6 to 8 hours

FROM MAY, 2009, p. 68

Gallery of Ideas
BUST UP CONCRETE

FROM JULY/AUGUST, 2009, p. 32

Tearing up concrete yourself can save you a ton of money. Hiring a contractor just to demolish a 12 x 14-ft. patio could cost you $1,400 or more. If you do it yourself, it'll cost you only about $400. You might think that demolishing concrete is backbreaking, brainless work. But that's only half true. There's more to it than just swinging a sledgehammer. And a bit of know-how can save you lots of time and sweat and possibly a visit to the chiropractor's office.

Project Facts
Cost: Approx. $400 for a 12- x 14-ft. patio (equipment rental and concrete disposal)
Skill level: Beginner
Time: At least 1 day

6 Outdoor Structures & Landscaping

IN THIS CHAPTER

SHARPEN YOUR **LAWN MOWER** BLADE

You wouldn't take care of grass that's too long by tearing off the end of each blade, would you? But that's exactly what a dull lawn mower does, leaving the torn grass vulnerable to sun damage and disease. You could sharpen your mower blade with a file (it takes forever!), a rotary tool or a bench grinder, but we'll show you how to do the job with an angle grinder. It's fast and easy. If you don't own a grinder, you can buy one for about $60 and use it for all kinds of other tasks too.

To sharpen your lawn mower blade, you'll need a socket or wrench to fit the blade nut. Tough nuts may call for a breaker bar and/or a penetrating lubricant. You'll also need two clamps, a block of wood and, of course, an angle grinder with a metal grinding blade.

Start by disconnecting the spark plug wire (**Photo 1**).

Next, place a piece of plastic (a sandwich bag works well) under the gas cap to prevent gas from leaking out of the vent hole when you tip the mower. Tip the mower so the side with the carburetor faces up.

Clamp a 2x4 block to the side of the mower to keep the blade from turning while you loosen it. Mark the "grass side" of the blade so you don't reinstall it upside down. Use a socket wrench or a breaker bar to turn the nut counterclockwise to loosen it (**Photo 2**). If it's stubborn, soak it with penetrating oil for a half hour and try again.

Clamp the blade securely in a vise or to the edge of your workbench. Prepare for grinding by putting on your gloves, face shield, hearing protection and a long-sleeve shirt. Before you start grinding, hold the grinder against the blade and tip it up or down until the grinding disc is

1 Pull the wire from the spark plug. Remove the gas cap, put a piece of plastic over the opening and replace the cap. This will help prevent gas spills when you flip the mower to access the blade.

GAS CAP

SPARK PLUG WIRE

PLASTIC BAG

2 Clamp a block to the lawn mower skirt to stop the blade from spinning while you unscrew the nut. Use the longest wrench you can find to loosen the nut. It's likely to be very tight.

MARK GRASS SIDE OF BLADE

3 Grind the blade carefully with an angle grinder to remove nicks and dents and restore the edge. Make several light passes to avoid overheating the blade.

LAWN MOWER BLADE

METAL GRINDING WHEEL

ANGLE GRINDER

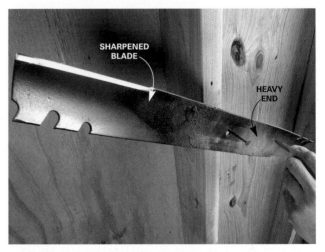

4 Balance the blade on a nail after you've sharpened both edges. If one side is heavy, it'll drop. Mark the heavy side so you'll know which end to grind. Grind a little off the heavy side and hang the blade on the nail again to recheck it. Repeat this process until the blade hangs level.

SHARPENED BLADE

HEAVY END

aligned with the angle on the blade. Try to maintain this angle as you grind. Keep the grinder moving and apply only light pressure so you don't overheat the blade or grind away too much (**Photo 3**). If you overheat the metal, it'll turn dark blue or black and become brittle. Then it won't hold an edge. Your goal is to remove the nicks and dents and create an edge that's about as sharp as a butter knife. A razor-sharp edge will dull quickly and chip more easily.

Make several passes across the blade with the grinder, checking your progress frequently. You don't want to grind off more than necessary. If your blade has a lot of nicks and gouges, try this: Start by holding the grinder at a right angle to the blade and grinding the edge of the blade flat to remove the nicks. Be careful to use light pressure and

move quickly. It's easy to burn the thin edge. After you've removed the nicks, go back to grinding at the correct blade angle.

If your blade has deep nicks or is cracked, bent or worn thin, don't sharpen it; buy a new one. You'll find the best selection at stores that sell and service lawn equipment. Take the old blade with you to get an exact match.

If you don't grind away the same amount of metal from both sides, the blade can become unbalanced. You can buy a special blade balancing cone or simply hang the blade on a nail (**Photo 4**). Correct an unbalanced blade by grinding a little metal from the blunt end of the heavy side of the blade until it balances on the nail. Make sure the marked side is toward you when you reinstall it and that you tighten the nut securely.

WHEN **POWER PAYS**

Rental tools that save time and toil

by **Rick Muscoplat**

Doing things yourself is supposed to save money. So starting a job by spending money on rental equipment might seem like a step in the wrong direction. But before you bypass your local rental center, consider how much time and strain you can save with the right tools. You might find that spending $50 to avoid 10 hours of backbreaking labor is a bargain. The right equipment also lets you tackle jobs that you would otherwise have to pay a pro for. And don't forget the fun factor. Some of the tools we tried are more fun—and a lot cheaper—than an all-expense-paid trip to Vegas or Disneyland.

We rented the most popular outdoor power equipment and put it through its paces so we could give you tips based on actual experience. Overall, each machine did its particular job as advertised. Here are our favorites:

> **CAUTION:** Be careful when using a chain saw from the lift. Position the bucket so you don't hold the saw any higher than necessary or lean outward from the bucket. Cut slowly and make sure that falling branches won't land on the machine or slide down the boom. Wear complete protective gear, including hard hat, goggles, chaps, leather gloves and steel-toe boots. If you're unsure of how to trim a tree, call in a pro. And stay away from power lines!

Boom lift. $200 per day

A boom lift can take you to new heights to trim trees, paint your exterior or apply siding and soffit material. Even if you climb ladders like a monkey, this machine will still save you tons of time. Plus, it's much safer than working on a ladder. If you rent it for a week, expect to pay about $800. Make sure the rental fee includes a safety harness, or rent a harness separately.

A typical boom can hoist you 37 ft. into the air and pivot 360 degrees. Picking the right parking place is critical. You'll need firm, level ground, 20 ft. of clear overhead space to raise the bucket and 5 ft. of clear space around the sides for the outriggers. Since you'll be towing it into position with your truck (it's too heavy to move by hand), plan your route to minimize lawn damage. Then unhitch it from your truck and drop the outriggers. Protect grass or asphalt by placing large scraps of wood under the outriggers. Hook up your safety harness, hop into the bucket, and take a few minutes to familiarize yourself with the operating controls. There are fast and slow icons on the controls. You'll want to use the slow buttons until you get used to operating the boom. The battery-powered boom will run for about eight hours before needing a recharge.

Posthole digger. $50 for 2 hours

Digging postholes for a fence or footing holes for a deck is usually the most time-consuming, back-breaking part of the project. The solution is a power posthole digger—but not just any model. "Two-man" diggers that are supported by hand are hard to handle. They toss you and your partner around, especially in hard soil. A one-person trailer-mounted model (shown above) is much easier to use. Just move it into position, start it up and tip the auger into the soil. The weight of the machine keeps it drilling straight down with minimal guidance from you. But you'll need extra muscle to move it to the next hole, especially if you're on a hill. Use your lawn tractor or truck if you're working solo. Or, remove the auger to lighten the load and move it by hand. Always block the wheels on hills before drilling. It takes longer to move the unit than it takes to drill holes. If you're drilling on a flat surface, plan on eight holes per hour.

Power trencher. $100 for 4 hours

Digging a trench for cable or gas lines means hours or days of hard labor. But a power trencher can do all that digging for you in a fraction of the time. This trencher can dig down 24 in. (other models can dig to 36 in.) and is self-propelled, so you don't have to pull it. Steering it around curves is still a workout, however. Also be aware that rocky soil and tree roots can jam the trencher and cause the tires to dig ruts in the grass. So don't try to power your way through a jam. Shut down the unit, clear the jam and then restart. On hills, start at the top and work your way down. However, before you start ripping up your yard, call 811 to get all the utility lines marked (go to call811.com for more information). Be sure to call at least a few days ahead.

Tip Reserve the machine you want a few days in advance. Popular equipment is in scarce supply, especially on weekends.

Backpack blower. $25 for 2 hours

A typical electric leaf blower throws out about 70 cu. ft. of air per minute (cfm). A commercial-grade backpack unit throws out an enormous 465 cfm. With all that extra power, you can clear leaves faster, of course. But a backpack blower will also do things a smaller blower can't: It will peel wet leaves off the ground, blast out debris that's stuck in cracks and move a mountain of leaves in one pass. And with the gas engine strapped to your back, you can do it all more comfortably than with a handheld model.

Do it yourself and save $150

Stump grinder. $35 for 2 hours

There's no need to pay a pro $150 or more to grind out a stump. With a rented stump grinder, you can do it yourself in a few minutes. For a stump that's no more than 18 in. in diameter, rent a light-duty grinder that's mounted on a trailer. For bigger stumps, rent a heavy-duty self-propelled monster like the one shown here ($80 for two hours). Make sure you remove any rocks around the stump to avoid breaking the teeth on the grinding wheel (the rental center will charge you big bucks for broken teeth). Work the grinding wheel side-to-side and advance slowly over the stump. Then repeat the process, digging deeper each time. In most situations, two hours is plenty of time to pull the grinder home, chew up the stump and return the grinder.

Walk-behind loader. $120 for 4 hours

A typical front-end loader makes quick work of moving piles of gravel, sand and dirt. But it won't fit through most fence gates or other tight spots. Worse yet, the wheels dig into your lawn every time you make a turn. Instead, rent a walk-behind, track-style machine with a loader attachment. Unlike other loaders, this one is easy to master—you'll operate it like a veteran after only a few minutes of practice. This version (the Toro Dingo) fits through a 35-in. opening and runs on grass-friendly rubber tracks. The bucket can move tons of material in a four-hour rental period. Follow the safety directions for the maximum bucket lift height, or the unit can tip over (don't ask how we learned this). The bucket is great for moving gravel or soil but not for digging. If you want to dig holes, rent a backhoe attachment instead.

Brush cutter. $50 for 4 hours

If you've left "the back 40" unmowed for too long and Mother Nature is taking over, don't waste time—and possibly wreck your lawn mower—by mowing down the brush. Instead, rent a machine designed specifically for clearing tall weeds and saplings (up to 1-1/2-in. in diameter). This self-propelled monster knocks the brush over and whacks it to bits with its machete-like blade. It moves quickly, even at its lowest speed (1.8 mph), so you can clear a large area in a few hours.

Pro-grade chain saw. $65 per day

If you only have one tree to fell and cut up, it's certainly not worth investing in a $350 chain saw. And you'll be sorely disappointed if you attempt the task with a small, underpowered chain saw. So rent a pro model for the entire day for only $65. It'll have more power, cut faster and tire you less. For chain saw safety tips, go to **thefamilyhandyman.com** and search for "chain saw safety."

BRUSH BLADE

Weed trimmer with a brush blade. $30 for 2 hours

If you want to cut saplings and brush without mowing down everything else, rent a commercial-duty trimmer with a brush blade. It will slice through saplings up to 1-1/2 in. in diameter. The shoulder harness carries the weight of the gas motor.

Just tap the blade against the base of the sapling. Don't swing it like an ax—that can destroy the drive shaft. To avoid bogging down the machine, make repeated jabs rather than a single cut. If you have a large area to clear, rent the trimmer for a whole day (about $50).

Get what you pay for

You can rent most power equipment for two- or four-hour periods or by the day. Here are some tips to help you make the most of the rental period:

- Ask about the cost of a trailer. It's usually not included in the rental price. If you use your own trailer, make sure it's rated to handle the weight of the machine and that your truck (and hitch) can tow the load.
- Remember that the rental period includes your drive time to and from your project. If the machine requires a trailer, also factor in time to unload the machine and reload it when the job is done. That can eat up 30 minutes or more of your rental time.
- Ask about delivery services. Having the rental center deliver and pick up the machine may cost $85 or

more. But since the rental period won't include drive time, loading or unloading, you have more time to actually use the equipment. Delivery service may save you money in the long run.
- Make sure the rental center staffers show you how to start and use the equipment. Then try it yourself before you drive away. That way, you avoid learning and making mistakes during the rental period.
- Be ready to use the machine the minute you get home. You can waste a lot of money letting the rental equipment sit idle while you mark posthole locations or clear rocks away from tree stumps.

OUTDOOR STRUCTURES & LANDSCAPING

New Tools&Gear

WATER-SAVING TIMER

A garden hose uses 5 to 7 gallons of water per minute. How many times have you gone to bed forgetting to shut off the lawn sprinkler? (Look at your water bill sometime—this matters!)

This Vigoro digital timer costs $35 at Home Depot. If you want to take it a step further, go for the Vigoro Wireless Moisture Sensor & Digital Water Timer ($40). Attach it to the hose spigot and stick the moisture sensor in the ground. The timer automatically turns the water on and off at preset times. The moisture sensor "talks" to the timer, so it doesn't water if the ground is already wet. The timer and sensor run on batteries.

You'll still have to move your hoses, but if you place a sprinkler in the flower garden, the sensor will take care of the rest. Both models are available at Home Depot.

MOISTURE SENSOR

NO-SWEAT GARDEN CART

Fully loaded wheelbarrows and garden carts are hard to push and easy to tip over. But Neuton's battery-powered Garden Cart makes hauling a snap! Turn the key and press a lever, and the self-propelled cart totes loads up to

200 lbs. It has two forward speeds (fast and slow) plus reverse. The front wheels are set under the cart for easy dumping, and a single back wheel pivots for great maneuverability.

The $320 price includes the 12-volt battery and charger (plug it into any outlet). Accessories that increase the hauling capacity are extra—the rails shown here cost $50. Buy it at Neuton's Web site or at drpower.com (item No. 22721).

**Neuton, (800) 798-2921.
neutonpower.com**

AUTOMATIC-START WEED TRIMMER

My wife will mow the yard with a walk-behind mower, but she refuses to use the trimmer for the finish work. That's because she has trouble starting it— a lot of priming and five or more pulls before it fires up. So I bought her Ryobi's trimmer with TouchStart. Its rechargeable 12-volt battery lets you start the trimmer with the push of a button— easiest start ever. Am I a great husband or what?

STARTER

The trimmer has a straight shaft, which the company says is better for getting into hard-to-reach areas. It also has a generous 18-in.-wide cutting swatch. The trimmer is available at Home Depot for $180.

Ryobi, (800) 525-2579. ryobitools.com

PROPANE-POWERED WEED TRIMMER

The trend in lawn and garden equipment has been environmentally friendly engines. That's why you've seen more four-stroke engines lately (they run cleaner than a two-stroke).

But Craftsman's new weed trimmer doesn't need gasoline— its four-stroke Lehr engine runs on propane. There's no gas to mix and store, no stale gas to gum up the engine, no gas emissions and no power cords to hassle with. I own this trimmer and I love it. It starts on the first or second pull, with no engine priming or choking. Five attachments are available (not included) for turning the trimmer into an edger, blower, cultivator, brush cutter or pruner.

PROPANE CANISTER

The trimmer uses the small propane canisters that portable grills use. The 16.4 oz. canisters cost $3 at home centers and hardware stores. Craftsman says one canister will power the trimmer at full speed for two hours, but I've actually trimmed for more than four hours (with a lot of idling). At $180, the trimmer costs more than most other models, but it runs clean. It's available at Sears stores (item No. 79211).

Craftsman, craftsman.com

Voted the most innovative tool by readers

BUY CONCENTRATED LAWN CHEMICALS

Save $$$

Manufacturers are always selling convenience, but that convenience costs a lot. With lawn chemicals, you're always going to save by buying concentrates and mixing your own solution. But only mix as much as you need because the shelf life is short, especially if you use tap water. Tap water isn't acid neutral and can deactivate the chemicals. So it's best to use distilled water if you think you'll have leftover solution. That'll help keep the mix effective.

Concentrate: $26 (plus free water)

Premixed: $54 Savings: $28

Do's&Don'ts

PRUNE FOR **HEALTHIER BUSHES**

Too often, bushes become eyesores because they're ragged and scraggly, misshapen, too big and full of ugly dead wood. And you're left with the difficult chore of digging them out and planting expensive new ones. But a half hour of pruning once or twice a year will prevent this problem. A simple trim will make your bushes and small trees more attractive, encourage better flowering and growth, and maintain their ideal size. The following tips will guide you through the basics.

Do it yourself; save $40 per hour!

Make a chart of the types of bushes you have

Every bush has a characteristic shape and size, and for each there is a best pruning technique to bring out the maximum beauty of its flowers, branch color and structure. Some require little pruning; others more. For the best pruning results, identify all your bushes and learn about their unique attributes. Bushes vary widely by region, so the most reliable way to identify the ones you don't recognize is to take a clipping to a nursery. Usually the nursery will have reference books with a photo of the characteristic shape and can tell you the mature size, as well as special pruning instructions. Keep the key information on a rough sketch of your yard. Tip: You can prune almost everything in early spring. Just be sure to get to it!

Cut out dead, damaged, diseased and deranged branches

Some arborists call these the 4 Ds. Start with the dead and damaged branches, because they make the plant look bad, and encourage rot and disease. Also cut out wilted, dried or diseased branches as soon as you spot them, to remove the disease before it spreads. "Deranged" includes a broad range of branches that cross (the rubbing wears away the bark; **photo at right**), loop down to the ground or simply look out of character with the bush (stick out at an odd angle or grow

CROSSING BRANCH

alongside the trunk). This pruning also thins out the bush, opening its interior to more light and air, which encourages fuller, healthier growth.

Prune out about one-third of the branches of bushes that grow from canes

Cane-type bushes, such as forsythia and hydrangea, usually send up new canes from their roots every year. In general, prune out the oldest (larger) wood to control the bush height. It's also OK to trim out newer canes to thin the interior of the plant and let in light as well as to control

LARGE OLDER CANE

its spread. If one of these bushes has gotten too big and out of control, you can often cut off all the canes and the roots will send up new shoots. You'll have a nice new bush in a year or two. Note: All bush categories have exceptions to these rules. So know your plants!

Clip off branch tips to promote small-branch growth and denser foliage

This "heading off" technique channels more growth energy to smaller side branches, which will then fill in vacant areas. Make this cut at a side branch or 1/4 in. beyond a bud (**top photo**). Be selective and watch the results from the previous year to help gauge future growth. It works best on bushes and trees that grow mostly from one or a few stalks, as opposed to bushes that continually send up new shoots (suckers), like lilacs and forsythia.

First year

BRANCH TIP

Second year

SIDE BRANCHES

Don't trim new growth with hedge shears!

It's tempting to grab the hedge shears and shape a bush by cutting off the branch tips. This "flattop haircut" approach may look fine for a year or two, but it stimulates growth on the outermost branches, forces the bush to grow into an unnatural shape (your idea rather than the plant's) and fails to control size. The bush actually grows larger and becomes more difficult to bring back to size without being ruined. The exception is hedge-type bushes.

HEDGE SHEARS

Remove entire branches to shape the bush and control its size

If neglected, many bushes get too big and dense. While the foliage might look OK this year, next year it just might be too big to prune back without butchering it. Instead, it's better to control size and shape by selectively pruning out a few entire branches each year. Cut them at a larger branch or the trunk. This also opens the plant to light and encourages healthy growth from the interior.

BRANCH TO PRUNE

FORK

Do's&Don'ts

Prune evergreens lightly

Unlike cane-type bushes, evergreens and other "non-sucker–type" bushes grow from their existing stems. They develop a more permanent branch framework and usually need less pruning. If your land-scaping was well planned, these bushes, especially evergreens, will grow to fit their spot with relatively little help. They'll need only a light annual pruning to remove dead branches and to control size and shape.

Make pruning cuts just beyond the branch "collar"

The branch collar is the bark swell that encircles the branch. If left intact, this collar will soon grow over and cover the wound. Don't leave stubs. They'll rot and might become diseased.

Don't force a big bush to conform to a small space by pruning

It can be done, but it's easier to pull out an overgrown bush and plant one that will mature at a size that better fits the space.

HandyHints®

SECOND-STORY BIRD FEEDER

We love to look out our second-floor window and watch the birds at our feeder. To make refilling the feeder easy, I attached a small pulley to the soffit of the overhang, threaded some thin nylon rope through it and attached one end of the rope to the bird feeder using an S-hook. After refilling the feeder, we hoist it back up to its spot so it's ready for the birds' next meal. I secure the rope down below by wrapping the end around a cleat attached to the siding.

PULLEY

CLEAT

PULLEY

CLEAT

STOP LUMBER FROM WARPING

If you store lumber in a pile long enough, especially treated wood, it's bound to twist and bow. That's one reason lumber loads are stored with steel banding. You can use this same idea at home by stacking your lumber, wrapping the ends with rope and using a narrow board to twist it tight, just like a tourniquet. Then screw down the board to the top board on the pile until you're ready to work on your project. Or easier yet, if you have ratcheting-type cargo straps, use those instead. Set your lumber on blocks rather than on the floor. That'll help too.

OUTDOOR STRUCTURES & LANDSCAPING

HandyHints®

EASY HOSE DRAINING

I've tried a lot of different ways of draining my hoses before storing them each fall. I've rolled them around on the hose reel. I've lifted them hand-over-hand over my head, and I've dragged them way over to my side hill and let them drain down the slope. These all work, but I think I've found the easiest way yet. Duct-tape the end of your air compressor nozzle to the hose end and turn on the compressor. Job done.

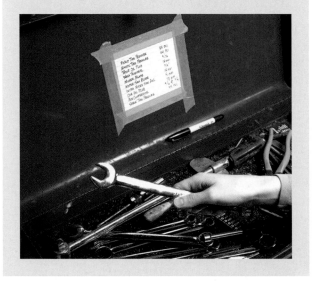

DUCT TAPE

PLEXIGLAS "WINDOW"

CURE NEWSPAPER DELIVERY ANXIETY

If your newspaper comes at a different time each day, it's hard to know whether it's been delivered unless you hoof it out to the box and look inside. That's fine in nice weather, but it's no fun in the rain and cold. Here's how to stay warm and dry: Use a jigsaw to cut off the back of the newspaper delivery box. Replace it with a piece of clear Plexiglas, attaching it with a bead of silicone around the back edge of the box. Then all you have to do is look out your window to see whether the day's headlines are in the box waiting for you.

MEMORY SAVER

It's almost impossible to keep all the different wrench and socket sizes for my lawn mower, snow thrower and leaf blower straight. Not to mention the different tire pressures on my bikes, cars and trucks (the little writing on the tires is impossible to read). So I keep an ongoing list of these items (and lots more) taped to the inside top of my toolbox. When it comes time to do the job, my list is right where I need it—with the tools! Now I don't spend extra time trying to remember what goes with what.

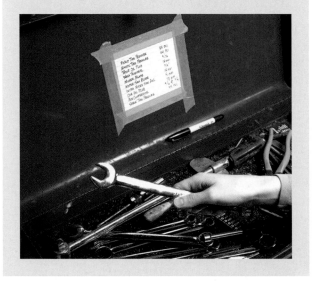

BIRDSEED CATCHER

To stop wasting birdseed and keep it off the deck or yard, screw a plastic plant saucer (20¢ at home centers and nurseries) onto the bottom of your bird feeder. You'll catch most of the seeds that those slovenly, wasteful birds kick out. And those seeds cause a real mess, especially when they start sprouting. To avoid cooking up a dish of bird-seed mush, cut a slit or two in the plastic for drainage.

PLANT SAUCER

FENDER WASHER

InstantProject

2-HOUR, $25 CAMPFIRE BENCH

Need outdoor seating in a hurry? This simple bench, based on author and ecologist Aldo Leopold's classic design, can be constructed in a couple of hours. All it takes is two boards and 18 screws, for a cost of less than $25.

Cut the legs from a 2x8 x 10-ft. piece of rot-resistant wood (**Photo 1**). Cut the seat and backrest from an 8-ft. 2x8.

Lay out and assemble the sides as mirror images, using the seat and back pieces for alignment (**Photo 2**). Join the legs with three 2-1/2-in. deck screws and construction adhesive. Predrill all the screw holes with a countersink bit to avoid splitting the wood. Finally, set the sides up parallel to each other and glue and screw the seat and back into place. Finish the bench with a coat of exterior oil or stain.

CUTTING LIST

(All from two 10' 2x8s)
Rear legs: 2x8 x 17-1/4" (22-1/2-degree cuts)
Front legs: 2x8 x 36" (22-1/2-degree cuts)
Seat: 2x8 x 42"
Back: 2x8 x 45"

1 Starting at one end of a 10-ft. board, make the same 22-1/2-degree cut five times to create the four legs.

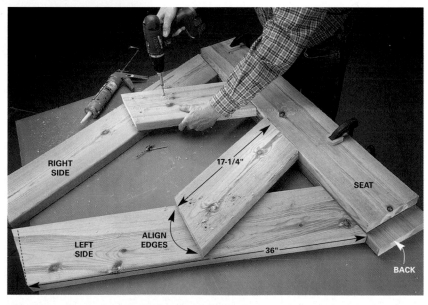

2 Clamp the seat and back to the workbench as a stop, then predrill, glue and screw the rear legs to the front legs.

BACKYARD PROBLEM SOLVERS

When it comes to solving problems, there's no substitute for real-world experience. So we asked our veteran hands-on yard and garden experts to share their best solutions for frustrating outdoor problems.

by **Rick Muscoplat**

Problem: Dead zones in your lawn

Last summer, I spilled some fertilizer and killed a patch of grass. When I reseeded the spot, nothing happened. When I laid sod over it, the sod died. Do I need to hire an exorcist?

Solution:

You're up against contaminated soil, not demons. And whether the contamination is from fertilizer or doggy doo-doo, the solution is simple. First, turn the soil over. Drive a spade deep into the ground and flip clumps of soil over. That buries the most contaminated top layer of soil deep in the ground where the contaminants will dissipate before new roots grow down that far. Then flood the area with a garden hose for at least 15 minutes. The water will drive contaminants deeper into the soil. Now you're ready for seed or sod. Be sure to water the new grass daily until it's established.

Seed dead spots only after you've turned and soaked the soil. Otherwise, soil contaminants left by fertilizer spills or pets may kill the new grass.

Apply tons of pulling force to shrub roots using a jack. Place plywood scraps under the jack and jack stand so they don't sink into the ground.

Problem: Stubborn shrubs

I need to remove some shrubs but don't have a 4x4 truck or access to TNT. How can I get the roots out without hours of digging and chopping?

Solution:

Use leverage. Start by digging around the base of the shrub and cutting all the roots you can get at. Then lay scraps of plywood on each side of the shrub. Set a jack stand or concrete blocks on one side and set up your jack on the other. Lay a beam across them and tie the root to the beam with a chain. You'll apply hundreds of pounds of pulling force, so both the beam and the chain must be strong. Use a 6-ft. 4x6 or 6x6 for the beam and a chain for towing cars.

Raise the jack, stopping to cut the roots as they become exposed. If you max out the height of your jack before all the roots are free, add a few blocks to increase the beam height.

> **CAUTION:** Before cutting the roots, reduce tension on the chain to prevent injuries from recoil. Wear eye protection.

Problem: Invasive plants

I love my lilies and black-eyed Susans, but they're taking over the garden and choking out other plants. Can I stop the invasion?

Solution:

Many plants multiply by dropping seeds and by sending out roots that establish new plants. A layer of mulch will prevent the seeds from taking root. But to stop those aggressive roots, you need a solid barrier. Replant the spreading plants inside underground "corrals." The plastic corrals should extend at least 10 in. below ground to prevent the roots from sneaking under them. This trick won't work with plants such as strawberries or mint that spread above ground.

Cut the bottom off a plastic pot or pail and set the container in the ground. Replant spreading plants inside it to hold in the roots.

Problem: Landscape fabric that wanders

Every spring I have to fix open seams between sections of landscape fabric in my planting beds. Is there a way to make the fabric stay put?

Solution:

Landscape fabric staples are the answer. You'll find them right next to the fabric in stores, but most people don't bother to use them. Make sure the edges of the fabric overlap by at least 3 in. And don't skimp on the staples; place them about 16 in. apart. A bag of 10 staples costs about $2.

Yank the fence post out of the ground after you've broken off enough concrete to lighten the load.

Problem: Rotting fence post

I have a rotting fence post that needs replacement. How the heck do I get that concrete pier out of the ground?

Solution:

It's not complicated, but you'll definitely work up a sweat. First, dig a semicircular hole the same depth as the concrete, around one side of the pier. Make the hole large enough so you can get a good swing at the concrete with a sledgehammer. When about half the concrete is broken off, you and a helper should be able to lift the post out of the hole. Sometimes the post breaks off during lifting. In that case, tie a rope around the pier to lift it out.

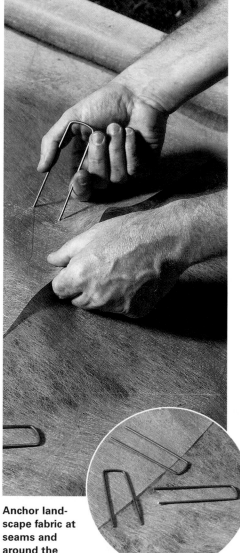

Anchor landscape fabric at seams and around the perimeter with staples. In hard soil, start the staples by hand and then push them in with your foot.

Problem: Noisy air conditioner

My central air conditioner's outside unit is so loud that it's driving me—and my neighbors—crazy. Can I deflect the noise with an enclosure?

Solution:

Fencing one or all sides of an air conditioner's outside unit (the condenser) can deflect noise. But experiment first: Prop up plywood around the unit so you can judge how much good a fence will do. If you decide to build a fence, keep it at least 3 ft. from the unit to allow airflow. For the best sound reduction, overlap fence boards instead of leaving gaps between them.

Aside from a fence, there are a few other approaches you should consider:

■ If your condenser is older, the best solution is a new unit. Newer designs are dramatically quieter than those produced just a few years ago. And they save money. A high-efficiency unit might cut your cooling bills in half and pay for itself in three or four years. The downside, of course, is the initial cost. Expect to pay at least $1,500 (installed).

■ If you already have a newer condenser, the worst noise is probably coming from the compressor. (Fans on newer units are very quiet.) Contact the manufacturer to find a sound blanket for your model or buy a universal blanket ($60 at brinmar.com and other online retailers; search for "compressor sound blanket"). Installation is easy. Don't bother putting a blanket on an old unit—you'll still hear the noisy fan.

1 Unscrew and lift off the top panel. The heavy fan motor is mounted on the panel, so have a helper hold it while you install the blanket.

2 Wrap the sound blanket around the compressor. Position the blanket so it doesn't touch the surrounding coils and won't obstruct the fan blades.

> **CAUTION:** Shut off all power to the unit. Turn off the thermostat inside the house, switch off the breakers at the main panel and pull out the fuse block at the outside disconnect box.

Problem: Heavy potted plants

I like to move pots around so I can always have flowers in bloom on my deck. But those big pots are heavy. Should I take up weightlifting?

Solution:

Buy a bag of foam packing peanuts instead ($12 at office supply stores). Fill the pot one-third to one-half full of peanuts, cover with landscape fabric and then add soil. This cuts the weight and saves money, since peanuts cost less than good potting soil. However, a smaller amount of soil means more frequent watering. To slow evaporation, cover the soil with wood mulch.

A foundation of foam peanuts makes pots easier to move and improves drainage.

RemodelResources

COZY AND FUNKY BIRDHOUSES

Aren't these cool? Designed by the artist J Schatz, these colorful and durable ceramic Egg Bird Houses have a 1-1/8-in.-diameter "door" to attract chickadees, wrens and smaller birds while keeping out larger birdhouse squatters like sparrows. Available in eight glossy colors, they sell for $135 each and are sure to create birdhouse envy in your neck of the woods. To order, visit the Web site.

jschatz.com, (866) 344-5267

WEATHERPROOF ALTERNATIVE DECKING

Alternative decking materials are a great option for homeowners who want the look of wood without the upkeep. But like real wood, most composite decking materials weather and fade over time. The Trex Escapes collection introduces a new Trex product that, according to the manufacturer, won't fade or change color over time and features improved stain, scratch and mold protection. Trex Escapes comes in three colors: Pewter (gray), Sahara (beige) and Acorn (brown). The decking sells for $3 to $4 per linear foot and is widely available at home centers and lumberyards. For help finding a dealer, visit the Web site below.

trex.com, (800) 289-8739

COMPOSITE PAVERS—BEAUTIFUL, LIGHTWEIGHT AND EASY TO INSTALL

Traditional stone, brick and concrete pavers are beautiful, but they're heavy and hard to install, and you need to rent specialized tools to cut them. Their colors fade in the sun, leaching can make concrete look chalky, and water absorption can erode the surfaces. New VAST engineered composite pavers, made from up to 95 percent recycled tires and plastics, are an innovative alternative to these materials.

Unlike traditional pavers, VAST pavers are engineered to withstand moisture, cracking and UV damage in all climates. They're as tough and durable as traditional concrete pavers, but you can cut them with standard cutting tools, and at a third the weight, they can be used in decks and rooftop patios

as well as sidewalks, pool areas and driveways. VAST pavers are set into a patented grid system that automatically aligns the pavers and cuts installation time in half.

With prices starting at $7 per sq. ft., the cost is comparable to that of traditional pavers, and they're available in a variety of natural and custom colors. Visit the Web site to find a dealer.

vastpavers.com, (612) 234-8958

LIGHTS THAT WON'T BLOW OUT

■ Candela lights (**photos, left and right**) can do everything an ordinary candle can do—except blow out in the wind or set the house on fire if left unattended. These portable, rechargeable LED lights are equally at home on the deck and on the bedside table. They light instantly when lifted from the charging platter and start recharging as soon as they're put back. The lights, which last up to eight hours on a charge, turn on automatically during power failures. They are available in sets of two, four and eight in a variety of styles ($39 to $129).

■ This portable lantern (**photo, right**) can illuminate your nighttime stroll or your dinner table when you're eating out under the stars. The Luau portable lamp ($199) is a rechargeable LED lantern that lasts from 6 to 10 hours on a charge. Dim it or turn it off to conserve the charge until you need it. You can also take it along camping and use it to light up the tent while you snuggle in a sleeping bag. Who says roughing it has to be…rough?

vessel.com, (877) 805-1801

FIRE PIT TABLES FOR EVERY BUDGET

Move over, fire pits—fire pit tables are the hot new thing. Light a fire in the middle of the table and then set drinks and dinner around the edge. It's a perfect way to linger outside during chilly evenings. Prices start at $100 and head up to the stratosphere depending on whether you choose a model that heats with wood or opt for a pricier one that uses propane, natural gas or special gel fuel canisters. There are dozens of fire pit tables to choose from. A good place to start is firepits.com, which offers a range of styles and prices as well as customer reviews.

firepits.com, (800) 420-7910

OUTDOOR STRUCTURES & LANDSCAPING

Question&Comment

A few readers disagreed with our advice to use cocoa bean mulch for paths (March '09, p. 40). They warned us that cocoa bean mulch can be fatal to dogs. However, our research found that while the mulch can cause sickness, rumors of canine deaths from consuming cocoa mulch are "highly suspect" (Journal of the American Veterinary Medical Association, June 1, 2006). The article concludes: "The odds of dogs dying from eating the fresh mulch are low, but those suspected of ingesting it should be examined by a veterinarian."

FIND BURIED CABLE

I'm putting in my own sprinkler system. The utility company marked its lines but obviously not my underground cable to the garage. How can I trace that line?

You can't just find the exit conduit from the house and the entry point at the garage and assume the installer buried the cable in a straight line between the two points. The most accurate method is to rent a buried cable locator (about $45 per day) from a tool rental company that handles construction equipment. Also get a spray can of marking paint ($5).

The locator tool can detect live voltage or can be set up to "induce" a signal onto the buried cable. Just follow the setup directions with the tool.

Even though you've marked the buried cable, always turn off the power to the garage before you dig in the sprinkler pipe.

Find where the cable enters the garage and "sight" back to the house.

DETECTOR

Then find the exact route with a buried cable locator. Swing the detector probe over the suspected area until you hear the strongest signal. Then mark the path with spray paint.

GreatGoofs®

Right deck, wrong house

I'm a carpenter who specializes in building decks. When the secretary of our company gave me the address and paperwork to build a deck for a customer, I drove to the house and got started. Two and a half days later, the beautiful new deck was finished.

Oddly enough, our company secretary told me that she'd been getting calls from an angry homeowner wondering why we hadn't started her deck yet. Well, you guessed it. We built the deck at the wrong house—a rental property that was vacant during the construction. The owner was happy to get a free deck and even hired us to build a couple more at his other properties. But it'll take a lot more decks to make up for that costly mistake!

Hot tub dash

My wife and I installed a new hot tub in our yard and were anxious to use it. On a very dark night, we decided to go for an inaugural skinny dip. We got halfway to the tub when the motion sensor fixture flooded the area with bright, show-you-in-all-your-glory light. We ran back toward the house and ended up falling in a heap on the ground. We don't forget that light anymore—or our towels!

Just add concentrate

I serve on our homeowners' association board and oversee the landscaping. Last spring, I decided to spot-spray the dandelions with weed killer. I poured 10 ozs. of concentrate into a measuring cup, emptying out the weed killer bottle. I washed out the bottle and put it in the recycling bin, then grabbed my 4-gallon backpack sprayer and spent the rest of the morning treating dandelions in a four-block stretch.

When I got back to my garage with my empty sprayer, I saw the measuring cup with 10 ozs. of weed killer concentrate still sitting on the workbench. So I got to spend my afternoon spraying the same weeds—this time with weed killer, not just water.

Digging into trouble

I was building an addition onto our house and needed to dig a trench for the footings. I enlisted a few friends with shovels, and we worked all day digging out the rocky soil. When the building inspector showed up for the footing inspection, he told me that I needed a crawl space for the addition—not just a footing—meaning I had to dig out the entire area.

I hired an excavator, who showed up with his skid steer and promptly began filling in my hard-dug trench so he could get to the addition area. I not only did all that digging for nothing but also used up my free labor capital getting my friends to help me—and I hadn't even started building anything yet.

Gallery of Ideas

FROM MAY, 2009, p. 32

WEEKEND WATERFALL

Project Facts

Cost: About $500, plus the stone

Skill level: Intermediate to advanced

Time: 1 to 3 weekends

DOLLAR-SAVVY SHED

Project Facts

Cost: $1,800

Skill level: Advanced

Time: At least 6 to 8 days, with a helper or two

FROM JULY/AUGUST, 2009, p. 44

FROM MAY, 2009, p. 48

ADD CURB APPEAL WITH A BRICK BORDER

Project Facts

Cost: $6–$10 per linear foot

Skill level: Beginner to intermediate

Time: 1 weekend

CHEAP & SIMPLE PATHS

Project Facts

Cost: Varies

Skill level: Beginner

Time: 1 weekend

FROM MARCH, 2009, p. 38

To order $3 photocopies of complete articles for the projects shown here, call (715) 246-4521, email familyhandyman@nrmsinc.com or write to: Copies, The Family Handyman, P.O. Box 83695, Stillwater, MN 55083-0695.
Many public libraries also carry back issues of *The Family Handyman* magazine.

New Tools&Gear

FLAME-RESISTANT CLOTHES

When you're working around fire, using torches or causing sparks to fly, you don't have time to worry about a wardrobe malfunction—like your clothes catching on fire. Buy Riggs Workwear flame-resistant clothing from Wrangler and put your mind at ease. The shirts ($70) and jeans ($65) are made of fabrics that are treated to protect against fire and burns. Wrangler says the clothes will self-extinguish almost immediately once the source of the fire is removed.

The clothes feel, look and fit like traditional jeans and shirts, and will remain flame-resistant for the life of the jeans if proper cleaning directions are followed.

Wrangler, (888) 784-8571. riggsworkwear.com

POWER TOOL FOR EVERYDAY CUTTING

The Skil Power Cutter (about $40) does a great job of cutting through that practically impervious plastic packaging that holds toys and other products hostage. The Power Cutter's rotating blade cuts most materials up to 1/4 in. thick, including vinyl flooring, cardboard, vinyl siding and chicken wire.

The Power Cutter slices through cardboard like butter and makes short work of cutting boxes down to size to fit in the recycling bin. Once you have the tool in the house, you'll find a zillion uses for it—like helping your kids cut foam core and tagboard for school projects.

The 3.6-volt lithium-ion battery will hold a charge up to 18 months, so it's always ready to go. Buy it at home centers or amazon.com.

Skil, (877) 754-5999. skiltools.com

New Tools&Gear Hodgepodge

AUTOMATIC LIGHT DURING POWER OUTAGES

Energizer's Twin Light Center has a home base recharging unit with a light that automatically turns on during power outages. Once you find it in the dark, just grab one of the two "light sticks" and you can wander all over the house. The lights are always charged (provided you keep them parked in their home base). No more hunting around a dark house for candles, matches or working flashlights!

The sticks provide 5 to 10 hours of light, depending on how many bulbs (two or four) you choose. And if they go dead, you can power them with three "AAA" alkaline batteries for 18 more hours of light. Buy it at Target for $45 (No. 10849453).

Energizer, (800) 383-7323. energizer.com

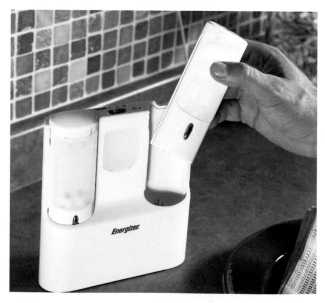

A BATTERY-POWERED HAMMER

I realized that the Craftsman Hammerhead was popular when my local Sears store was sold out the first two times I stopped in to buy one. The 12-volt lithium-ion battery-powered auto hammer pounds in nails up to 3-1/2 in. long in seconds—the high-speed, high-torque motor delivers a whopping 3,600 impacts per minute. The magnetic head holds nails with heads up to 7/16 in. wide in place to start them, so you can keep your fingers safely out of the way. The nail sleeve automatically retracts during use to set the nail flush with the work surface.

The Hammerhead is the tool to reach for when you're working in tight spots and don't have enough room to swing a hammer, or working on a material that you don't want to mar with hammer-head dents. It's also a good tool for novices who don't feel confident using a hammer. But the Hammerhead is loud—very loud—so you'll want to use hearing protection. Buy this $99 tool (No. 11818) at Sears stores or sears.com.

Craftsman, craftsman.com

The tool most desired by female readers, as ranked by Powerhouse

PRESSURE DIAL KNOB

QUICK-ADJUST, LOCKING PLIERS

The downside to most adjustable pliers is that you have to slide open the jaws to an approximate setting before you use them. You also have to constantly adjust the locking screw.

Whiteford Tools' Self Adjusting Locking Pliers solves that problem by automatically adjusting the jaws for you. Grip the pliers onto the object, slide the center lock closed, then turn the pressure dial knob to increase the gripping pressure (the manufacturer says that one-half turn increases the grip by 400 percent). When you're done, turn the knob in the opposite direction and release the lock.

The jaws open as wide as 1-5/8 in. We found that the pliers easily handle nuts and bolts, but they don't grip bare pipe as well as locking pliers with arc-shaped jaws. Buy the pliers on the company's Web site for $25, plus shipping.

Whiteford Tools, (800) 343-9532. whitefordtools.com

LEVEL THAT TRANSFERS MEASUREMENTS

Sola's Picture Hanging Level ($30) has four brackets that slide along the level to mark locations for nails, brackets or wall anchors. The level makes quick work of transferring mounting points from an object onto the wall, without any measuring. Just place the level against the object, slide the brackets over the mounting holes, then hold the level on the wall and make your marks. You'll appreciate this tool every time you hang pictures, towel bars, shelves or anything else that requires precise mounting locations.

This isn't a picture-hanging gimmick tool (we've seen lots of those lately). This is a well-made 31-in. straightedge that does double-duty as a traditional level. It's available at Rockler stores and rockler.com (item No. 25958).

Rockler, (800) 279-4441. rockler.com

SLIDING BRACKET

PORTABLE, BATTERY-POWERED GRINDER

Hitachi's 4-1/2-in. angle grinder is the perfect go-to tool for grinding metal or for cutting tile, metal or rebar when you don't want to hassle with a cord. Once you own the grinder, you'll find yourself reaching for it instead of a hacksaw, recip saw or corded grinder—and saving a lot of time.

Don't think the cordless grinder won't deliver—the high-torque motor cranks out 9,100 rpm to handle tough jobs. And it's lightweight (4.2 lbs.) and quieter than corded

models. The downsides: It's more expensive than a corded model and needs to be charged. If you already own an 18-volt Hitachi tool, you can use that NiCad, NiMH or lithium-ion battery and just get the grinder itself for $100. The grinder with one lithium battery and a charger costs $200. If you need help locating a retailer, visit the Web site.

Hitachi, (800) 706-7337. hitachipowertools.com

CHARGER

HandyHints Hodgepodge

TOWEL KNEE PADS

I don't tile very often, but when I do, I like to use something to protect my knees. If you don't have knee pads,
you can easily make them yourself. Just duct-tape old bath
towels to your knees. You might look a little funny, but it
sure beats destroying your pants, and it's a lot easier on
your knees.

OLD BATH
TOWEL

DUCT
TAPE

SPRAY FOAM TUBE CLEANING

We all do it, so don't feel bad. You forget to clean
the plastic tube and nozzle after using half a can of
spray foam. Do you go to the store a month later
when you need more foam? Nope! Just push a
12-gauge wire into the tube and shove out the dried
foam in a single piece, then clean out the clogged
nozzle with a toothpick or small finish nail. Now go
ahead and use the leftover foam.

MINI BELLOWS FOR THE GRILL

A strong puff of air can be mighty useful for getting a fire started in the grill. Taking a deep breath and blowing hard works, but that gets old fast. An easier way is to just rinse out an old squeeze bottle (such as a ketchup bottle), fill it with air and squeeze as needed.

EASY GLUING FOR SMALL REPAIRS

When you're gluing small items like a broken earring or teacup, it can be tough to keep them clamped and still while the glue is setting up. To hold everything together during the repair, embed the parts in reusable adhesive tack ($3 at hardware stores and home centers). The pieces will stay right where you put them, so you can apply the glue and let it dry undisturbed.

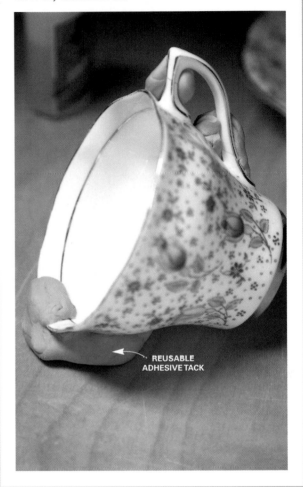

REUSABLE ADHESIVE TACK

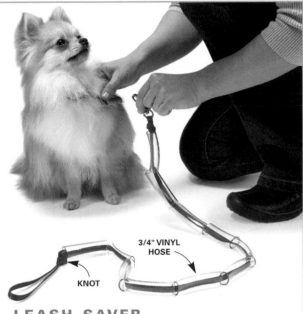

3/4" VINYL HOSE

KNOT

LEASH SAVER

When you have a puppy or a dog that chews on its leash, protect the leash with 3/4-in. vinyl hose (about 75¢ per foot at home centers). Cut the hose into 3-in. pieces and thread them onto the leash until you reach the end. Cutting the vinyl into pieces makes it slide more easily over the leash and also keeps the leash pliable. It's just too bad they don't make vinyl hose big enough to cover a pair of slippers!

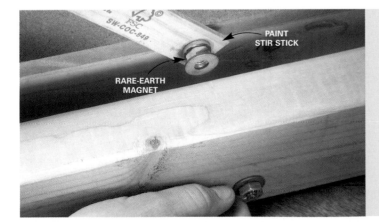

PAINT STIR STICK

RARE-EARTH MAGNET

MAGNETIC STICK TRICK

In a hard-to-reach area, it can be frustrating to get a nut into place when you need to thread on a bolt from the other side. Here's a slick trick. Glue a small rare-earth magnet to the end of a paint stir stick, attach the washer and nut to the magnet, and use the stick to hold them while you thread on the bolt.

Q&C Hodgepodge

WHO'S AT THE DOOR?

I've heard about these high-tech front door monitoring systems that let you see who's at the door. How much do they cost and are they hard to install?

Inexpensive door video phones have been around for years. But most of them hook up to a single dedicated unit inside the house, forcing you to run into the kitchen (or wherever you install the viewer) to answer the door. The viewing screens are usually pretty small, and the video cameras flip out in extreme weather. But newer devices are more reliable and they allow you to view the door video on any TV in the house and answer the door from any phone.

To install a system like this, you'll have to pull Cat5e wiring and coaxial cable from your cable or satellite box and telephone entrance point to the front door. Then install an RF modulator, splitters and combiners so you can distribute the door video to an unused channel on your home's existing cable or satellite wiring. The controller box is what rings your house phones when a visitor presses the doorbell button. Set the controller to ring a distinctive pattern for the door.

The model shown here is the Viking Compact Entry Phone, model E-50 ($490). To install it, you would also need the C-200 phone controller ($182), plus other components based on your particular TV setup, bringing the total cost to about $800. Contact

twacomm.com for installation instructions and a list of components for your particular application (877-389-0000).

Installing a system like this is a lot of work, but when you finish, you'll be able to answer the door from any phone in the house (wired or portable) and view the visitor from any TV.

Install the E-50 door phone in a single-gang electrical box at your front door. Aim the video camera to get the best viewing angle.

WHAT GLUE FOR GLUING WHAT TO WHAT?

I'm never quite sure what glue to use when attaching different materials. Is there an "adhesive bible" of some sort?

Stop guessing and head right to this Web site: thistothat.com. Enter the two materials you want to bond and the site will present the recommended adhesive(s). Click on the adhesive. The site will then give you additional information like drying times, pricing and availability.

GreatGoofs®

Chair fit for a sucker

Last year my husband volunteered to build a king's throne for our son's school play. He used scrap lumber and red velvet fabric from a couch that someone had thrown out. After the play, this awful red-velvet monstrosity cluttered up our garage for months. Then I put it in our yard sale for $25. A guy took one look at it and immediately told me that if I'd hold it until he came back with a pickup, he'd give me $50.

Sure enough, he came back that afternoon with his truck and gave me the money. After loading it up, he told me that the chair was a rare antique and actually quite valuable. When I told him that no, my husband had made it from scrap lumber and recycled fabric for a school play, his jaw dropped to the sidewalk.

GET RID OF ANTS

Kill ants in your house and yard (without stepping on them) — $25 is all it takes

by **Brett Martin**

Wait! Don't step on that ant! Stomping on every ant you see won't solve your ant problem. In fact, the ants scurrying across your kitchen floor might be the key to wiping out the entire colony—ridding your house of these six-legged pests once and for all.

In this story, we'll show you how to kill ants in and around your house. In most cases, you can put an end to your ant problem for less than $25 with products from a home center or hardware store. On the following pages, we'll show you what products to use and where to use them to wipe out the ants.

I.D. the ant

Start by identifying the type of ant in your house so you can find out its nesting habits and have a better idea of where they're living (they may be nesting outdoors). Take a close-up photo of the ant and e-mail it (or snail mail it) to your local university extension service (enter your state's name and "university extension service" into any online search engine). The extension service will tell you the type of ant you're dealing with and where it nests. It may give you fact sheets about the ant species and maybe even some advice on getting rid of that particular ant species.

Keep it clean

A clean house is your first defense against ants. Sweep up food crumbs, wipe up spills, take out the garbage and don't leave dirty dishes sitting around the house. This takes away the ants' food source. Spray vinegar mixed with water around bowls of pet food to keep ants from feasting there.

1 Disrupt the ant trail so more ants won't follow it inside. Mix vinegar and water, then spray it where you've seen ants to cover the ant scent.

PEANUT BUTTER

HONEY

FRENCH FRIES

2 Test the ants to find out what type of foods they like. Set out sugar or honey, fried food and peanut butter, then see which food attracts ants. Use whichever food they prefer for bait.

3 Place liquid ant bait stations in areas where you've seen ants, like under the sink and along walls, to make it as easy as possible for the ants to take the toxic bait back to the nest.

4 Look for water-damaged areas in the house and places where water has recently leaked to find the ant nest. Spray the nest with an indoor insecticide.

5 Spray an indoor insect killer in places where ants can enter, including windows and doors, holes in exterior walls and cracks in the foundation.

6 Spray outdoor insecticide on the foundation walls, and on and under the first course of lap siding to keep ants from entering the house.

7 Look for ant nests or tunnels in the foundation or siding. Spray the area with an insecticide to kill the ants.

Erase their trails

Where you see one ant, you're bound to see others. That's because ants leave a scented trail that other ants follow. Sweeping or mopping isn't enough to eliminate the scent. Instead, mix 1 part vinegar with 3 parts water in a spray bottle, then spray wherever you've seen ants in the past (Photo 1).

This will stop outdoor nesting ants that entered the house to forage for food (ants that come inside are not necessarily trying to establish a nest). But vinegar and water won't stop ants that are already nesting indoors. You'll need to kill them with ant bait (see the next step).

Wipe out colonies

When you see an ant, your first impulse is probably to step on it. But don't. You'll kill it, but for every ant you see, there may be hundreds more hiding in the house. The ones you see are scout ants, foraging for food to take back to the colony. Use these scouts to wipe out the entire colony.

Prebait ants in areas you've previously seen them (Photo 2). Ants' tastes change during the year. They usually prefer protein in the spring and sweets or fatty/oily foods in the summer. Once you know what the ants like, buy and set out ant bait that's geared to their taste (Photo 3). Look on the bait package for words like "controls both sweet and grease eating ants."

Expect to see more ants (initially) when you set out the bait. That's a good thing. It means more ants are taking the bait (which is toxic) back to the colony where they'll share it with the rest of the ants, including the queen, and kill them. There might be thousands of ants back at the nest.

Liquid bait works best for many sweet-loving ants. Other ants prefer solid baits. Terro is one brand of liquid bait ($8 for a six-pack). If you still have ants after two weeks, replace the bait containers. If that doesn't work, it's time to hunt down the nest.

Hunt down the nest

Sometimes the solution to an ant problem is getting rid of their nest. If you're dealing with carpenter ants, which can do structural damage to your house, it's vital that you wipe them out ASAP. Finding the nest may not be easy and takes some detective work.

Ants generally prefer damp areas, such as framing or flooring that's soft and spongy from a plumbing or roof leak. Start by looking for areas with water damage (Photo 4). Attics, bathrooms and exterior walls are obvious candidates. Visit **thefamilyhandyman.com** and search for "find leaks" to learn how to identify and fix leaks.

Cut small holes in water-damaged walls to track down the ant nest. (You're going to have to repair the walls anyway.) When you find the nest, spray it with an insecticide that contains bifenthrin, permethrin or deltamethrin (look on the label). Ortho's Home Defense Max is one brand ($5 for 24 ozs.). Be sure to fix the water leak and replace damaged wood.

If you can't track down the nest, hire a pest control service. Pros spend about 80 percent of their time hunting down nests. Their fees start at about $150, but tough cases with multiple treatments can cost $400 or more. Find pros by looking under "Pest Control Services" in the phone book.

Spray entry points

After ridding the house of ants, take steps to ensure they don't come back. Caulk and seal holes, and then spray insecticide around doors and windows (Photo 5). Use an insecticide that contains bifenthrin, permethrin or deltamethrin. Spray a 4-in.-wide band along entry points, just enough to wet the surface. Once dry, the spray leaves an invisible film that repels ants so they won't enter the house.

Each spring, spray the insecticide to guard against ants.

8 Spray a lawn and garden insect killer on the grass within one day of mowing. Also spray on trees and shrubs. Spray on a calm day to prevent drift.

9 Apply fire ant bait using a broadcast spreader. Fill the spreader over the driveway or a tarp to catch the granules that fall through the spreader.

10 Trim back trees, shrubs and plants so they're at least 6 in. from the house, roof and deck. This eliminates bridges for ants to reach your home.

But keep in mind that this only works to keep ants out—it won't kill ants that are already inside, and it can actually interfere with the use of ant baits.

Spray on a barrier

If you're still getting ants in your house after spraying interior entry points, spray a 12-in.-wide band of insecticide on the foundation and siding (**Photo 6**). Use an outdoor insecticide that says "barrier treatment" on the label. Bayer Advanced Home Pest Control is one brand ($9 for 1 gallon).

Destroy exterior nests

If you frequently see ants in the same area on the siding, there's probably a nest in there (**Photo 7**). Look for holes in the siding where ants are crawling in and out. The holes are often located between bricks where mortar has fallen out, under lap siding or in cracks in stucco. Once you locate the nest, or the vicinity of the nest, spray the area with an insecticide containing bifenthrin.

Kill ants in your yard

Anthills are eyesores in yards, and the ants can ruin outside dining. If you only have ants in a certain area, like along your sidewalk, spot-treat the area with an outdoor insecticide. Liquid or granules work fine. For large-scale ant problems, use a lawn and garden insect killer that contains bifenthrin as the active ingredient. Ortho's Bug-B-Gon Max is one brand ($11 for a 32-oz. concentrate that covers up to 16,000 sq. ft.). The spray will also kill other insects (read the label for a list). First mow the grass, then spray the insecticide on the entire lawn (**Photo 8**). Spray in the early morning or late afternoon when the ants are most active. If ants are still building mounds after six weeks, treat the lawn again (the insecticide works for up to six weeks). You won't kill every ant in your yard (nor would

you want to!), but spraying will eliminate most of them and stop the annoying mounds.

Kill fire ants with bait

Fire ants are found in the Southeastern United States and Southern California. Standard insecticides are much less effective at killing fire ants. You need a special product that's designed to wipe out these biting critters, like Amdro's FireStrike Ant Bait ($24 for a 5-lb. bag that treats 10,000 sq. ft.). Apply the granules with a broadcast spreader (**Photo 9**). Fire ants carry the granules, which they think are food (it's actually toxic bait) back to their mounds. The ants share the bait and die. A longer-lasting alternative is Garden Tech's Over 'N Out! ($23 for a 10-lb. bag that treats 5,000 sq. ft.) This granular insecticide keeps killing fire ants for up to a year. As with other baits, it may take a few weeks for you to see full results.

Eliminate safe havens

Once you kill the ants in your house and yard, take steps to ensure they don't come back. Trim back bushes, shrubs and trees that brush against your siding or roof and provide a bridge for ants to reach your house (**Photo 10**). Keep a 3-in. to 6-in. clearance space between the soil around the foundation and the bottom row of siding to prevent ants from nesting in the siding (and make sure the soil slopes away from the house). Avoid stacking firewood next to the house. Firewood makes a perfect retreat for ants.

Ants like bare spots in the yard and they like to build nests under layers of thatch. Maintaining a healthy lawn is one way to discourage ants. If anthills pop up in bare areas, spray the mound with insecticide and plant grass in the bare spots. Rake the lawn or bag the grass when you mow to eliminate thatch.

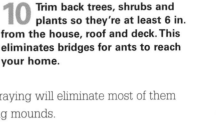

DollarSavvy Hodgepodge

RENTING ISN'T ALWAYS SMART

Sometimes it makes sense to rent—but not always. That's especially true if you're not quite sure how long a job will take. When's the last time you finished a job early? For example, say you think you'll need a trim gun, hose and compressor for two days at $80 a day. If it winds up taking you three days to trim out the basement, you could have bought the whole kit and caboodle for less than the rental cost.

Any tool that costs less than $100 is probably worth buying if you think you'll ever use it again. And even more expensive tools, such as a $250 tile saw, will pay for themselves in only a few days of rental. True, consumer-grade tools aren't always as rugged as rental tools, but you won't need that ruggedness for occasional use. Plus, with all those tools to lend, you'll be more popular with all your friends and relatives.

Rental cost for three days: $240

Price of a brad nail/ compressor kit: $200

DON'T CHANGE FLUORESCENT BULBS UNTIL YOU HAVE TO

Some people think fluorescent tubes have to be changed when the ends of the tubes turn black. Not true. Continued use doesn't harm the starting ballast or significantly affect light output. Leave them alone until the bulb starts flickering or takes a long time to fire up. Then stick in a new bulb, because at that point the old one will damage the ballast.

HALF-PRICE BLADES — SAVE $12

You don't have to be a professional drywall hanger to go through a lot of utility blades. Do-it-yourselfers go through dozens in the house, shop and garage. And most DIYers use the same dull blade for too long and make all their cutting jobs a whole lot tougher. So why not just cough up the cash for a 100-count package of blades? You'll use them eventually—and save 50 percent by buying in bulk.

100 blades in bulk: $12

100 blades in 5-count packs: $24.50

STOP GIVING AWAY MONEY!

The average American family chugs its way through 900 aluminum cans a year, or 2.5 cans every day. In the past year, hauling them to the recycler would have yielded $12 to $33 depending on the fluctuating price of aluminum. If you're the average family, maybe that's not enough money to worry about. But if your family members are super slurpers, maybe you should stop hauling cans out to the curb and giving them away. Crush them as they're used, and when you've amassed a mountain, haul them to a nearby recycler that pays for scrap and cash in. Make the most money by taking them in when the price is high; call the recycler once in a while to check on the price. Look under "Recycling" or "Scrap Metal" in the phone book to find the nearest yard.

And if you're having your aluminum siding replaced, tell the installer that you'll haul it away—right to the recycler. This chunk of cash would otherwise go into the installer's pocket.

USE THE TOLL-FREE NUMBERS FROM YOUR INSTRUCTION MANUAL

This tip could save you a ton of money or be completely worthless, depending on the company. But the next time something breaks, get out the instruction manual or go online to find the toll-free help line. You could get a knowledgeable person who can help you troubleshoot your problem and save on professional repair bills. Or you might get the part you need for free— especially if your product is still under warranty.

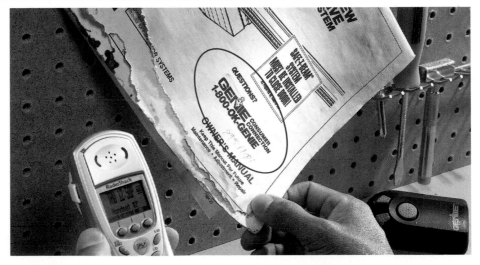

Gallery of Ideas

money-saving

These 8 articles will help you save money—around the house, and when doing business.

To order $3 photocopies of complete articles for the projects shown here, call (715) 246-4521, email familyhandyman@nrmsinc.com or write to: Copies, The Family Handyman, P.O. Box 83695, Stillwater, MN 55083-0695. Many public libraries also carry back issues of *The Family Handyman* magazine.

IN THIS CHAPTER

PROPER WAY TO TORQUE LUG NUTS

Did you know there's a right and a wrong way to tighten lug nuts? Most people think "tighter is better." Not true. Overtightening lug nuts is the No. 1 cause of brake rotor lateral run-out (warp). Warped rotors cause pedal pulsation and can increase your stopping distance. Overtightening is also a great way to break wheel studs. The stud itself doesn't cost much ($3), but the labor to press out the old stud and insert the new one can cost $50 to $75.

Spin the lug nuts on by hand. *Never* coat the stud with grease, oil or anti-seize. Lower the jack only enough to bring the tire into contact with the road. Tighten each nut to one-half of the specified torque. Then lower the vehicle completely and tighten each nut to full torque.

1 Consult your owner's manual or a shop manual and set your torque wrench to one-half the recommended torque specification.

2 Reset the wrench and tighten each nut to full torque. Move the socket from one nut to the next in a star-shaped sequence.

LOCKING → COLLAR

EXTRA LONG NEEDLE-NOSE PLIERS

In the old days, you could see the ground from the top of an engine compartment. Today, you can't see down more than 6 in. past crammed-in engines. So whenever you drop a nut or bolt, you can be sure it won't fall to the ground for easy retrieval. Oh, no, it'll likely hang up in some little nook just out of reach. And that's just one case in which these 16-in. needle-nose pliers will come in handy. The assortment includes traditional straight needle-nose, angled nose, offset and rounded nose (for pulling hoses and cables).

Astro Pneumatic No. 9415 four-piece 16-in. Needle-Nose Pliers Set, $27. tooldiscounter.com

Reach into unreachable places with this set of needle-nose pliers. Move parts into position or pluck fasteners from deep and dark crevices.

PLIERS FOR TIGHT SPOTS

They're not the jaws of life. But when you're in a tight spot and can't get a grip, these flexible head pliers can really save your bacon. The jaws flex a full 180 degrees, and the handles are spring-loaded for easier grabbing. **SK No. 89103 three-piece set of Flexible Head Pliers, $38 (lineman's pliers, diagonal cutters, needle-nose pliers). tooldiscounter.com**

AIR CHISEL HAMMER BIT— BACK BY POPULAR DEMAND!

Plunk this baby into your air chisel and you've got an air hammer that will knock just about anything loose or pound it back into place. When we showed how to use this hammer bit to loosen rusted-on receiver hitches, we found ourselves buried in mail from readers wondering where to buy one.

Grey Pneumatic No. CH117, 1-in. hammer bit, $8. tooldiscounter.com

Car&Garage

NEVER LOSE SOCKETS AGAIN!

Load these socket holders and take all your sockets right to the job. Magnets hold the sockets in place. Pick one color for metric, the other for SAE. No guesswork.

Lisle Socket Holders:

- No. 40120 for 1/4-in. sockets (red), $11
- No. 40130 for 1/4-in. sockets (green), $11
- No. 40200 for 3/8-in. sockets (red), $14
- No. 40210 for 3/8-in. sockets (green), $14

tooldiscounter.com

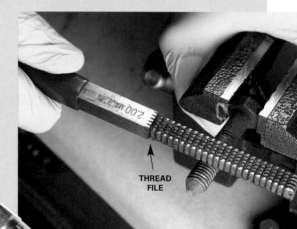

PICK ONE COLOR FOR METRIC . . .

. . . AND THE OTHER FOR SAE

RESTORING STRIPPED THREADS IN NUTS AND BOLTS

No matter how careful you are when you reinstall old rusty nuts and bolts, someday you're going to strip some threads. Of course it will happen on a critical bolt, on a Sunday night when all the stores are closed. That's when a thread restoration kit pays for itself. A full set (metric and SAE) costs less than $60 and can put those nuts and bolts back into service. The rethreading tools look like traditional taps and dies. But instead of cutting new threads, they reshape them to original condition.

To restore bolt threads, start by finding the thread count (SAE) or pitch (metric). Hold the thread file against the bolt threads until you find the size that matches. Clamp the bolt in a vise, engage the thread file grooves with the bolt threads and push the file (**photo right**). That "resets" the threads enough so you can screw on a rethreading die (apply a few drops of oil first). Use a rethreading tap to restore threads on nuts or threaded engine component holes. Don't try to rethread the entire bolt, hole or nut in one operation. Insert the rethreading tap or die and rotate a few turns, then back it off a full turn. That will dislodge the debris from the teeth.

THREAD FILE

RETHREADING TAP

Clean rusty or stripped threads with a thread restoration die. Use a rethreading tap on nuts and threaded holes.

Kastar 48-piece Rethreading Kit No. 971, $58 from tooldiscounter.com

REPLACE BURNED-OUT DASH LIGHTS

You've probably replaced burned-out headlights and taillights, but if you've backed away from replacing burned-out dashboard lights because you thought the job was too complicated, you're now out of excuses. We'll show you how to remove the trim panels and instrument cluster on a 1999 Ford Taurus. But you can apply these disassembly tips to almost any vehicle. Pick up several packages of new bulbs at an auto parts store before you start the project (replace all the instrument cluster bulbs at the same time), and plan on devoting about two hours to the job. You'll save about $80 by doing this yourself.

Removing dash trim panels is actually easy. The hard part is figuring out which panel to remove first. That's where exploded diagrams from a shop manual really pay off (see "Online shop manuals," p. 235). Online factory manuals offer the most detailed diagrams and cost as little as $10 for a three-day subscription. If you hate reading shop manuals, at least follow these two important tips: First, remove the bottommost trim panel; we had to remove the Taurus radio to get to the bottom trim panel screws (**Photo 1**). A lower panel always hides the screws for the panel above it. And second, if a panel won't pop out, don't pull harder. You must have missed a retaining screw, so look harder.

Then pry at a corner of the instrument cluster trim with a non-marring tool. Buy a set of nylon pry tools ($5) or wrap electrical tape around the end of a butter knife (screwdrivers can damage the dash). Insert the tool and use a quick snapping motion to dislodge the spring clip panel fasteners.

Disconnect the negative battery terminal before removing any electrical connectors. Then remove the connectors from the switches and controls and lift out the panel. Every electrical connector has a lock/release tab. Release it before trying to pull off the connector. Next remove the instrument cluster bezel (plastic window) to access the cluster retaining screws. Tilt the cluster forward and disconnect the electrical connectors (**Photo 2**). Remove the cluster, turn it over and locate the bulb sockets. Remove the old bulbs and insert the new ones (**Photo 3**). Handle them with a clean rag or gloves to keep skin oils off the glass. But be careful. Miniature bulbs can shatter and slice your fingers if you squeeze too hard trying to get them out of their sockets. If the bulb won't budge, use a small screwdriver to pry it out.

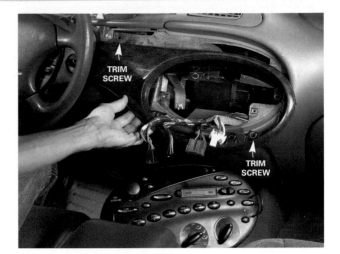

1 Pull the radio (if required) using a set of radio removal tools ($5 at any auto parts store). Then remove the bottommost trim panel screws and pop off the panel to reach the screws for the panel above.

2 Remove the instrument cluster screws and tilt the assembly out far enough to reach the electrical connector and speedometer cable (older vehicles).

3 Twist the bulb socket a quarter turn and pull straight out. Swap in a new bulb.

AUTO & GARAGE

Car&Garage

PRY BARS THAT WORK

Bust anything apart with these heavy-duty pry bars.

When you've got to move a big hunk of metal, you need lots of leverage. That's where a good pry bar set earns its keep. With three lengths to choose from, this set lets you "persuade" just about any automotive component into or out of place. The long handles give plenty to hang on to, and the chrome striking caps can withstand the hammer blows when more force is needed. This is a tool gearheads probably wouldn't buy for themselves, but would appreciate on the next repair job.

MASTER CYLINDER RESERVOIR

OTC No. 8203
three-piece pry bar set, $40.
12-in., 18-in. and 24-in. bars with chrome striking caps on handle ends.
tooldiscounter.com

FOUR-WHEEL-DRIVE CLUNKS

When I put my truck into four-wheel drive, I feel clunking or jumping when turning. Am I doing something wrong, or am I using 4WD when I shouldn't be?

This happens when you drive a "part-time" 4WD vehicle on dry pavement. Trucks with "full-time" 4WD don't have problems on dry pavement because they have a center differential that allows for differences in rotation between front and rear tires. But part-time 4WD trucks don't. When you drive it on dry pavement and make turns, the front wheels rotate at different speeds than the rear wheels. At that point, something's got to give. Either your tires will skip on the dry pavement, causing a "hopping" sensation, or you'll hear clunking. Use part-time 4WD only on wet or icy roads. If you're in 4WD and hit an extended patch of dry pavement, shift into 2WD.

HOIST YOUR BIKE TO MAKE ROOM FOR YOUR WHEELS

Surveys show that one of the major reasons buyers back away from a motorcycle purchase is that they'd have to park one of their cars outside to leave space for the bike. If you're facing that dilemma, consider installing a motorcycle storage lift. It'll lift your bike, four-wheeler or riding mower high enough to fit your car underneath it.

The Loft-It system from Tivan uses an electric motor and stainless steel cables to lift a bike (up to 1,200 lbs.) on a 4 x 8-ft. platform. The 7-amp, 110-volt motor plugs into an ordinary receptacle, so you won't have to call an electrician for special wiring. The motor senses the load and won't operate if you exceed the maximum lifting weight. You can install it yourself in about two hours with hand tools and a drill.

During biking season, either load the platform with your snow toys or fold it up against the wall. Loft-It costs $1,995 plus shipping. For more information and to locate a dealer, visit loft-it.com.

Run your bike onto the platform and flip the elevator switch. Once it's up and locked, restake your claim to the stall by parking your car under it.

SHORT
SCREW

SNAP
CLIP

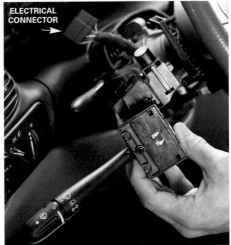

1 Remove the screws from the bottom half of the steering column cover and note the length, thread style and location of each screw. They have to go back in the same place. Disengage the plastic snap clips and separate the two halves of the steering column cover.

ELECTRICAL
CONNECTOR

2 Remove the switch retaining screws and pull out the switch. Disconnect the electrical connector.

FIX INTERMITTENT-WIPER AND TURN SIGNAL PROBLEMS

Once known as a turn signal or blinker switch, this lever now also controls headlights, high beams, emergency flashers, wipers and washers. No wonder it's now called the multifunction switch (MFS). Unfortunately, the MFS has a fairly high failure rate. The two most common failures are a broken turn signal "canceling" mechanism that won't shut off the "blinkers" after a turn, and a partial or complete loss of intermittent wiper control. To fix these two problems, you'll need a shop manual, a digital multimeter and possibly some Torx bits.

On most late-model vehicles, the MFS is located under the plastic covers behind the steering wheel. In that case, you can do this repair in about an hour and save almost $100 by doing it yourself. But some older vehicles require the removal of the airbag and steering wheel, and that's a job for a pro. Refer to a shop manual to see where your MFS is located (see "Online shop manuals," p. 235).

Always disconnect the negative battery terminal and wait 15 minutes for the airbag system to power down before starting work on the steering column. Then remove the screws and lift off the plastic covers.

The MFS is usually held in place by hex-head or Torx screws. Remove them, pull out the switch and disconnect the electrical connector. If the problem is a broken canceling mechanism, you must replace the entire MFS (auto parts store or dealer). If the problem is faulty intermittent wiper operation, use a multimeter to check the connectors on the back of the MFS for resistance (ohms) readings for each setting on the intermittent wiper dial. Then compare them with the manual. If the resistance readings are off, the shop manual will tell you to replace the MFS. But you may be able to save big bucks ($90 to $200) by disassembling the MFS and cleaning the variable resistor contacts yourself. Search the Internet for "multifunction switch repair." If you can't disassemble the MFS or the cleaning doesn't work, replace the entire unit and reinstall the covers.

3 Connect a multimeter to the wiper contacts on the switch to check the resistance readings. Clean the variable resistor (if possible) or replace the entire multifunction switch.

MULTIFUNCTION
SWITCH

AUTO &
GARAGE

Car&Garage

REPLACE A LEAKING HEATER HOSE

Leaky, crimped-on heater hoses can be replaced with new, expensive ($50 and up) assemblies. But you can replace just the leaky section. It's simple and cheap to do with a short matching length of hose (about $10) and a new worm-drive clamp. (You should reuse the factory spring clamp, but you can't reuse the old crimp ring.) Check with a local auto parts store to locate replacement molded hose

sections. Or bring in the leaking section and see if the staff can visually match it to a stock hose for another vehicle.

If you can't find the proper molded hose, slide a Goodyear E-Z Coil ($10) over a straight section of hose and bend it to the proper angle for your application. The coil will maintain the angle and prevent the hose from collapsing at the bend.

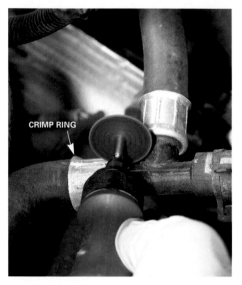

CRIMP RING

FACTORY SPRING CLAMP

WORM-DRIVE CLAMP

1 Cut through the crimp ring with a rotary tool and cutoff wheel or a close-quarters hacksaw.

2 Slip on the new hose and secure it with worm-drive hose clamps.

NEVER INFLATE TIRES TO THE MAXIMUM PRESSURE!

My neighbor tells me he's getting much better gas mileage since he inflated his tires to the maximum pressure shown on the tire. Can this be true?

Never assume that the *maximum* air pressure shown on the tire's sidewall is the same as the recommended tire pressure. Filling to the maximum pressure *always* means you're overinflating your tires. The *recommended* tire pressures for your car are printed on the driver's door or doorpost decal.

Your neighbor's dollar savings based on increased gas mileage are short term. He will pay far more in the long run when he replaces his tires, suspension parts and shock absorbers, all of which will wear out prematurely. Worse yet, he's risking his life and the lives of his passengers.

Overinflated tires carry the entire weight of the car on the middle portion of the tread. On wet roads, the center tread can't pump the water out to the sides

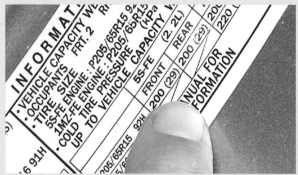

(think of a squeegee with a bulge in the center). So they're more prone to hydroplaning and also more likely to skid in a stop or in a turn, and blow out on hard bumps. The bottom line: Overinflation is foolish and dangerous. Always follow the inflation pressures shown on the car, not the tires.

SERVICE YOUR "TUCK-UNDER" SPARE TIRE LIFT NOW!

Most trucks, vans and SUVs stow the spare tire under the vehicle. It's a great space-saving idea, but one that doesn't always work well in the real world. The corrosive brew of road salt, mud and sand usually eats away at the tire lift's metal components, rendering the lift unusable when you need it most. Picture yourself with a flat tire at the side of the road—in a storm, of course.

You can prevent that nightmare by checking your spare tire lift right now, in the comfort of your garage. If you don't know how to lower the spare tire, consult your owner's manual. Check to make sure you still have the factory cranking tools. Now is the time to get any replacement parts.

Start by raising your vehicle and supporting it with jack stands. Try lowering the spare tire. If it's stuck, shoot spray rust penetrant through the wheel openings to saturate the lift. Then lightly tap on the T-bar with a hammer to set up vibrations and break up the rust. After several rounds of spraying and tapping, the lift should free up. Lower the tire and move it out of the way. If it still doesn't budge, insert a long screwdriver or pry bar into the wheel hub opening and force the release latch open. That may ruin the latch, but replacing it now is a heck of a lot better (and cheaper) than dealing with it on an emergency basis.

Coat all rusted parts with rust converter and allow them to dry. Then apply waterproof marine grease to all the working parts of the release latch. Yes, the grease will pick up road dirt, but it'll also repel water and keep the latch from binding in the future.

Finish the job by checking the air pressure in the spare tire and restowing it. Perform this quick maintenance exercise once a year and your spare tire will never let you down. For flat tire tips and hints, go to thefamilyhandyman.com and search for "flat tire."

1 Soak a stuck spare tire lift with rust penetrant. Tap the T-bar to set up rust-busting vibrations.

2 Coat the release latch with rust converter. When it's dry, coat the components with marine grease.

Car&Garage

PUT THE BRAKES ON HIGH
AUTO INSURANCE COSTS

Everybody wants to save on car insurance. But most people can't figure out how to do it without either reducing coverage or increasing the deductibles. We got some better advice from a seasoned insurance expert who's worked with dozens of major insurance companies.

Insurance laws vary by state, so some of these cost-saving methods may not apply in your area. But if you follow these tips, you should be able to save an average of $300 per year, or possibly more, on your car insurance. We'll work with a model of a two-car household with two 57-year-old adults and one college-age driver. This household's annual premium is $2,300 based on one accident and one speeding ticket.

1 Pay in advance. Save $60

You pay *lots* extra if you're paying your car insurance monthly. Find out the least expensive pay-period—usually six months. If you have the cash, you could save even more money by paying the full year's premium in advance (check with your agent).

2 Pay promptly. Save $15 to $50

Some companies offer attractive incentives for paying the invoice within 10 days, rather than taking the full 30 days. We're not telling you to pay your mortgage late so you can pay the insurance company early. But if your insurer offers a "prompt pay" discount (ask for one), it may be worth your while to reprioritize your bill payment schedule. If you're temporarily short on cash, it may even make sense to pay with your credit card.

3 Complete a "senior driver" training (and refresher) course. Save $200

Most insurance companies offer a discount for each driver 55 and older who takes an authorized driver safety education program (some states mandate this discount). The initial course is eight hours, and some companies (and states) allow you to take a four-hour online version ($20 per driver). Classroom rates vary. You'll be a safer driver and can pocket the savings every year. For more information, contact your insurance agent, AARP, AAA or your local adult education center, or search the Internet for "senior driver education."

4 Kid at college? Save $400

This one's a no-brainer. If your kid is away at college, minus the family car, your insurance rates will be lower. Tell your agent that your kid is at school and work out arrangements for those few days when he or she is home. If your student has a car at school, you should still notify your agent. The rates may be lower based on the school's location.

5 Change jobs or retire? Save $60

If you drive 20 miles to work every day, you're paying a higher premium than people who drive only 5 miles. So if you get a new job closer to home, tell your agent immediately. Also, if you're lucky enough to retire, tell your agent so they can reclassify you as a "pleasure driver." You'll see a drop in your premiums in both cases.

6 Track your tickets.
Save $100

Insurance companies check your driving record regularly and increase your premium on the very next bill if they find a traffic violation. But they're not always so quick to reduce your premium later when the violation falls off your record. So keep track of the dates of your tickets and ask for a reduction once your record is "clean" (usually three years, but check with your state's Department of Motor Vehicles).

7 Avoid small claims.
Save $200

If you get a small dent or other minor damage on an older car, think twice about filing a claim and getting it fixed. To avoid rate hikes, it might be worth your while to just live with it if there are no safety issues. And if you have towing coverage on your policy and use it to get your jalopy towed every six months, be ready for a 10 percent rate increase on your next renewal. Buy a roadside assistance plan (available from AAA, AARP and other vendors) instead. It's cheaper.

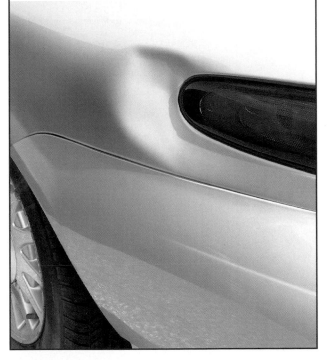

9 Drop collision and comprehensive coverage when it makes sense.
Save $300

Let's face it—old cars (10-plus years) aren't worth much. So at a certain point it doesn't make sense to keep paying for collision and comprehensive (C&C) coverage. Find the "book" value of your vehicle on the Internet (nada.com, edmunds.com or kbb.com) or at the library. Then add up the annual premiums for C&C. Chances are, you're paying for the full value of the vehicle every three years. If you're comfortable accepting a low level of risk, cancel your C&C coverage and put that money away. You'll probably come out ahead.

10 Install an alarm.
Save $100 to $200

The discount varies by location, the make and model of the alarm, and the theft likelihood of your particular vehicle model. But insurance companies give the largest discounts for installing a "stolen vehicle recovery" system like MobileGuardian, LoJack, VehicleRECOVER or GM's OnStar. These systems can locate a stolen vehicle within minutes and prevent a total loss. The discount alone may pay for one of these systems in just a few years.

You can learn more about these systems by visiting lojack.com, vehiclerecover.com and mymobileguardian.com.

8 Shop early.
Save $50

Everyone should shop around for new insurance rates every three years. Insurance companies reward early shopping (30 days before renewal is perfect) by giving better rates. Last-minute shopping (less than 10 days before the policy expires) makes insurance companies think you're irresponsible, and that will be reflected in a higher quote.

AUTO & GARAGE

Car&Garage

CHANGE YOUR OWN OIL—MAKE $40 AN HOUR

Changing your own oil isn't brain surgery—you probably did it yourself years ago. But with some oil change shops now charging upward of $70, it's time to get back under the car and start saving big bucks.

You'll save at least $25 and possibly $40—in less than half an hour. Plus, you won't be pressured into buying overpriced add-ons (like wiper blades and PCV valves) *every* time you go in for a change. We'll show you how to change your oil fast and painlessly. And we'll show you some tips you may *not* know about.

Buy the right oil and filter

Before you head off to the auto parts store, consult your owner's manual for the type and weight of oil specific to your vehicle. *It's especially important to follow the carmaker's recommendations for oil viscosity.* That's a big change from the old DIY days. Late-model engines rely on oil pressure to regulate valve timing and apply the proper tension to the timing belt or chain. Substituting your personal pref-

erence for the manufacturer's recommendations can result in engine damage, poor performance and even a "Check Engine" warning.

In the old days, oil filters were all pretty much the same inside. But not anymore. If your owner's manual recommends extended oil change intervals (every 6,000 miles instead of 3,000 miles), you *must* buy a filter that's rated to go the distance. In other words, don't fill your engine with expensive synthetic oil and then spin on an economy filter—it won't last. Check the filter box, ask the store clerk, or check the filter manufacturer's Web site to make sure the filter you buy is rated for extended oil change intervals.

Changing oil the fast way

If you get all your ducks in a row, you'll be done in about 20 minutes. Start by spreading plastic sheeting on the ground. Then drive your car on top of it. That will eliminate all oil spill cleanup work since you can just toss the entire sheet when you're done, or keep it for the next change if

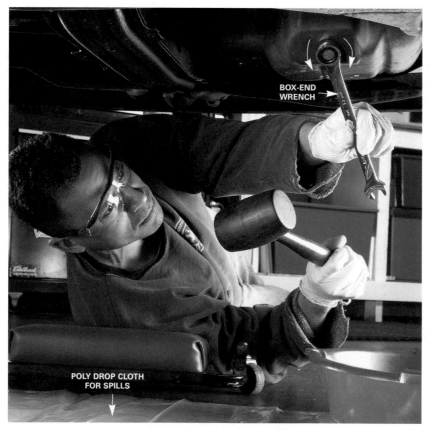

1 Unscrew the plug and quickly pull it out and away from the oil stream. Clean the drain plug and install a new gasket (if required).

2 Crank off the old oil filter and make sure the rubber gasket comes with it. If not, peel it from the engine.

you're lucky enough to go spill-free. Jack up the car, set the jack stands in place, and lower the car. If you're on asphalt, place squares of plywood under the jack stands for support.

Place all your tools on a tray or in a box so everything you need is in one place. That means a box-end wrench for the drain plug, a rubber mallet (Photo 1), a filter wrench, a drain pan and the new filter. Before you slide it all under the car, open a new oil bottle and smear clean oil on the new filter's gasket. Then you're ready to start the job.

Remove the drain plug and get the old oil flowing. Then remove the oil filter and install the new one. Once the old oil is down to a trickle, install a new gasket on the plug (if required) and tighten it by tapping the box-end wrench with the rubber mallet. Wipe the drips with a rag and you're done under the car.

FILTER PLIERS

BAND WRENCH

CAP WRENCH

EXPANDABLE CAP WRENCH

STRAP WRENCH

Different oil filter wrenches work best for different cars. Select the one that gives you the most room to maneuver.

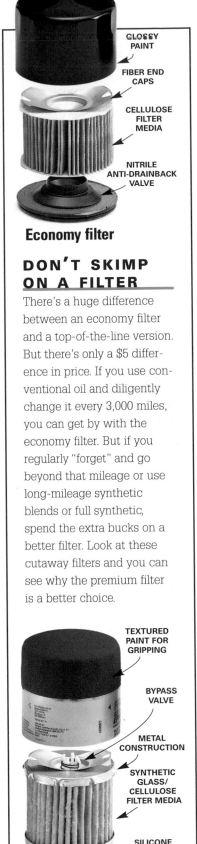

GLOSSY PAINT

FIBER END CAPS

CELLULOSE FILTER MEDIA

NITRILE ANTI-DRAINBACK VALVE

Economy filter

DON'T SKIMP ON A FILTER

There's a huge difference between an economy filter and a top-of-the-line version. But there's only a $5 difference in price. If you use conventional oil and diligently change it every 3,000 miles, you can get by with the economy filter. But if you regularly "forget" and go beyond that mileage or use long-mileage synthetic blends or full synthetic, spend the extra bucks on a better filter. Look at these cutaway filters and you can see why the premium filter is a better choice.

TEXTURED PAINT FOR GRIPPING

BYPASS VALVE

METAL CONSTRUCTION

SYNTHETIC GLASS/ CELLULOSE FILTER MEDIA

SILICONE ANTI-DRAINBACK VALVE

Premium filter

3 Refill the engine using a funnel and recap the bottle (to prevent spills) before you toss it into the recycling bin.

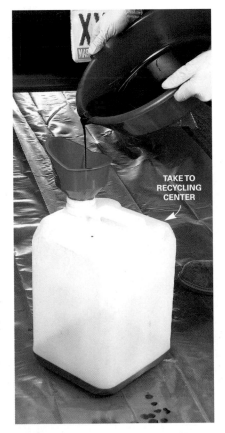

TAKE TO RECYCLING CENTER

4 Pour the used oil into a large jug. Fill the engine and run it until the dashboard oil light goes out. Wait a few minutes. Then check the dipstick and add oil if needed.

Car&Garage

PLAY MP3 TUNES ON YOUR RADIO

If you want to play your MP3 (or iPod) tunes through your car radio, you have two choices: an FM adapter or an MP3 adapter that installs permanently inside your dash. The in-dash MP3 adapter powers (and recharges) your MP3 player, provides better sound quality and eliminates the constant channel switching required by the FM adapter.

In-dash adapters are available in models to fit almost every factory radio made since 1992. The unit for our Toyota Camry cost about $135. The installation was a cinch and took less than an hour. But one warning: If you already have an external CD changer, you'll have to give it up. That's because the MP3 adapter plugs into the CD changer port in the back of the radio.

MP3 adapters are radio-specific, so take a mental (or actual) snapshot of your radio before you go to the adapter manufacturer's Web site (one source is neocaraudio.com). Next, download radio removal instructions ($4) from carstereohelp.com. We followed its instructions and had the radio out in 10 minutes (with no broken parts).

The most time-consuming part of the job is finding a good route for the MP3 player cable. You can route it through an opening under the dash and out to the console or glove box. Or you can hide the cable by routing it directly to the console (drill a hole in an inconspicuous location). We decided not to install an MP3 mount (they alert thieves that you have theft-worthy gear in the car). If you want one, check out "device holders" at proclipusa.com.

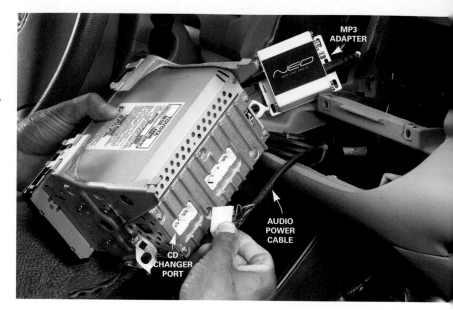

1 Plug the MP3 adapter into the external CD changer port on your factory radio. Use zip ties to secure the adapter to a recess behind the radio.

2 Route the combination audio/power cable to a convenient location near your console and plug in your MP3 player. Test the radio and adapter before you remount the radio.

FILL TIRES WITH NITROGEN—OR NOT?

The dealer service guy tried to talk me into filling my new tires with nitrogen for $39.99. He made lots of claims about how much better it is than air. I'm skeptical. Is this a scam?

No, it isn't a scam. Everything the dealer said about nitrogen is true. It leaks less than compressed atmospheric air (because nitrogen molecules are larger than oxygen molecules) and reduces rubber oxidation. But that doesn't mean nitrogen never leaks. The problem is that once you commit to a nitrogen fill, you must stick with it for the life of the tire. The instant you add compressed air, you negate all the benefits.

Since you still need to check and refill your tires, and since nitrogen is hard to find, you'll be married to the dealer forever. And that's not good if they're not conveniently located.

Even though nitrogen really is better than regular old air, it's doubtful you'll ever see enough of a benefit to justify the $39.99 investment. Your tires will probably wear out from normal driving long before the important benefits of nitrogen really kick in. But if you drive less than 5,000 miles per year and plan to keep your tires for 10 years (and don't mind hanging out at the dealer), nitrogen is definitely worth it. By the way, the green caps on tire valve stems indicate the tire is filled with nitrogen.

PREVENT LICENSE PLATE THEFT

When gas prices are high, nasty people have been known to steal someone else's license plates, fill their own cars with gas, drive off without paying and let the gas station cameras capture the stolen license plate number. Install a set of locking fasteners (aka security screws) to stop the crooks before they get their sticky fingers on your plates. The screws are cheap ($4 a set), easy to install and available in a style to fit your vehicle. The kits come with a security wrench; keep it in a safe place so you can change plates when they expire.

licenseplateshop.com

LOCKING FASTENERS

4 REASONS TO BUY A BETTER CREEPER

If your idea of changing your own oil is to grab a piece of cardboard and slide under the car, it's time to get with the program: Save your back and invest in a creeper. They range in price from $20 to $200, but you don't need to spend a fortune. You can get a darn good creeper for about $50 (**photo right**). Here are the four features to look for in a creeper:

1. A sturdy backboard reduces stress on your upper and lower back muscles. Economy models are built with a thin sheet of plywood. Look for a reinforced backboard that will support your back and shoulders.

2. Steel wheels make for rough riding and they get stuck in every crack. Rolling off your creeper to free up a stuck wheel is a real drag. Shop for a creeper that has urethane ball-bearing wheels.

3. Make the best use of limited workspace with a low-profile design. Recessed wheels get you closer to the ground and give you more room to maneuver tools and parts.

4. Wood creepers absorb oil, coolant and fluids, making every spill last a lifetime. Instead, look for a creeper with a heavy-duty chemical- and oil-resistant fabric and firm padding.

ONLINE SHOP MANUALS

Go to alldata.com OR go to nastf.org/i4a/pages/index.cfm? pageid=3292 and click on the brand of your car.

BUDGET CREEPER
Lisle No. 98102
36-in. Economy Creeper, $37 from menintools.com

PREMIUM CREEPER
Lisle No. 96302
42-in. Low Profile Creeper, $50 from tooldiscounter.com

PLYWOOD BACK; ONLY 36" LONG

LOW PROFILE; STURDY PADDED BACK; 42" LONG

STEEL WHEELS

RECESSED URETHANE WHEELS

New Tools & Gear

NEW CLASS OF CHORE BUSTERS

KUBOTA RTV1100

KUBOTA

As easy to drive as a golf cart, all-terrain vehicles or utility work machines can handle the heavy lifting for outdoor chores.

BOBCAT

BOBCAT 2300 4x4 W/SNOW BLADE

Several companies now offer utility vehicles for tackling extra-heavy-duty work. These versatile, easy to operate workhorses are designed for folks living on large acreage, hobby farms or traditional farms. The vehicles are like a pickup truck, compact tractor and all-terrain vehicle rolled into one tough machine. Some have all-wheel drive for cruising through mud and snow and up steep hills, and some will even dump the load.

The vehicles can do more than just haul—attachments are available for snow plowing, mowing, and lifting materials with a pallet fork or bucket. Heating and air conditioning options are available for the cab.

The utility vehicles range in price from about $6,500 to more than $15,000, plus attachments. Sure, they're expensive, but the alternative is buying job-dedicated power gear one piece at a time, each with its own engine.

Bobcat, bobcat.com
John Deere, deere.com
Kubota, kubota.com

PERFECT PARKING EVERY TIME

A tennis ball hanging from a string is a classic way to indicate where to stop your vehicle in your garage. But if you're looking for a solution that's equally low-tech but less obtrusive, try the Parking Target from Innovative Products International. An adhesive backing holds the 1-1/4-in.-tall, 3-1/2-in.-wide and 16-in.-long strip to the floor. When your front tire bumps against it, you stop the car. Genius!

The Parking Target is ideal for crowded garages where it's a tight fit between the toolbox or workbench in front of the vehicle and the garage door in back. It's available for $14 on the company's Web site.
Innovative Products International, (303) 765-2252.
parkingtarget.com

SQUEEGEE AWAY WATER SPOTS

The Ultimate Paint Squeegee from Griot's Garage showed up at our office on a rainy day, so we went to the parking lot to try it out. It made short work of wiping the water off vehicles, especially the windows. When you wash your car or truck, you can use it along with a towel for much faster drying—without water spots.

The thick squeegee blade is super soft closed-cell foam, so it conforms to the shape of your vehicle and doesn't squeak like other squeegees. The squeegee (item No. 82187) also works great for wiping down tile walls and the shower door after a shower. Buy it at the company's Web site for $15.

Griot's Garage, (800) 345-5789. griotsgarage.com

INSTANT TRAYS WHERE YOU NEED THEM

The Magnetic Tool Cribs from Griot's Garage stick to metal surfaces, like your toolbox or vehicle, to provide instant trays right where you need them. They'll hold all your fasteners, parts and tools while you work in the shop or under the hood.

Each tray is held in place by large magnets, which are coated so they won't scratch paint. The set of four ($40; No. 77549) are 4-1/2 in. wide, 1-1/8 in. deep and range in length from 5-7/8 in. to 12-1/8 in. Buy them at the Web site below.

Griot's Garage, (800) 345-5789.

griotsgarage.com

"CLAW" BIKE STORAGE

Several types of bike storage products, from a simple hook in a rafter to elaborate floor-to-ceiling racks, are available at home centers. Some work great, others not so well. Gladiator's Claw is in the first category. It fastens to a rafter with two screws, then holds a bike rim to suspend the bike from the ceiling. The Claw uses a plunger system—press the tire against the plunger pad and the hook arms wrap around and hold the rim. Press the pad again to open.

The Claw can hold up to 75 lbs., and the rubber-coated arms won't scratch your rims. Although the Claw is admittedly expensive at $40, it's durable and easy to use. Find retailers on the company's Web site or buy it on amazon.com.

Gladiator GarageWorks, (866) 342-4089.

gladiatorgw.com

New Tools&Gear

AFFORDABLE, POWERFUL IMPACT WRENCH

One of my favorite "go-to" tools is a 1/2-in. electric impact wrench. Simply put, it'll take care of problems and speed up jobs like no other tool can. I use mine for driving lag screws, changing tires on vehicles, and loosening nuts and bolts that are so stubborn even a breaking bar can't break them free. And since it's electric, I don't have to hassle with hooking up a compressor and running air hoses. I've had my impact wrench for more than 20 years, and it cost me a whopping $250.

But the Kobalt 1/2-in. heavy-duty impact wrench only costs $140, *and* it comes with a 12-piece set of SAE six-shouldered sockets, rugged enough to handle the enormous 420 ft.-lbs. of torque the wrench generates. (If you buy a set of metrics to fill out the set, be sure you get ones that are rated for impact wrenches.)

Kobalt, kobalttools.com

JACK STANDS

3-TON JACK KIT LIFTS VEHICLES FAST

If you're still using the jack from your trunk to lift your car, you know what a slow process it is. Check out the Kobalt 3 ton garage combo kit, which can safely jack up a vehicle in seconds. The kit consists of a heavy-duty floor jack and a pair of jack stands. Jack stands are crucial for safety if you're working under the car. But what really makes this combo kit special is the $125 price tag. A floor jack and jack stands of this quality typically cost a couple hundred bucks or more

Voted the best value for the money by readers

when bought separately. The only downside: The jack is super heavy and hard to carry, so it's only for your garage. The kit is available at Lowe's stores (item no. 89476) and lowes.com.

Lowe's, (800) 445-6937. lowes.com

WASH-AND-RINSE NOZZLE

Forget about mixing soapy water in a bucket for washing your vehicles. Spend $15 on Griot's nozzle and car wash dispenser instead. Fill the soap reservoir with up to 3 ozs. of car wash soap, then spray it on the vehicle. Give the dial on top a quarter turn to change from soapy water to plain water for rinsing. Ten spray patterns let you choose the spray you want. The padded handle is so comfortable that you'll want to open your own car wash. You can order the nozzle (item No. 92526) by phone or buy it directly on the company's Web site. **Griot's Garage, (800) 345-5789. griotsgarage.com**

GARAGE DOOR UPGRADES

If you're in the market for a new garage door, consider upgrading to an energy-efficient model. You'll reduce your energy bills, and you may also qualify for a homeowner's tax credit equal to 30 percent of the cost of the garage door! (Visit energystar.gov for details on the tax credit.)

Clopay's Classic Line Collection Premium Series garage doors (model 9203 shown at left) now feature three layers of polyurethane insulation foam sandwiched between galvanized steel layers with a thermal break. Single doors start at $750 and double doors at $1,300. The added insulation nearly doubles the thermal protection offered by older insulated garage door models and bumps the R-value up to a whopping R-17.2.

Other Clopay garage door collections with the same three-layer insulation option include the Coachman Collection (shown below, $1,200 for a single door and $2,400 for a double door), the Gallery Collection and the Grand Harbor Collection. Clopay's Web site provides detailed information on all these collections. It also includes a free interactive Web tool that lets homeowners upload a digital image of their home to "try on" garage door designs in a variety of materials and colors to find the perfect match. **clopaydoor.com, (800) 225-6729**

AUTO & GARAGE

BURGLAR-PROOF
YOUR GARAGE

by **Jeff Gorton**

Garages make easy targets for all types of thieves, whether it's teens who steal beer from your garage fridge or professional burglars who start by "garage shopping" and then return the next time you're away to clean you out.

In about one-fifth of home breakins, the thief enters through the service door on the garage. We spoke to a specialist in burglary prevention to come up with this list of things you can do to keep out the crooks. All the strategies are simple, fast and cheap, and will really enhance your security.

Don't leave your remote in the car

Thieves know right where to look for your garage door opener remote—clipped to the visor in your car. To avoid giving them easy access to your garage, take the remote with you when you leave the car. The handiest way to do this is to replace your big remote with a small keychain version ($30 to $40 at home centers or where you bought your garage door opener). Match the remote to the brand and year of your opener. Then follow the instructions for programming it.

If you've lost the remote for the garage door opener, it's possible that it has ended up in the wrong hands. To be safe, follow the instructions that came with your opener to reset the code, disabling the lost remote.

Disable the overhead door

When you go away on vacation, unplug the garage door opener. If you don't have an opener, padlock the latch or disable the door by putting a bolt through one of the holes in the garage door track. This will prevent someone from coming in through the overhead door while you're away.

Scare away thieves with motion detector lights

Replacing existing light fixtures with ones that have a built-in motion detector is an easy way to make your garage and house more secure. Burglars will be reluctant to jimmy open a door or window when they're working under a bright light. Or you can add a standalone motion detector that connects to your existing lights. If you live in a cold climate, don't use compact fluorescent bulbs in the light fixture. They take too long to light in winter, giving thieves extra time for their mischief.

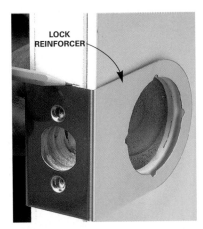

1 Prevent the door from splitting by wrapping it with a metal lock reinforcer. Mark the edge of the door and chisel a shallow recess so the reinforcer is flush to the door's edge when it's installed.

2 Reinforce the weakest link on your service door by installing a heavy-duty strike plate with extra-long screws that penetrate the framing at least 1 in.

Fortify the service door

For a service door, the solution is to install a good-quality dead bolt and reinforce the doorjamb and hinges to resist a brute-force attack. The best dead bolts have an ANSI Grade 1 rating, but even a Grade 2 lock will provide above-average security. Look for the rating on the package. But even the best dead bolt won't help if the doorjamb and door aren't reinforced. Before installing the dead bolt, strengthen the lock area of the door with a metal sleeve (**Photo 1**). Then install a strong strike plate that's securely attached to the wall framing with long screws (**Photo 2**). Heavy-duty strike plates are available at home centers and hardware stores.

Hinges that are installed with the usual wimpy 3/4-in. screws are nearly as easy to kick in as a wimpy door latch. So while you've got the drill and screws handy, remove one of the short screws nearest the weather stripping from each hinge and replace it with a 3-in. screw (**Photo 3**). If you have an attached garage, use these same methods to reinforce the door from the garage into your house. Also make sure to keep this door locked; otherwise, a burglar who gains access to the garage can walk right in.

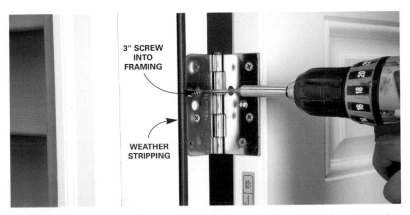

3 Strengthen the hinge side of the door by replacing one of the screws in each hinge with a 3-in.-long screw that penetrates the framing.

AUTO & GARAGE

Cover windows to stop prying eyes

To prevent burglars from "casing the joint," cover glass so they can't "window shop." Use curtains, shades or blinds. Or apply a translucent film to the glass that obscures vision but still lets in light. Plastic film like this is available in several patterns and costs $8 to $15 for an average-size window. You'll find it in the window covering department of home centers as well as at full-service hardware stores and window covering retailers. It's also available online (search for "privacy window film"). Installation is simple. Follow the instructions included with the film you purchase.

RAZOR KNIFE   PLASTIC WINDOW FILM

Bar the windows to prevent break-ins

If they can't simply enter through an open door, burglars will often try to come through windows because most are relatively easy to pry open or break. Breaking a window is their last choice because of the noise. Luckily it's not difficult to eliminate this possible entry point. First, make sure to lock windows if possible. If you have windows that you don't open, screw them shut. But for the ultimate window security, add strong bars across the window so that thieves can't get in even if they pry open the window or break the glass.

Ready-made bars are available, but it's easier and cheaper to use a few lengths of 1/2-in. steel pipe (**photo left**). Use either precut and threaded pieces of 1/2-in. steel pipe or measure for the lengths you need and have the pipe cut and threaded at the hardware store. Space bars every 6 to 8 in. Get two tees, two 3/8-in. washers and two 3-1/2-in. x 3/8-in. lag screws for each bar. Thread a tee onto each end of the pipes. Then attach the pipes to the framing by running a lag screw through a washer, then through the tee and into the framing. Expect to spend about $8 per bar.

TEE   LAG SCREW

1/2" STEEL PIPE   WASHER

Keep the garage door closed

Leaving the garage door open is practically an invitation to burglars, not to mention that you're really presenting a storefront window display of your possessions to anyone driving by. But if you're like a lot of other people and tend to forget to close the door, or have kids who forget, there's an easy solution. Install a device that signals your garage door opener to close the door after a predetermined amount of time. One brand is Garage Butler (about $60; garagebutler.com; 918-274-1037). You can set the amount of time that elapses before the door closes, or override the control if you want the door to remain open. It takes about an hour to install the sensors on the garage door track and the keypad that connects to the opener control. One more point: When you're leaving for work, don't just hit the remote button to close the door and then drive away. Wait until it closes to make sure it doesn't reopen. ⌂

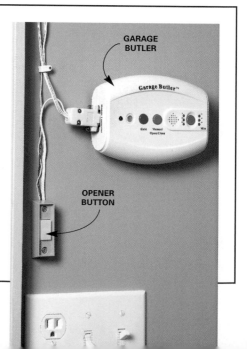

GARAGE BUTLER

OPENER BUTTON

Question&Comment

HEAT A GARAGE

I'd like to heat my garage so I can work on projects in the winter. But I don't know what type of heater is best or what size to get. Can you give me advice?

We recommend a ceiling-mounted, gas-fired, forced-air unit heater. Some installers recommend infrared heaters because they heat objects instead of air. You'll be warmed and so will the floor (if it's free of vehicles). But you won't be happy with the cold tools inside your tool chest. Infrared heaters are no more energy efficient than forced-air heaters, and they cost about twice as much.

The least expensive alternative is a portable kerosene or propane heater. But they're a poor choice. They require ventilation (think "open door") and pump gallons of water vapor into your garage. That means working with a constant cold draft and putting up with smelly exhaust and burning eyes. Then there's the issue of rust on your tools from all that humidity. Kerosene and propane heaters just aren't a good solution if you work in the garage regularly.

So bite the bullet and buy a ceiling-mounted, forced-air unit heater that's rated for residential use (building inspectors won't OK an industrial unit in a residential garage). Plan to spend $500 to $650, plus the cost of professional installation. Advanced DIYers can install a unit heater, which involves gas lines, venting and electrical work. But don't skip the permits and inspections. An improper installation can kill you. Check with the inspector to see if it's even legal in your area to perform your own gas hookups.

If you'll be working on wood projects or using spray finishes, choose a heater with a separate combustion chamber. They burn fresh outside air instead of the dust or paint-laden air inside a garage. There's a slight fire danger using a conventional heater, and the dust and paint particles will cause burner problems that require service calls.

Some unit heaters are more compact than others and can be mounted within 1 in. of the ceiling. So review the dimensions of the heater and calculate the installed height to ensure proper headroom.

To help size the heater and estimate monthly energy costs, consult modine.com/hotdawg and ultimate-garageheater.com. Most residential garages require heaters with a capacity of 30,000 or 45,000 Btu. Your heater size depends on the garage's square footage, ceiling height and insulation, so don't guess. And don't oversize your heater—especially if you intend to leave it on (even at a reduced temperature) all winter. An oversize unit heater cycles too often and wastes energy.

If you have an attached garage, mount the thermostat on the common wall between the garage and the house and away from the heated airflow. In a detached garage, mount it on the wall below the heater.

Mount the unit heater in a corner and aim it at a 45-degree angle toward the garage door. Point the louvers down. Locate the thermostat away from the airflow.

GAS SHUTOFF

FURNACE POWER SWITCH

THERMOSTAT

HandyHints®

SPRING CLAMP

1-1/2" PLASTIC PIPE

HANG-IT-HIGH HELPER

This classic handy storage hint makes the most of hard-to-reach areas in your garage. Use this homemade extension pole to hang items in high or awkward spots. Attach a spring clamp to the end of 1-1/2-in. plastic pipe, and use the crotch between the handles of the clamp to lift items on or off a hook or nail.

GARAGE CEILING TRACK STORAGE

If you store stuff in big plastic storage bins and you need a place to put them, how about the garage ceiling? Screw 2x2s to the ceiling framing with 3-1/2-in. screws spaced every 2 ft. Use the bins as a guide for spacing the 2x2s. The lips on the bins should just brush against the 2x2s when you're sliding the bins into place. Then center and screw 1x4s to the 2x2s with 2-in. screws. The garage ceiling is a perfect place to store light and medium-weight seasonal items like holiday decorations and camping gear.

3-1/2" SCREW

2x2

2" SCREW

1x4

CAR DOOR PROTECTOR

Here's a way to prevent dings in your car doors and dents in your finished garage walls. Use a pool noodle toy ($3) instead of a regular door guard ($20). Just make a slit in the noodle with a utility knife, run a Bungee cord or a rope through the middle and attach it to screw eyes on the garage wall. Now that's using your noodle!

SCREW EYE

STUD

Gallery of Ideas

FROM SEPTEMBER, 2009, p. 32

THE NEATEST GARAGE ON THE BLOCK

Project Facts

Cost: About $200

Skill level: Beginner

Time: 1 weekend

This system is very simple and fast to build, plus you'll find everything you need at a home center or hardware store.

BACK-DOOR STORAGE CENTER

Project Facts

Cost: $150 per cabinet

Skill level: Intermediate

Time: 3 hours per cabinet

If you have an attached garage, the door to your house often ends up being a dumping ground. Customize these cabinets to handle your family's clutter.

FROM SEPTEMBER, 2009, p. 42

FROM SEPTEMBER, 2009, p. 21

GARAGE FINISHING TIPS

Project Facts

Cost: Varies

Skill level: Intermediate to advanced

Time: Varies

Convert your drafty, dingy, dusty garage into a bright, comfortable workspace.

To order $3 photocopies of complete articles for the projects shown here, call (715) 246-4521, email familyhandyman@nrmsinc.com or write to: Copies, The Family Handyman, P.O. Box 83695, Stillwater, MN 55083-0695. Many public libraries also carry back issues of *The Family Handyman* magazine.

AUTO & GARAGE

TFH BEST

BEST
WORKBENCH UPGRADES

Our favorite ways to add storage, convenience and handy features to any workbench

by Jeff Gorton

To find the best ideas for simple workbench upgrades, we sampled the workbenches of our staff and pro friends. No matter what kind of workbench you have, you can add one or all of these improvements to make your bench more functional and fun to use.

The largest project here, the three roll-out drawers, only requires one sheet of 3/4-in. plywood and less than a day to build. The rest of the projects require even less time and materials. You could build any of these projects with basic carpentry tools and a circular saw, drill and jigsaw. But a table saw will simplify the process by adding speed and accuracy. And, of course, a pneumatic trim nailer would be handy for building the shallow drawers and for tacking together the roll-out drawers before you strengthen them with screws.

1 Easiest add-on drawers

These roll-out drawers are easy—you don't even have to mount them to the bench. They're just sturdy boxes that ride on 2 in. casters. Measure from the floor to the bottom shelf of your workbench and subtract 3-1/4 in. to figure the height of the boxes. Then subtract 3/4 in. from this measurement to determine the height of the drawer front, back and sides. Next, decide how many drawers you want and calculate the widths. Allow for a 1/2-in. space between drawers.

Cut the parts and screw them together. Then measure the width and length of the box and cut the bottom. Screw on the bottom and cut a handhold in the front of the drawer with a jigsaw. Finish up by screwing 2-in. fixed (not swiveling!) casters to the bottom of the drawer as shown.

Build basic plywood boxes and screw on the casters. Carefully align the casters parallel to the box sides so the drawers roll smooth and straight.

2 Our favorite 15-minute workbench accessory

This tool tray is so simple to build that you can have it mounted in about 15 minutes, start to finish. It's a great place to keep small, commonly used tools handy but off the benchtop. And it keeps pencils and other small tools from rolling or getting knocked off the bench and landing on the floor where you can't find them.

Building the tray couldn't be simpler. Just cut a 1x4 and two 1x3s 24 in. long and nail the 1x3s to the sides of the 1x4. Cut two pieces of 1x3 5 in. long and nail them to the ends to complete the tray. Screw the tray to the end of your workbench and you'll never waste time searching for a pencil again.

③ Our favorite convenience feature

Every bench needs easy-access storage for all the odds and ends that would otherwise clutter the benchtop. These shallow drawers, which mount directly under the benchtop, fit the bill perfectly.

There's no fancy joinery on these drawers. And the special pencil drawer slides simplify mounting. We used 22-in.-deep drawer slides and built the drawers 22 in. deep to match. The drawer slides (No. KV8250; $24 a pair) are available from wwhardware.com (800-383-0130).

You can build the drawers up to about 30 in. wide, but remember to allow a few inches of space on each side for the mounting hardware. Rip strips of 3/4-in. plywood or solid lumber to 3-1/4 in. wide for the front, sides and back. Cut the sides 22 in. long and the front and back pieces 1-1/2 in. less than the desired width of the drawer. Glue and nail the sides to the front and back. Then measure the width and length of the drawer and cut a bottom from 1/4-in. plywood. Glue and nail the bottom to the assembled frame. If you're careful to cut the bottom piece perfectly square, your drawer will be square. Or you can hold one side and the drawer front against a framing square while you nail on the bottom.

Photo 1 shows how to attach the drawer slide. Line up the bottom of the slide with the seam between the drawer bottom and drawer side. If you don't have 2x4 crosspieces under your bench, add them in the location of the drawer hardware. Then prop up the drawer in the right spot and screw through the brackets into the crosspieces (Photo 2). Finish by cutting drawer fronts that are 1-1/2 in. longer and 1/2 in. taller than the drawer. Attach the drawer front from the back with 1-1/4-in. screws driven through the front of the drawer box.

1 **Mount the drawers with special "pencil drawer" slides. These slides include hanger brackets, so you don't have to build extra parts just to attach the drawer slides.**

PENCIL DRAWER SLIDE

2 **Prop up the drawer and screw it to the underside of the workbench. Add crosspieces if there's nothing to screw into.**

ADDED CROSSPIECE

TEMPORARY SUPPORT

Best benchtop space-saver

When you want to use the whole top of your workbench, a permanently mounted vise or grinder just gets in the way. Free up space by mounting your grinder and vise to a double-thick piece of 3/4-in. plywood and hanging them on the end of your workbench until they're needed.

Cut four 20-in.-long x 12-in.-wide pieces of 3/4-in. plywood. Glue and nail them together in pairs to make two 1-1/2-in.-thick slabs. Transfer the location of the mounting holes on your vise and grinder to the plywood. Use a 1-in. spade bit to drill a 1/2-in.-deep recess at each hole location. Then drill through the plywood with a 3/8-in. bit and mount the tools with 3/8-in. bolts, washers and nuts. Position the recess on the side of the plywood opposite the tool to ensure a flush surface.

We screwed a double-thick piece of 3/4-in. plywood to the end of the workbench to make a sturdy mounting plate, but your workbench may not need this. Any strong, flat surface will work. Drill two 1/2-in. holes into each tool holder and mark matching hole locations on the mounting plate. Drill 3/8-in. holes at the marks and attach 3/8-in. bolts with nuts and washers. We recessed the nuts in the mounting plate so the tool holders would sit flush, but this isn't necessary.

Most versatile hold-down system

You don't need a super-expensive vise or fancy clamps to hold large projects while you work on them. An inexpensive woodworker's vise paired with shop-made bench dogs will do the trick. We ordered this Adjustable Clamp medium-duty vise online ($45 from 7corners.com; 800-328-0457). You may have to cut and notch your workbench to make the vise fit. The goal is to align the top of the jaw flush with the top of the bench. If your workbench is less than 3/4 in. thick, reinforce it by gluing and screwing a 2x4 block underneath the vise area. Then drill 1-in. holes 1/2 in. deep to recess the mounting bolt holes, and bolt the vise to the top of the workbench.

You can extend the versatility of your woodworker's vise by drilling a series of 3/4-in. holes 4 in. apart in your bench-top. Drill the holes in a line at a right angle to the clamp jaws and centered on the sliding steel dog built into the vise. You can buy plastic or metal bench dogs to fit the holes, or make some simple plywood and dowel dogs like ours.

To make a bench dog, rip a scrap of plywood to 2-1/2 in. wide. Set your miter saw to 10 degrees and cut a 2-1/2-in. length from the strip of plywood to form a 2-1/2-in. square with one beveled side. Drill a 3/4-in. hole in the center of the plywood square and glue a 4-in. length of 3/4-in. hardwood dowel into the hole. The short side of the bevel should be on the side with the dowel extending from it. Face the beveled side of the bench dog toward the piece you're clamping. The bevel keeps the workpiece from sliding up and over the dog.

6 Our favorite double-duty bench stop

Here's a simple add-on that can do double duty as a stop or outfeed support for your miter saw. Elevate the sliding piece of plywood slightly above the work surface and use it to keep your work from sliding backward while you're belt sanding. Or adjust it upward to match the height of your miter saw bed and use it as a support for long stock.

Cut a piece of plywood 8 in. wide x 20 in. long. Then mark 3/8-in.-wide slots 2 in. from each end and 1 in. from the top and bottom. Drill 3/8-in. starter holes and cut the slots with a jigsaw as shown below. Use the completed bench stop as a pattern to mark the bolt locations.

We screwed 5/16-in. x 4-1/2-in. hanger bolts into our thick workbench top, but you may have to use another method on your workbench. Hanger bolts have wood threads on one end and machine threads on the other. Drill a 7/32-in. starter hole. Then thread two nuts onto the bolt and tighten them against each other. Now place a wrench on the outermost nut and screw in the hanger bolt. Leave 1-1/4 in. of the bolt protruding. Remove the nuts. Mount the bench stop to the bolts with washers and wing nuts.

3/8" HOLE

Cut slots in a piece of 3/4-in. plywood and attach it to your bench with bolts and wing nuts. Drill 3/8-in. starter holes. Then cut the slots with a jigsaw.

5/16" x 4-1/2" HANGER BOLT

3/8" SLOT

⑦ Simplest support for long boards

Have you ever needed to hold a long board or door on edge to work on it but struggled to find a good method? If you have a woodworker's vise, adding this board jack is an easy solution. The board jack shown hooks onto the beveled support strip and slides along it to adjust for the length of the workpiece. The 3/4-in. dowel adjusts up and down to accommodate different widths.

Start by ripping a 45-degree angle on a 1x3 board or strip of plywood. Screw the strip to the front of your workbench (**photo right**). Then build a board jack like the one shown. Drill 3/4-in. holes every 6 in. and insert a 4-in. dowel in the hole to support your work. Adjust the length of the stand-off to hold the board jack plumb on your workbench.

3/4" DOWEL →

3/4" HOLE →

BOARD
JACK

STANDOFF
↓

Mount a board jack to the front of your workbench and use it with your vise to support your work. Screw a beveled strip to the front of your workbench. Then build the board jack and hook it over the top to support your work.

OUR FAVORITE
PAINTING GEAR

by Brett Martin

Here at *The Family Handyman*, we spend a lot of time painting. In this story, we'll share the painting tricks and tools we use every day. These ideas and products will not only save you time but also eliminate a lot of hassles—like moving unwieldy ladders and spreading out massive drop cloths. All of the products mentioned here are available at paint stores and home centers.

Our favorite floor protector

If you're only painting walls and not the ceiling, don't bother spreading a drop cloth across the entire floor. Just cover the perimeter with a narrow canvas drop cloth ($13 for 4 x 12 ft.). A 3- or 4-ft.-wide strip provides enough space for your ladder and materials, and plenty of room to stand on. It's easier to set up and move than a large square, and it fits conveniently in doorways. We use canvas drop cloths instead of plastic because they're easy to spread out and they stay in place without tape. And they're not slippery!

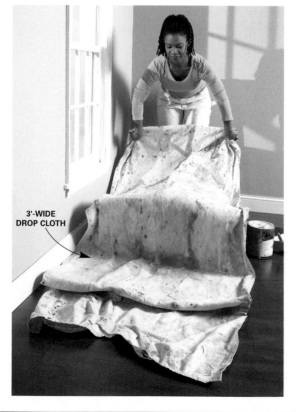

3'-WIDE DROP CLOTH

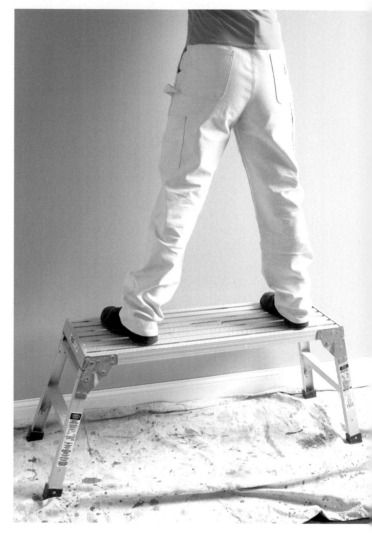

Our favorite product for painting up high

We discovered this work platform five years ago—and we've been using it daily in our photo studio ever since. It's the perfect height to stand on to reach the top of 8-ft. walls, making it ideal for painting along ceilings. Truth be told, I spend a lot of time sitting on it too.

The platform gives you a wider standing space than a ladder and extends your reach, so you don't have to climb down and move it as often. When you do need to reposition it, you'll find the aluminum platform lightweight and easy to carry. The legs lock in place, keeping the platform stable while you work, and fold up for easy storage. It also costs less than most ladders. The Tricam model (WP-20-B; tricamindustries.com) costs $38 at Menards, and the Werner version (AP-20-MP6; wernerladder.com) costs $43 at Lowe's and Home Depot.

Our favorite rollers for a lint-free paint job

Sure, you can buy a 99¢ roller cover, but then you'll waste time picking fuzz out of your freshly painted walls because the cover will shed as you use it. Cheap covers also get matted easily, which changes the texture of your painted surface. It's much smarter to spend at least $5 to get a quality cover that will give you a consistent texture, without shedding lint. More-expensive rollers also hold paint better than cheap covers, so you don't have to reload as often. Look for covers that say "woven" or "lint-free" on the packaging, or ask a paint store employee for help picking one.

NO-SHED ROLLER COVER

Our favorite tool for cleaning paintbrushes

PAINTER'S COMB

A $5 painter's comb helps remove caked-on latex paint that won't wash off your paintbrush bristles. And after washing, the comb helps straighten the bristles so they don't fan out as the brush dries.

A good paintbrush will last a lifetime if you take care of it. Here's how: After painting, while your brush is still wet, wipe it on newspaper to get rid of excess paint. Then stick the brush in a bucket of warm, soapy water (any liquid soap will do) and slosh it around to wash out the paint.

Hold the brush under running water and run the painter's comb through it, especially near the ferrule, to remove dried paint and buildup. When the water coming off the brush is clear, the brush is clean. Comb the bristles again to get them straight and let the brush air-dry. Finally, to keep the bristles straight, wrap it with heavy paper (like a grocery bag) and hang it from a hook or store it flat.

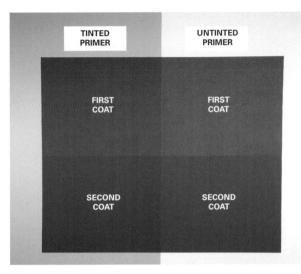

TINTED PRIMER

UNTINTED PRIMER

FIRST COAT

FIRST COAT

SECOND COAT

SECOND COAT

Our best tip for superior coverage

Some vibrant paint colors, especially oranges and reds, don't cover existing paint colors well. If you're painting over a light color, it might take three, four or even five coats. And even then the color might be off. Try a tinted primer instead.

Have the paint store tint your primer gray. Prime the walls or woodwork with the gray primer, then one coat of paint (two at the most!) will cover nicely. It will also give you a "truer" color, one that's closer to the paint chip you chose at the store. Tinted primer also works great for covering varnished woodwork that you want to paint.

Primer is less expensive than paint, so you'll save money applying primer and then paint instead of rolling on two (or more) coats of paint. Primer also adheres better to the wall and improves paint durability.

TINTED PRIMER

Our favorite (fast!) roller cover cleaner

The Roller Washer ($25) does the impossible: It gets roller

covers clean—and does it in five minutes. Just insert the cover into the tube, screw the cap on, attach it to a faucet and flush out the paint with water. Call (585) 335-9119 or send an e-mail to rollerwasher@frontier.com to find out where to get one in your area.

ROLLER WASHER

Our best tip for opening paint cans

You can open a paint can with a screwdriver, but it'll leave

dents in the lid as you pry it off, making it tough to reseal the can to keep the paint fresh. A paint can opener is designed so the tip slides under the lid and lifts it off without damaging it. And it costs less than a buck!

PAINT CAN/ BOTTLE OPENER

Our best tip for smooth paint

If you want a sleek finish but don't want to use spray equipment, buy foam rollers or mohair roller covers. Unlike standard rollers, foam and mohair don't lift the wet paint as they roll it on, creating a bumpy texture. Use them to paint doors or anything else that requires a smooth finish.

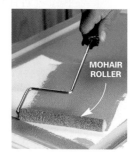

MOHAIR ROLLER

You can't go wrong with either cover—it's all about preference. Find mohair covers ($5 and up) at paint stores and amazon.com.

Our favorite paint pail

When you're painting with a brush, don't paint from the can. A can is awkward to hold and the grooves get full of paint. It's also hard to tap your loaded brush against the sides of the can to knock off the drips. Instead, check out the HANDy Paint Pail ($10; handypaintpail.com).

It's a simple concept—a small pail with a handle along the side—that makes paint easy to carry when you're painting trim or cutting in on walls. A magnet holds the brush out of the paint to keep the handle and ferrule clean. But what sold us on it are the disposable pail liners ($5 for a six-pack). When you're done painting, just take the liner out and throw it away—cleanup is a breeze!

Our favorite poly—no brush required!

We're big fans of wipe-on poly ($6 per qt.) and use it in our studio and shops. It gives you an impeccable finish—no brushstrokes, drips or streaking—and you can coat a dresser in about 15 minutes. You can also get into crevices without worrying about runs. The poly dries quickly, so airborne dust doesn't cause bumps in the finish, and you can recoat in a few hours. The drawback is you usually need several coats. Minwax (minwax.com) and Watco (watco.net) are two brands. ⌂

Question & Comment Special

HOME CARE MYTHS— BUSTED!

by Rick Muscoplat

No "Best of TFH" collection would be complete without some good, old-fashioned myth busting. We talked with top-notch experts to get the scoop on these "holy grail" myths and misunderstandings. You'll be surprised by what we found—and you'll save money by following their advice.

MYTH.

Leaving my computer on all the time makes it last longer.

This myth had some basis 20 years ago when hard drives bit the dust early from frequent on/off cycles. It's no longer true. From a power-use standpoint, leaving it on ALWAYS uses more power than shutting it off—even when it's in "sleep" or "hibernate" mode. Leaving it on also increases your risk of catastrophic damage from power surges—even with a surge protector. So turn off the power strip or unplug your computer when you're not using it.

MYTH.

Laundry bleach is the best product to remove mold and keep it from returning.

EPA researchers compared 12 over-the-counter cleaning products with diluted household bleach. They used each product to clean the mold on individual samples of painted and bare gypsum drywall. Then they stored the samples under ideal mold growing conditions and monitored them to see how much mold returned. Diluted bleach scored the worst on bare (unpainted) drywall. It fared better on painted drywall, but not as well as the leading cleaning product, full-strength Lysol All-Purpose Cleaner Orange Breeze. The researchers also tested the cleaners on wallpapered samples and mold-inhibiting paints. To read the research paper, go to springerlink.com and search for "wallboard microbial."

MYTH.

Cheese is the best bait for mousetraps.

Cheese isn't on any mouse's "top-10 list." They'll only eat it if nothing else is available. Plus, cheese hardens after sitting out for a while, making it easier for mice to "steal" the bait without setting off the trap. The perfect bait is actually peanut butter or bacon, or a blend of peanut butter and

bacon grease. Mice can't resist the smell and taste. So wipe that on the trip mechanism to get the greatest number of "catches."

BACON

PEANUT BUTTER

POLYURETHANE CAULK

ELASTOMERIC STUCCO PAINT

1-1/2" NAP

MYTH.

Duct cleaning is something that should be done regularly.

Most homes never need duct cleaning. There are some exceptions, however. If you find mold, or rodent or insect nests in the ducts, eliminate the source of the contamination or infiltration and have the ducts professionally cleaned and disinfected. Expect to pay $350 to $1,000 for a thorough job that includes scrubbing the ducts with special brushes. Avoid cheap duct cleaning "specials" for $100 or less. Those low-cost services usually just blow compressed air through the ducts. That gets the loose dust moving, but it doesn't clean the mold or rodent or insect residues.

MISUNDERSTANDING.

You should never paint stucco.

Ordinary house paint seals the pores on stucco. And as the stucco expands and contracts, the paint cracks, breaking the seal. Then water enters the stucco, gets trapped inside, and pretty soon the paint starts to delaminate. It doesn't take long before you're left with sections of bare stucco and patches of paint—not a pretty sight.

However, you can use elastomeric paint, which is formulated for stucco. It expands and contracts with the stucco and resists cracking (one brand is Valspar Duramax Elastomeric Exterior Masonry and Stucco Paint, $26 per gallon). Elastomeric paints also breathe, allowing moisture to get out. The best part: DIYers can apply it themselves.

If you don't want to paint your stucco, consider hiring a contractor to "fog" it. Fogging contractors use a special spray gun that combines a colorant with a thin cement slurry. Fogging is much faster and cheaper than dashing and lasts almost as long.

COPPER

STANDARD GALVANIZED PIPE NIPPLE

DIELECTRIC UNION

MISUNDERSTANDING.

A dielectric union is all I need to protect my water heater from electrolysis/galvanic action.

Anytime you join two dissimilar metals (such as copper and galvanized pipe) and add water, you create a flow of electrons

DIELECTRIC NIPPLE

(electrolysis or galvanic action), that eventually destroys the galvanized pipe. For decades, plumbers have used an insulated dielectric union to prevent the damage. A dielectric union does provide a small measure of protection. But it's not enough to prevent the complete failure of the galvanized pipe (**top photo**).

Lab tests show that a 3-in. dielectric nipple (starting at $9) reduces current flow by 85 percent over the use of a dielectric union alone. So, next time you install a water heater, install a dielectric nipple in addition to a dielectric union. Buy them at a plumbing supply store or contact the manufacturer (perfectioncorp.com) at (800) 544-6344 to find a local distributor.

MYTH.

You should twist the wires before you put on the wire nut.

This advice comes right from the wire nut manufacturers. You do NOT have to twist the wires before applying the wire nut. Most high-quality wire nuts incorporate a square-cut spring-steel wire that literally bites into the copper wires as you twist it on. The spring wire expands and contracts as the electrical wires heat and cool, keeping them tightly bound. Continue twisting the wire nut even after it "hits bottom." Keep turning the nut until the wire insulation is twisted 1-1/2 in. past the wire nut.

Note: Some lighting fixtures come with wire nuts that don't have a spring-steel wire insert. Toss those freebies and use only high-quality wire nuts that have a wire insert.

MYTH.

The best time to water grass is in the evening so the water doesn't evaporate.

Evening watering does reduce evaporation, allowing the soil to soak up and hold more water. But it also sets up the perfect growing conditions for mold and other lawn diseases. The best time to water your lawn is in the early morning hours as the sun is rising. Late riser? Use a watering timer.

By the way, an impact sprinkler is the most efficient type of sprinkler. Avoid sprinklers that shoot fine spray or streams into the air—the water evaporates quickly.

IMPACT SPRINKLERS

HUGE MYTH.

Setback thermostats don't save money.

Sure, the furnace has to pump out a lot of BTUs to bring the house back up to the daytime temp. But studies have proven beyond a doubt that the fuel savings during the setback period far outweighs the cost of raising the temp again. Set the temperature back at least 5 degrees at night and 10 degrees during the day (when no one is home) and you'll save 20 percent on your heating/cooling bill (raise the temp by the same amount for cooling in summer). That will more than pay for the cost of the setback thermostat in the first year. 🏠

ShopTips™ Special

OUR **6 FAVORITE** SHOP TIPS

by **Travis Larson**

You can find me in my shop a good five times a week. Sure, having satellite TV and the Golf Channel might have something to do with it. But I actually do a lot of woodworking out there too. For this "Best of TFH" collection, I'm sharing six of my favorite shop tips. A few are oldies, the rest brand new, but in any case, I hope you find a few that help you out.

3/4" PLYWOOD

CORK TILE

SANDPAPER

1 Reusable sanding blocks

Foam sanding sponges are a great invention. They excel at sanding curved surfaces or drywall-taped inside corners, but at $3 apiece, they're not practical for sanding large, flat surfaces. Make your own reusable sanding blocks for about 35¢ each for the initial blocks and about 16¢ for rebuilt ones. Here's how:

Cut six blocks from scrap 3/4-in. plywood for each sandpaper grit you commonly use. Make them 2-1/2 in. x 4-3/4 in. Spray adhesive on both a square of cork tile and

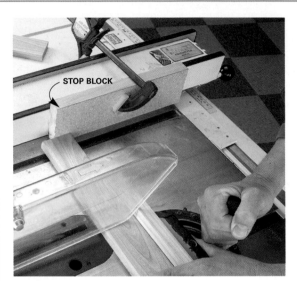

STOP BLOCK

2 1-in. crosscutting stop block

Here's an old tip that's worth repeating. When you're crosscutting on a table saw, set the cut length with a block clamped to the fence. Don't ever use the fence directly. That's a good way to get a board kicked back right at you. Ruptured organs and broken ribs—or worse—are a very real possibility.

Instead, clamp a block of wood to the fence before the blade. Then the end of the board will be free of the fence during and after the cut. If you make a block that's exactly 1 in. thick, you can set the fence scale at 1 in. greater than the length you're after. No tricky fractions involved.

10 of the blocks. One 12-in. cork tile ($5) will face 10 blocks. Stick 10 of the blocks to the cork and cut the cork flush with a utility knife. Then spray adhesive on a sheet of sandpaper. One sheet will face six blocks. Stick the sandpaper on six of the blocks cork side down as shown. Cut the sandpaper flush with the cork, and label the blocks.

When you wear out all six of a set of sanding blocks, soften the adhesive with a hair dryer, peel off the old sandpaper and apply new.

3 Stair gauge cutting guide

Stair gauges are usually used to lay out stair jacks. You clamp them to a carpenter's square to match the rise and run of a stair jack and then mark

the notches. But if you put them both on the same tongue of a carpenter's square, the combination makes a great crosscut guide for circular saws. Pick up a pair for less than $5 at any hardware store or home center. Clamp the square in place so it won't slide around while you're cutting. You wouldn't like that one bit.

STAIR GAUGE

4 Try a drafting square

When you need an accurate square in the 2- to 3-ft. range, your options are limited. Drywall squares are notoriously inaccurate and cumbersome. Carpenter squares involve that nagging hassle of having to hook them onto the edge of your workpiece. If you have a drafting square lying around, drag it out to the shop. Or, go to an art supply store and pick one up ($5 or more). They're very accurate and you'll find yourself grabbing it nearly as often as you do the tape measure.

5 No more glue stains

To prevent stains caused by oozing glue along joints, clamp the pieces together without glue. Put tape on the joint, then cut along it with a sharp blade. Separate the pieces, apply the glue and clamp them together again. The glue will ooze onto the tape, not the wood. Peel off the tape before the glue dries.

6 Clamp small stuff with hot glue

When you have to cut, shape, file, sand or finish something small, reach for your hot glue gun and glue the piece to a pedestal stick. The hot glue will hold just about anything as well as or better than any clamp ever could—if using a clamp is even possible. When your project is complete, try to pop it loose with a putty knife, but don't use too much

force—you might tear out the wood or break the piece.

You have two options for breaking the grip: cold and heat. First, try sticking the workpiece into the freezer for an hour or so. Frozen glue will usually give way with very little force. If that doesn't work, try a hair dryer to soften the glue. Still stuck? Reach for the heat gun. But warm the piece slowly and from a distance to avoid scorching the wood or damaging the finish.

OUR **FAVORITE** HANDY HINTS

Bed leg boot

How many times have you stubbed your toe on your metal bed frame? Ouch! Here's a creative way to protect your piggies. Cover the bare metal leg and wheel with a foam beverage can holder. It'll save your toes and prevent carpet dents and hardwood floor scratches to boot!

FOAM BEVERAGE CAN HOLDER

PLASTIC WRAP

GARBAGE BAG

Spatter-proof painting

When you're painting, it's hard to work around sinks, pipes, toilets and light fixtures without getting paint on them. Painter's tape works at the edges, but it doesn't protect against drips and spatters, especially when you're using a roller. The next time you paint, wrap these obstacles with plastic wrap, a garbage bag or aluminum foil. Cleanup will be quicker, these products conform to any shape, and one of them is always on hand.

Microwave cleaner

Cleaning baked-on food and spills in your microwave is always an issue, so we thought it was time to run this classic tip again. Partially fill a measuring cup or coffee cup with water and add a slice of lemon. Boil the water for a minute, then leave the door closed and let the steam loosen the mess. After 10 minutes, open the door and just wipe away the mess.

CD DISPENSER

Handy string dispenser

Using a ball of string or twine can be awkward, especially when you pull on the end and the ball rolls out of your hand and halfway across the floor. Here's an idea to make it easier. Use a CD dispenser and stick the ball of string right on the spindle. Drill a hole into the top of the plastic cover, run the string out of the hole and you've got an easy way to control exactly how much string you take each time.

Portable paint colors

Here's a classic tip. Every time you paint a room a new color, dip a stir stick into the can and let it dry. On the stir stick write the name of the paint, the brand, the color number, the sheen and the room that was painted. When you need to match the color or find a complementary one, just grab the stir stick and take it along with you to the paint store.

Easy spackling

Removing wall anchors can leave behind deep holes to fill. Instead of using a putty knife and going back to the can each time, put the spackling compound in a plastic bag. Then just cut a notch in one corner and squeeze the compound into the hole. If it's too thick, add a bit of water and knead the bag to mix it in.

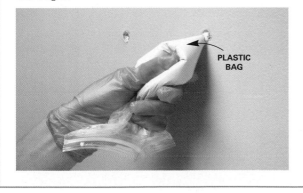

PLASTIC BAG

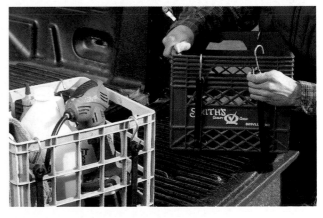

Stay-put storage crate

A lot of pickup owners keep a milk crate in the back of their truck to hold things like a tow rope and emergency gear. The crate tends to slide around unless you attach it to a tie-down loop in the truck bed. Solve the problem by wrapping rubber cords around the crate to give it some traction. The crate won't slide around, and you've got a great way to store cords, tools and supplies. 🏠

New Tools & Gear
Special

OUR FAVORITE
TOOLS UNDER $100

by **Brett Martin**

The editors of *The Family Handyman* enjoy talking about tools. We attend trade shows and talk to tool companies to stay abreast of the latest products and trends. But we also have our favorite tools—ones we've been using for years—and we wouldn't trade them for anything. This collection showcases our favorite tools that cost less than 100 bucks. They're available at home centers or online.

Versatile angle grinder cuts almost anything fast

An angle grinder excels at grinding down metal or masonry, but it's a must-have tool because it can do so much more.

My favorite use for an angle grinder is as a tile saw. Fitted with a diamond blade ($13), it'll cut just about any stone or ceramic tile. And the relatively small blade is perfect for the intricate cuts needed for outlet openings or the curved holes around a shower faucet.

Grinders cut metal fast too—all you need is a metal cutting wheel ($3). With wire wheels and brushes ($18 for a set of three), you can strip paint from metal or remove rust from wrought iron. For occasional use, a $40 to $50 angle grinder will work fine for all these jobs.

Go-through-anything hammer drills

"If you're going to buy a corded drill, get a hammer drill," said Joe Jensen, set builder for *The Family Handyman* and home improvement contractor. "It does everything a traditional drill does, but the hammering action lets you drill through tough materials faster—without burning up the bit."

The drills use a hard, fast pounding action while drilling. When you don't want the hammer feature, simply turn it off and use the drill like a standard one. Hammer drills have dropped in price considerably in recent years. You can now buy one for $60 (the model shown, the Hitachi No. FDV16VB2, costs about $80 at Lowe's and online).

"I just used my hammer drill when I was remodeling my basement," Joe said. "The drill easily drove concrete screws into the concrete and drew the plates tight against the floor."

Clamp-in-place straightedge

"I picked up this special clamping straightedge at a tool sale 15 years ago and still find myself reaching for it whenever I want to make a perfectly straight cut with a circular saw," said Jeff Gorton, associate editor. "The built-in clamps adjust quickly to plywood or lumber—and they're great for cutting off the bottom of doors."

Different lengths of straightedges are available, from 24 to 99 in. The 24-in. model costs $35. The BORA Edge Clamp from Affinity Tool Works is one brand (borapro.com).

"Just slide the back clamp until it's snug against the wood, and then press down the lever to lock the straightedge in place," Jeff said. "The whole process takes seconds and leaves you with a securely attached straightedge with no protruding clamps to get in the way. The grippy rubber clamp feet even let you clamp at angles up to 22.5 degrees as a guide for angled cuts."

You can find clamping straightedges at rockler.com and amazon.com.

Voted "Favorite Tool" by readers! Also the tool readers are most likely to buy.

CLAMPS

Voted 2nd favorite product by readers

Forever filter for shop vacuums

"About 10 years ago, I bought a CleanStream filter. I've worn out two shop vacuums since then, but that filter lives on," said Gary Wentz, senior editor. "Aside from immortality, the CleanStream has two more advantages: First, it's easy to clean. You can rinse it off with water, but I usually just take it outside and tap it against a tree; 90 percent of the dust drops off in 90 seconds. Second, it's a HEPA filter. That means it catches fine particles like drywall and sanding dust that pass right through other filters."

You'll notice the difference in the super-durable filter material when you touch it—the slickness keeps debris from sticking. A sturdy aluminum core maintains the shape of the filter when you tap it to clean it.

CleanStream filters cost $20 to $36, depending on the model (be sure to buy the filter that fits your shop vacuum brand). You can find the filters at home centers, hardware stores or on the company's Web site at cleanstream.com.

Drive concrete screws fast

If you drive lots of concrete screws, save time with a concrete screw installation kit (one brand is Buildex Tapcon, buildextapcon.com). It contains the masonry drill bit and screw drive on the same shaft. Ordinarily, you'd have to chuck a bit into the hammer drill, drill the hole and then take out the bit and chuck in the driver to run the screw in. Or use two drills. But with this, you drill the hole and just slip the driver shaft over the bit and sink the screw with the attached screw drive. The whole operation takes about 30 seconds. You'll find the kit (about $22) near the concrete screws at home centers.

TOOLS **UNDER $15**

Speedy socket driver

Buy a socket driver at a home center and you can leave your slow ratchet in the toolbox. It lets you use sockets in your drill, which is a great way to increase your drill's versatility. And it's cheap, too—$4 for the 1/4-in. socket driver and $6 for the 1/2-in. version.

$4

$14

Cheap shock insurance

This $14 noncontact voltage detector may be the best value ever. Hold it in front of an outlet or switch and an LED light and alarm will let you know if the power is on. It's also a fast way to track down breaks in circuits. They're available at home centers.

$13

Grabber for tight spots

This flexible magnet pickup tool ($13) is perfect for reaching into tight spots to retrieve dropped parts. Get the version that keeps the magnet shielded until you need it, then extends when you press the handle (otherwise the magnet sticks to things you don't want it to). Some also have fingers for picking up nonmetallic items. Get one at auto parts stores or amazon.com (search for "flexible magnet pickup tool").

$11

Pull nails with nippers

Put $11 nippers in your tool belt anytime you're removing trim and you'll make quick work out of pulling the old nails—without damaging the wood's surface. The sharp jaws bite into the nail, holding it firmly as you roll the nippers back to pull out the nail from the back side of the trim. Buy them at home centers.

$5

Odd-shape gauge

Whenever you need to mark an irregular shape, a contour gauge ($5) is a lifesaver. When you press the gauge against an object, the pins conform to the object's shape. Then you lock the pins in place and transfer the shape to whatever you're cutting. They're sold at home centers.

Double-fast chalk line

Speed chalk lines don't look any different from standard ones. But you'll notice the difference when you rewind—they rewind up to 3-1/2 times faster than standard chalk lines. Look for "fast retrieval" or "high-speed" on the packaging when buying one. Speed chalk lines are available starting at $7 at home centers and amazon.com.

$7

Greatest GreatGoofs®

The best "genius idea gone wrong" goof

I worked for a contractor who said he liked to give the hardest job to his laziest worker because the worker would figure out the easiest way to get it done. The drawback is that labor-saving ideas often end disastrously. Here's one of our favorites.

While taking down an old chain link fence, my dad and I came across a stubborn corner post. The other posts weren't set in concrete, but since this was a corner post and wouldn't budge, we figured it must be cemented in. So we wrapped a towing strap around the post and looped the other end over the hitch on our minivan. The van didn't pull out the post right away, so my dad backed up, shifted back into drive and punched the gas. The post "budged" at the speed of a missile launched from a giant slingshot. With precision aim, it shot through the back window of the van and darn near went through the passenger seat. Next time we'll stick with shovels.

The most submitted goof of all time

We ran this goof in March 1997 and soon discovered that this mistake is universal: Dozens of readers have told us the same tale of woe. So for the sake of your wallet and your pride, please pay attention before you cut doors!

I needed to cut 1 in. off the bottom of a door so it would clear my new carpet and pad. I removed the door, put it on sawhorses, measured carefully, then made a very precise cut—off the top of the door. **Note:** See "Litter-box olympics," p. 281, for a very funny version of this goof.

The best "unexpected shower" goof

Readers often forget the cardinal rule of plumbing—never pour water down drains or flush toilets when working on drain lines. Here's a classic.

The drainpipe under our kitchen sink was leaking, so my husband said he'd fix it. After removing the pipe, he needed to run to the store to pick up some new parts. He said no one—repeat, no one—should use the sink until he got back. A few seconds later, I heard water gushing, so I ran into the kitchen. With water on his shoes and on the floor, and his face beet red, my husband explained sheepishly, "I thought I'd wash my hands before I went to the hardware store."

SPECIAL SECTION
BEST OF TFH

Car&Garage Special

5 AUTO FIXES THAT SAVE YOU CASH!

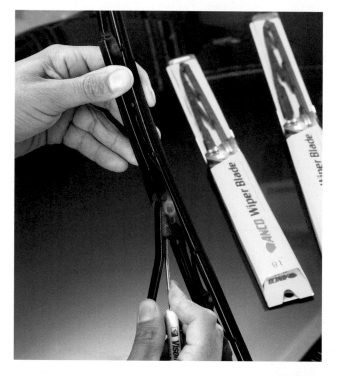

by **Rick Muscoplat**

Here are five of the best ways to save money on car maintenance. These are easy jobs that you can do yourself in minutes instead of overpaying at the oil-change joint. Do each one, as needed, throughout the year, and you'll leave about $175 in your wallet.

Replace the wiper blades

DIY savings: $20

It's easy to tell when your blades need replacing. Simply press the washer button and see if your blades wipe clean. If they streak, they're toast. The auto parts store will have lots of economy blades, but go with a name brand instead (ANCO, Trico or Bosch). They cost more than economy blades, but their higher-quality rubber wipes better, has better UV protection and lasts longer.

Follow the installation instructions on the package. Be sure you have a firm grip on the wiper arm once you remove the old blade. If it gets away from you, it can hit the windshield with enough force to crack it.

Shake your PCV valve

DIY savings: $12

This sounds complex, but it's not. Pull out your PCV valve every other oil change. In most cases, you'll find the valve on the top of the engine, connected to a vacuum hose. Some late-model cars don't have PCV valves, so don't beat yourself up trying to find it. Slide the vacuum hose off the valve and unscrew the valve. Then perform the world's easiest diagnostic test: Shake it. If it makes a metallic clicking sound, it's good. If it doesn't make noise or sounds mushy, replace it ($4). But don't replace it on appearance alone—all used PCV valves look dirty.

Need help locating your PCV valve? Buy a short subscription to an online

OLD PCV

factory service manual (oem1stop.com); rates start at $10 a day. Non-factory manuals are cheaper, but they're skimpy on instructions and diagrams for these kinds of repairs.

DIRT AND LEAVES

PASSES TEST

Replace your air filters

DIY savings: $30

Told that your engine air filter needs replacing? It may be true. But testing your filter is easy and replacing it is a brainless task—so do it yourself. Replace the filter ($12 to $20) based on its actual condition rather than the manufacturer's recommended service intervals. Checking its condition isn't rocket science. Just pull it out and give it a look-see (**inset photo**). If it fails the back-light test, replace it. While the filter is out, vacuum out the crud in the air cleaner box.

Remove the air filter and vacuum out any dirt. Then hold it in front of a shop light. If dirt blocks more than 50 percent of the light, replace the filter.

Change power steering fluid

DIY savings: $55

There aren't any test strips for power steering fluid, so you'll have to rely on the manufacturer's service recommendations or general rule-of-thumb (two years or 24,000 miles). Use the turkey baster method to remove the old power steering fluid. Suck out all the fluid (engine off) as shown. Then refill the reservoir with fresh fluid. Start the engine and let it run for about 15 seconds. Repeat the fluid swap procedure until you've used up the full quart.

Note: Never substitute a "universal" power steering fluid for the recommended type, and never add "miracle" additives or stop-leak products. They can clog the fine mesh filter screens in your steering system and cause expensive failures.

Swap out your brake fluid

DIY savings: $60

Some carmakers recommend replacing brake fluid every two years or 24,000 miles. Others don't mention it at all. But it's easy to test your brake fluid. Just dip a test strip into the fluid and compare the color to the chart on the packaging.

You can't do a complete brake fluid flush yourself, but you can do the next best thing—a fluid swap. This procedure won't replace all the old fluid with fresh, but you'll introduce enough new fluid to make a difference.

Use a baster to suck out the dark brown brake fluid (brake and power steering fluids are incompatible, so use a different baster for each). Squirt it into a recycling bottle. Refill the reservoir with fresh brake fluid as shown. Then drive the vehicle for a week to mix the new fluid with the old. Repeat the procedure several times over the next few weeks until the fluid in the reservoir retains its light honey color. Note: The brake fluid may damage the baster's rubber bulb, so don't suck the fluid all the way into the bulb. 🏠

POWER STEERING RESERVOIR

OLD BRAKE FLUID

Gallery of Ideas

money-saving

BEST KITCHEN APPLIANCE FIXES

FROM JUNE, 2009, p. 58

REFRIGERATOR

If your refrigerator or freezer compartment won't cool, there are several simple fixes to try before you call for service. Sometimes just cleaning the coils and vents is all it takes to get the fridge cooling again, but if that doesn't solve the problem, you can replace the evaporator fan and the condenser fan. If you get this far and the fridge still isn't cooling, it's time to call in a pro.

DISHWASHER

If your dishwasher runs, but the dishes aren't getting clean, be sure you're using the right amount of detergent, loading the dishes properly and using water that's hot enough. Other possible causes for dirty dishes are an insufficient amount of water in the dishwasher during the wash cycle, a clogged inlet screen or faulty inlet valve, and a stuck float. You can fix all of these problems yourself!

FROM JUNE, 2009, p. 60

FROM JUNE, 2009, p. 62

ELECTRIC RANGE

If one of your electric burners isn't heating, it could be a bad burner, a bad connection in the burner socket or a faulty switch. Check if it's the burner by replacing it with one that you know works. If that burner won't heat either, the problem is the burner socket or the infinite switch (the shaft of the infinite switch is what the burner temperature knob slides over).

GAS RANGE

If your gas range's oven won't light, first check the obvious: Is the oven plugged in and the gas valve open? If those check out, you probably need a new igniter, which you can install yourself. If it's a burner on your gas range that won't light, you may need to clean the spark igniter and unclog the burner holes. Another problem might be a faulty igniter control module.

FROM JUNE, 2009, p. 64

INSTANT PROJECTS: GET ORGANIZED!

BATHROOM SHELVING UNIT

For $50 or less, you can make these attractive and functional shelves out of oak or pine. (The shelves shown are made of cherry, which costs approximately twice as much.) All you need is a 6-ft. 1x4, a 6-ft. 1x6 and a 6-ft. 1x8.

FROM JUNE, 2009, p. 45

FROM JUNE, 2009, p. 46

ADJUSTABLE SPICE SHELF

This clever in-cabinet spice shelf puts your spices at eye level and leaves room for tall items below. Assemble the U-shaped shelf outside the cabinet and then set it on standard shelf pegs. Materials cost less than $10. Once you install it, you'll never have to go hunting for the nutmeg again!

FROM JUNE, 2009, p. 48

CABINET DOOR MESSAGE BOARD

This handy family organizer is made from dry-erase board (aka whiteboard) and a sheet of metal. Be sure to get steel instead of aluminum so your magnets will work.

FROM JUNE, 2009, p. 49

CUTTING BOARD RACK

Get your cutting boards off the countertop with this nifty rack. Materials cost less than $10! Just remember to mount the rack low enough so it doesn't bump into the cabinet shelf.

FROM JUNE, 2009, p. 54

LAUNDRY ROOM IRONING CENTER

Keep your laundry room tidy with the help of this $25 ironing center. All you need is a 10-ft. 1x8, a 2-ft. piece of 1x6 and a pair of hooks to hold your ironing board.

FROM JUNE, 2009, p. 52

TIE, SCARF AND BELT ORGANIZER

For $10 to $15, you can make this handy accessory organizer. Use a hole saw and a jigsaw to make the holes, slots and notches in the plywood. Sand everything smooth and apply several coats of polyurethane so it doesn't snag delicate items.

SPECIAL SECTION
BEST OF TFH

FAVORITE **GARAGE** **STORAGE** SOLUTIONS

RECYCLED-HOSE YARD TOOL ORGANIZER

Cut an old hose into 7-in. pieces, slit them, and nail them to the wall to make good holders for handled tools in the garage.

SAVE YOUR LAWN PRODUCTS

Leave a bag of fertilizer or weed killer open for long and it'll soak up moisture from the air and won't go through a spreader. Even grass seed could use an extra layer of protection from a moisture-wicking concrete floor. Place opened bags of lawn products in large resealable plastic bags ($1 at discount stores). The products will be free of clumps or pests when you need them.

DOUBLE-DUTY SHELF BRACKETS

Shelf brackets designed to support clothes hanger rods aren't just for closets. The rod-holding hook on these brackets comes in handy in the garage and workshop too. You can bend the hook to suit long tools or cords. Closet brackets cost about $3 each at home centers and hardware stores.

OVERHEAD STORAGE

Rakes, shovels, brooms and other long-handled tools seem to be in the way no matter how they're stored in the garage. Here's a rack that works: Cut two pieces of plywood about 12 in. x 48 in. and drill matching 2-in. holes in each, spaced about 6 in. apart. Mount the racks on crossties below your garage roof rafters.

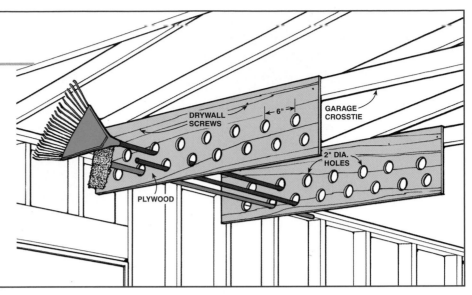

MOVABLE BIKE RACK

Tired of that darn bike hanging in your way? Build this movable bike rack from a 2x4 and a pair of bicycle hooks. Cut four 3-1/2 in. blocks, stack two on top of each other, and screw them together. Now screw them on the end of a 4-ft. 2x4 and repeat the process for the other side. Drill a hole in the middle of the stacked blocks and screw in the bicycle hooks. Lay the rack across your garage ceiling joists, and hang your bike from the hooks. When you need to get behind the bike, simply slide the entire rack out of the way.

2-MINUTE TOOL RACK

One way to get rid of clutter in your storage shed or garage is to screw 16-in. scrap 2x4s at a slight upward angle to each side of a wall stud. They will hold a wide variety of yard tools.

SPECIAL BONUS SECTION

SELF-STICK HOOK-AND-LOOP STRIPS

CLOSET POLE AND SHELF BRACKET

BIKE RACK

Closet pole and shelf brackets can keep your bikes up and out of the way of car doors and bumpers. Just screw the brackets to the wall studs. Line the pole carriage with self-stick hook-and-loop strips so it won't scratch your bike frame.

HANG-IT-ALL HOOKS

Those plastic hooks that plumbers use to support pipes make convenient hangers for just about anything. They're strong, cheap (25¢ to $1 each) and come in a range of sizes. Find them in the plumbing aisle at home centers and hardware stores.

5/16" THROUGH BOLT

BLOCKING

WYE

ELL

MORE OVERHEAD STORAGE

Stow bulky items overhead by cementing together a simple rack from 2-in. PVC pipes and fittings. Bolt the straight pipe to the ceiling joists to support heavy loads, and screw the angled pieces from the "wye" connectors into the cross brace to stabilize the whole rack. The PVC's smooth surface makes for easy loading and unloading.

SIMPLE YARD TOOL ORGANIZER

Create a simple long-handled tool hanger out of two 1x4s. On the first one, drill a series of 2-in. holes along the edge of the board. The trick is to center each hole about 1 in. from the edge. That leaves a 1-1/2-in. slot in the front that you can slip the handles through. Space the holes to accommodate whatever it is you're hanging. Screw that board to another 1x4 for the back and add 45-degree brackets to keep it from sagging. If you wish, pound nails into the vertical board to hang even more stuff. No more tripping over the shovels to get to the rakes!

WOOD BLOCK

2" HOLE

GARAGE STORAGE TUBES

Cardboard concrete-forming tubes are inexpensive ($7 at any home center) and provide a great place to 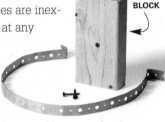 WOOD BLOCK store baseball bats, long-handled tools and rolls of just about anything. Rest the tubes on a piece of 2x4 to keep them high and dry. Secure each tube to a garage stud with a plumbing strap.

PVC TOOL HOLDER

Build this PVC rack to store your tools on the wall. Use a jigsaw to cut a 1-1/4-in.-wide notch down the length of a 2-in.-dia. PVC pipe. Cut several 3-1/2-in.-long sections with a hacksaw or miter saw, and drill two 1/8-in. holes behind the notch. Use 1-1/4-in. drywall screws to attach these pieces to a 2x4 screwed to the wall.

BUTTERFLIES&BIRDS

HOW TO BUILD
A **BUTTERFLY HOUSE**

Butterflies sometimes like to seek shelter. Invite them into your yard by building this simple house. It takes just a few hours and costs under $20.

The best material for your butterfly house is smooth or rough-sawn cedar; it's rot-resistant and weathers to a mellow gray. For durability, assemble the house using moisture-proof glue (like Titebond II) and galvanized nails. Make sure to hinge and latch one side so you can insert and maintain the long twigs and tree bark that butterflies use as a roost (**Figure A**, p. 275).

A jigsaw, drill and common hand tools are all you need, although a table saw (to cut angles and the wood to size) speeds up the work greatly.

To attract butterflies, locate the house in an area with lots of flowering plants, and mount it 2 to 3 ft. off the ground.

STEP-BY-STEP INSTRUCTIONS

1 Cut the parts to the sizes indicated in the **Cutting List**, p. 275, and the angles shown in the photos.

2 Lay out the entry slots on the front (**A**), drill the ends with a 3/8-in.-dia. bit, then cut the slots the rest of the way with a jigsaw (**Photo 1**). Smooth the sides of the slots with sandpaper.

3 Use a 7/8-in. spade bit to drill the holes for the support pipe in the bottom (**D**), and the bottom pipe stop (**E**).

4 Glue and nail the back (**A**) to the side (**C**). Glue and clamp the two support pipe stops together, then glue and clamp them to the back. Glue and nail the bottom (**D**) to the assembled back and side.

5 Glue and nail the false-front roof pieces (**F**) to the front (**A**), then glue and nail the front in place, and attach the roof boards (**B**). Use the door (**C**) as a spacer between the front and back when you attach the roof.

6 Trim the door, if necessary, so it fits loosely between the front and back. Align the door, and hammer in the two hinge pivot nails (**Photo 2**).

7 Use two pliers to bend a nail in half. Drill a pilot hole, then tap in this latch.

JIGSAW

3/8"-DIA. STARTER HOLES

1 Create the entry slots. Drill 3/8-in. holes for the top and bottom of each slot. Connect the holes using a jigsaw.

Figure A: Butterfly House Details

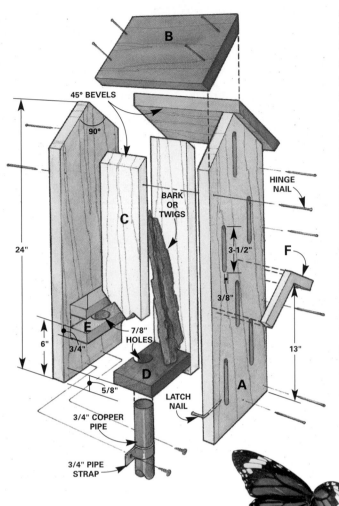

8 Insert the support pipe through the bottom and into the pipe stop. Drill pilot holes for the pipe strap screws, attach the strap (**Photo 3**), then loosen it and remove the support pipe.

9 Determine the best location and height for the house (keep it low). Hammer the pipe into the ground (protect the end of the pipe with a piece of scrap wood), then slide the house on the pipe, tighten the pipe strap and watch for your first fluttering houseguests.

MATERIALS LIST

ITEM	QTY.
1x6 x 10' cedar	1
4d galvanized casing nails	25
3/4"-dia. type L copper pipe*	1
3/4" copper pipe strap*	1
No. 8 x 1/2" pan head screws	2
Titebond II moisture-proof glue	small bottle
*Available at home centers	

CUTTING LIST

KEY	PCS.	SIZE & DESCRIPTION
A	2	3/4" x 5" x 24" cedar (front and back)
B	2	3/4" x 5" x 6-1/4" cedar (roof boards)
C	2	3/4" x 3-3/4" x 22-1/4" cedar (side and door)
D	1	3/4" x 3-3/4" x 3-1/2" cedar (bottom)
E	2	3/4" x 1-1/4" x 3-1/2" cedar (support pipe stop)
F	2	1/2" x 3/4" x 3-1/2" cedar (false front roof)

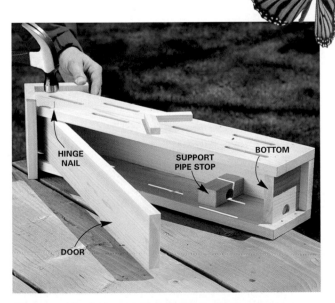

2 Assemble the house. Use straight nails for the door hinges and a bent one for the latch. (Note: Here the door is open so you can see the inside, but it's easier to align everything with the door closed.)

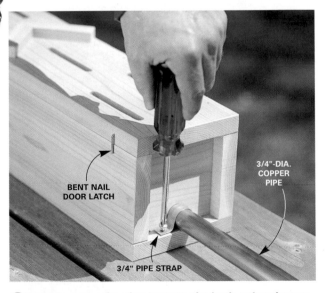

3 Loosely screw the pipe strap to the back, using the support pipe as a guide. Remove the pipe, pound it into the ground, then permanently tighten the strap around the pipe to prevent the house from spinning.

ATTRACTING & KEEPING BUTTERFLIES IN YOUR YARD

Picture yourself as a butterfly. Some family handyman built you a house where there was nowhere to make a living, no food for you or the kids, no heat, no water, no furniture, just a simple roof over your head. Even if it was a beautiful house, who'd want to live there?

About 572 species of butterflies inhabit the lower 48 states. Whether you live in the mountains, desert, tundra or jungle, there are butterflies looking for shelter.

Here are some tips for attracting them to your yard:

Location, location, location

Place their home in a shady area so it doesn't get too hot, but also near an open, sunny spot. Butterflies love the sun.

Food

To attract and keep a population, this is number one, much more important than the house. Most adults drink nectar from flowers. Providing a wide variety of flowers is best, but to find out what the butterflies in your area like, you'll need to do some research. Butterfly Bush and different varieties of milkweed (for Monarchs) are two examples of widely available butterfly "food." As you'll learn from your research, caterpillars won't eat the same food as adults—big surprise! The same research will tell you what they like too. Also consider a butterfly feeder. Fill it with homemade butterfly nectar, a substance similar to hummingbird nectar but weaker.

Heat

Butterflies love to bask on sun-warmed objects such as bricks and rocks. Include some of these materials in your garden plan.

Furniture

The inside of the house should have the butterfly equivalent of a La-Z-Boy. A butterfly's idea of kicking back is to nestle between tall vertical sections of bark with coarse chunks of bark for carpeting.

Water

Do you ever see large groups of butterflies around mud puddles or wet sand? They're drinking and absorbing minerals. You can create a butterfly watering hole by burying a bucket in the ground, filling it with sand or soil and soaking it with water.

Nix on the pesticides

Nonselective insecticides or even organic pest controls will kill your new garden pets. Remember— butterflies are insects too.

Butterflies may or may not decide to live in your butterfly house, but enhancing their habitat will go a long way toward attracting and keeping them in your new butterfly garden.

For More Information

■ Planning a butterfly garden, choosing plants, understanding butterfly behavior and more. butterflysite.com.
■ Plant suggestions for butterflies and caterpillars. butterflywebsite.com.
■ *Creating a Butterfly Garden,* by Marcus Schneck. amazon.com, $9.85.
■ *Beastly Abodes,* by Bobbe Needham. amazon.com, $6.

HOST A BUTTERFLY FESTIVAL

Love to watch butterflies fluttering among your flowers? To attract more, plant these butterfly favorites around your yard: purple coneflower, butterfly bush, milkweed, Joe Pye Weed and bee balm (monarda). To the average butterfly, your yard will suddenly look like a Las Vegas lobster buffet looks to someone coming off a month-long fast.

BIRDBATH LEVELER

Leveling a paver stone under your birdbath is a slick way to keep it from tipping over. It will also keep the water in the bowl level. Round or square paving stones like the one we're using are readily available at garden centers ($3 to $6).

Dig a hole about 2 in. deeper than the thickness of the paver. Spread and roughly level a 2-in. layer of sand in the hole. Set the paver on the sand and check it with a short carpenter's level. Lift one edge of the paver and add or remove sand to level it.

SQUIRREL STOPPER

Tired of squirrel banquets at your "squirrel-proof" bird feeder? Cut the bottom off an empty 5-gal. plastic water bottle with a jigsaw. Drill a hole through the neck of the bottle, slide the bottle over the pole and hang it from the feeder with a short length of coat hanger. You're in—and the squirrels are out of—business! It's rewarding to watch the little varmints climb inside the bottle and peer around in frustration with their beady little eyes.

Buyer's Guide

Look under "Water, Bottled and Bulk" in the Yellow Pages for a water bottle source. By the way, squirrel-proof feeders usually work great. Try oiling and adjusting the mechanisms first.

SPECIAL BONUS SECTION

NO MORE SPROUTING BIRDSEED

Birdseed that drops to the ground often makes a mess, kills the grass and then grows into an odd jumble of plants. A carpet scrap keeps the seed off, allowing the area to be neat and weed-free. To get rid of the hulls, sweep the carpet or shake it off in the garbage can. However, the carpet scrap will kill the grass underneath.

BIRDBATH CLEANUP

Stubborn stains in a birdbath are usually caused by chemicals in rain, tap water or well water as well as organic debris. Fill the basin with a quart of water, add 1/2 cup of household bleach, then scrub the basin with a wire brush until any gunk or discoloration disappears. (Use a soft scrub brush rather than a wire brush on shiny ceramic surfaces.) Take care that you don't splash bleach on surrounding vegetation. Rinse well to ensure the birdbath remains chemical-free.

BLEACH

WIRE BRUSH

WATER

CONCRETE BIRDBATH

BIRDSEED CATCHER

Do you have a mound of seeds and hulls on the ground at the base of your birdfeeder? It's not only ugly but also can kill the grass. To catch this debris, mount a plastic disc sled to the feeder pole. Cut a hole in the middle of the disc the same size as the pole. Slide the disc over the pole and place a hose clamp midway up to keep it in place. A short piece of an old rubber cord placed between the pole and the clamp will help hold the disc. Empty the disc each time you fill the feeder and you'll be able to grow grass or other plants under your feeder again.

YOUR DAUGHTER'S DISC SLED

SEED HULLS

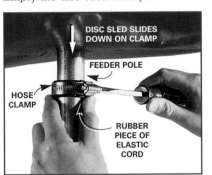

DISC SLED SLIDES DOWN ON CLAMP

FEEDER POLE

HOSE CLAMP

RUBBER PIECE OF ELASTIC CORD

ANT-PROOF YOUR HUMMINGBIRD FEEDER

If it bugs you that ants come to your humming-bird feeder and treat it like a picnic table, try this. Punch a little hole in the bottom of a shallow can and thread through the line that suspends the feeder. Tie a large knot in the line so the container rests on the knot. Seal the hole at the top and bottom with silicone caulk. Then punch a hole in a smaller can, slip that over the string and caulk it to the bottom of the first can. After the caulk hardens, pour in water and your feeder will be ant-proof. It acts like the moat around a castle. [A layer of cooking oil on top of the water will slow down evaporation.]

BIRD RETRIEVAL

A pet bird that gets loose can be difficult to recapture. Try closing the curtains and turning off all the lights. Birds don't usually fly in the dark, so it'll land and be easy to spot with a flashlight.

CrazyCritter GreatGoofs®

Catastrophe

While I was rolling the fridge in and out to clean behind it, the copper tubing to the icemaker got crunched. I decided to replace it with plastic tubing. I removed the old copper, pushed the new tubing through the floor and into the old saddle valve, and then gave it a try. Wow! Everything worked just fine (and on the first try). Suddenly I heard our cat dashing across the floor. I rushed into the kitchen and saw water spraying everywhere. After shutting off the water, I examined the tubing and saw that it was covered with tiny cat tooth marks. I immediately decided that I like copper better!

Between hornets and a hard place

Hornets had built a good-size nest in our porch light, so I rounded up a can of insecticide and a large cloth and waited until dark, when the pests would be in their hive.

That night I quickly wrapped the cloth around the light fixture to keep all the angry, buzzing hornets inside. But when I tried to grab the can of spray at my feet, I realized I couldn't reach down that far without letting go of the cloth—the only thing between me and an irate colony of stingers. Was I stuck!

Fortunately, it was summer and the windows were open. After I gave a few desperate yells, my wife came and rescued me from my potentially painful pickle.

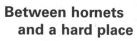

Litter-box olympics

We keep our cat's litter box in the basement. Much to my annoyance, the door to the basement often gets closed unintentionally and the cat can't get downstairs to do her business. To make life easier for the cat and us, I decided to cut a little archway in the bottom of the door so my cat could find her way to the basement and back even if the door was closed. After removing the door, hauling it to the workshop and cutting the archway, I brought the door back into the house to install it. Well, now I've got two choices: teach my cat to pole-vault, or go and buy a new door and start over. Yes, I cut the archway on the top of the door!

Cat'll call

After living in our old house for years, we decided to go all out and remodel the bathroom. Our dream was to install a Jacuzzi tub with a beautiful tile surround. After all the backbreaking work, we finally got to the fun part—setting the tile. We did a flawless job! Later that evening, we realized our cat was missing. After looking everywhere, we heard a distinct meow coming from the bathroom. Realizing that the sound was coming from the new tub surround, we carefully cut through the tile and cement board and found our cat alive and well. We made the best of a bad situation—our rescue hole became a maintenance access panel that we probably should have installed in the first place.

In the doghouse

Proud of my well-constructed doghouse complete with shingles and nameplate, I was ready for my German shepherd to move in. I had even attached an eyebolt to the doghouse to fasten the dog's leash to, since he's a bit rambunctious. On the trial morning of this new setup, I let the dog out, hooked up the leash and went back inside. A few minutes later, I went out to check on him. The dog and the house were gone! I looked in every direction and then across the street. There I saw him enjoying his new yard. The doghouse is now anchored to a concrete slab.

Doggone

One day last summer, I was working on our faulty electric garage door opener and my wife was outside training our new puppy. After a while, she decided to pick some weeds and slipped the dog's leash over the closest, most convenient spot, the garage door handle. Unaware of this, I finished the repairs and hit the opener button on the wall. When the door got about halfway up, I could hear the dog yelping and my wife screaming as the dog was hoisted up by the neck. Fortunately, the dog survived without injury and we've agreed to remove the outside door handle.

Painting faux paw

When my mother decided it was time to paint her living room, I told her I'd help. We took all the usual precautions like placing dropcloths and masking the trim to keep cleanup to a minimum. The painting was going fine until the cat decided to pay us a visit and proceeded to jump into the half-full roller pan. The cat freaked and ran a circle around the room and then dashed up the staircase. It wasn't hard to "track her down" and scrub the paint from her paws, but the rest of the cleanup job took several hours. We now keep the curious cat in another room while we paint!

Puppy art

While painting our side door, I spilled a few drops of paint. As I was getting a rag to clean it up, my son came home from school. He opened the storm door and just missed stepping in the can of paint. Unfortunately, our dog, which I had carefully shut outside, came trailing in right behind him. A big, hairy paw stepped right into the can of black, oil-based paint. To make matters worse, the dog got scared and ran as I yelled and chased him, hoping to keep him off the carpet. His paint-soaked paw made a disaster across the house. When I was between cleaning the floors and the black-pawed dog, my wife came home. Calling it "puppy art" didn't improve the situation.

Chirp, chirp

One evening last summer, just after going to bed, my wife and I heard a chirping sound coming from the hallway. In the morning I promptly changed the battery in the smoke alarm, thinking that would fix it. The next night we heard it again. The next morning I changed the batteries in the remaining smoke alarms. That night we heard it again. I assumed that the smoke alarms must be faulty, as they were several years old. I went to the home center the next day and bought three new alarms and installed them. Eager for a good night's rest, we went to bed. That night the periodic chirping continued. I called the home center and asked what the problem might be. After an extensive search, we found it—a lonely cricket. I coaxed it into a jar and put it outside. Now I'm sleeping better than ever. No crickets, and all that peace of mind from the new smoke alarms.

Warm birdbath?

We'd always used a well to water our gardens and clean out the birdbaths. However, I was having a pump problem and figured the time had come to connect my outside water to the city system.

I hooked up a valve, soldered some basement pipes and went outside to check my work. The water came out hot at first—because I had just sweated the pipes, I told myself. But to my surprise, the water stayed hot and then got even hotter.

Downstairs, I followed the pipe all the way back to our water heater. I had to spend the rest of my day redoing plumbing—or only the birds would have gotten a hot bath at our house.

Decorator flooring

My husband and I put a smooth, flawless coat of epoxy on our garage floor. Then we lowered the overhead door, leaving it high enough that it wouldn't touch the wet floor but low enough that the cat couldn't squeeze in under it.

The next morning I peeked into the garage and my eyes grew to the size of silver dollars! We didn't keep the cat out of the garage; we kept her in—all night! (She must have been hiding on top of the rafters.)

It's a goof we're unlikely to forget; hundreds of little paw prints across the floor's mirror finish remind us every day.

INDEX

Visit **thefamilyhandyman.com** to search five years of article archives.

ACKNOWLEDGMENTS

FOR THE FAMILY HANDYMAN

Editor in Chief	Ken Collier
Senior Editors	Travis Larson
	Gary Wentz
Associate Editors	Elisa Bernick
	Mary Flanagan
	Jeff Gorton
	Brett Martin
Senior Copy Editor	Donna Bierbach
Design Director	Sara Koehler
Senior Art Director	Bob Ungar
Art Directors	Becky Pfluger
	Marcia Roepke
Photographer	Tom Fenenga
Production Artist	Mary Schwender
Office Administrative Manager	Alice Garrett
Financial Assistant	Steven Charbonneau
Reader Service Specialist	Roxie Filipkowski
Production Manager	Judy Rodriguez

CONTRIBUTING EDITORS

Spike Carlsen	Rick Muscoplat
Duane Johnson	Jeff Timm
Bob Lacivita	Bruce Wiebe

CONTRIBUTING ART DIRECTORS

Roberta Peters	David Simpson

CONTRIBUTING PHOTOGRAPHERS

Mike Krivit, Krivit Photography
Ramon Moreno
Bill Zuehlke

ILLUSTRATORS

Steve Björkman	Bruce Kieffer
Gabe De Matteis	Don Mannes
Roy Doty	Paul Perreault
Mario Ferro	Frank Rohrbach III
John Hartman	

OTHER CONSULTANTS

Charles Avoles, plumbing
Al Hildenbrand, electrical
Joe Jensen, Jon Jensen, carpentry
Bruce Kieffer, woodworking
Bob Lacivita, automotive
Dave MacDonald, structural engineer
Costas Stavrou, appliance repair
John Williamson, electrical
Butch Zang, painting and wallpapering
Les Zell, plumbing